Beyond Anorexia
Narrative, Spirituality and Recov

Beyond Anorexia is a sociological exploration of how people recover from what medicine labels 'eating disorders', and the first book to focus exclusively on recovery. Beginning with her own autobiography, and drawing on conversations with over thirty other former sufferers, Catherine Garrett demonstrates that narrative is fundamental to social theory and to healing. She interrogates existing explanations of anorexia (and their related clinical practices) for the contribution they make to a theory of recovery, contrasting them with insights gained from her own research. Her central claim is that recovery is a 'spiritual' experience reconnecting the self with body, nature and society. She analyses spirituality and its relationship with formal religion along with its association with the ascetic rituals of eating disorders. Recovery is shown as the key to full understanding of anorexia, and the processes associated with recovery are explored in terms of embodied spirituality. Using the anthropological theories of Durkheim and van Gennep and contemporary theories of the body, Catherine Garrett reveals some of the social sources of recovery – the solution – which exist alongside the causes of the problem.

CATHERINE GARRETT was born in Sydney, Australia in 1948 and spent the second half of her childhood in Geneva, Switzerland. On her return to Australia, she attended Presbyterian Ladies' College, Sydney, studied history and philosophy at Melbourne University, taught primary students in Suva, Fiji and gained a Teaching Certificate at Sydney Teachers' College. During the 1970s, she taught in several primary schools, trained as a teacher of English as a Second Language, worked as a consultant in multicultural education and ran vegetarian cooking classes. In the 1980s, she returned to study at Macquarie University, obtaining an honours degree in sociology and women's studies. She is currently a senior lecturer in sociology at the University of Western Sydney, Nepean, where her research and teaching focus on the sociology of health, the body and the emotions, and gender relations. She has published widely in sociology, health and counselling journals.

Beyond Anorexia

Narrative, Spirituality and Recovery

Catherine Garrett

CAMBRIDGE
UNIVERSITY PRESS

PUBLISHED BY THE PRESS SYNDICATE OF THE UNIVERSITY OF CAMBRIDGE
The Pitt Building, Trumpington Street, Cambridge CB2 1RP, United Kingdom

CAMBRIDGE UNIVERSITY PRESS
The Edinburgh Building, Cambridge, CB2 2RU, United Kingdom
  http://www.cup.cam.ac.uk
40 West Street, New York, NY 10011–4211, USA   http://www.cup.org
10 Stamford Road, Oakleigh, Melbourne 3166, Australia

First published 1998

Printed in the United Kingdom at the University Press, Cambridge

Typeset in 10/12 Plantin [VN]

A catalogue record for this book is available from the British Library

ISBN 0 521 620155 hardback
ISBN 0 521 629837 paperback

Contents

Preface

To create stories of recovery from suffering is to be involved in healing. The people whose stories are included in this book knew that re-crafting their own narratives was a part of their emergence from self-starvation, compulsive eating, or bingeing and vomiting, and that without the stories of others for comparison and inspiration, their own would be meaningless. In the same way, sociologists can make links among many such personal experiences, to tell a broader story and offer greater possibilities for resolving the social problems we have come to know by their psychiatric label of 'eating disorders'. Medicine, psychiatry and psychology usually emphasize the causes of these problems and find them in the circumstances of individual lives. This book focuses on their resolution and finds it in the same society that gives rise to the problems in the first place. The very culture that provides the negative example of deliberate starvation and self-limitation also offers something else: life-affirming stories and actions; the myths and rituals that can prevent and overcome anorexia. To discover these, sociology must explore what people mean when they speak of their recovery as a 'spiritual' process.

This particular sociological quest is an alternative to the ideas of popular 'self-help' books, New Age spirituality, medical science and postmodern social theory; though it considers each in turn. It is not just a sociology of anorexia and recovery, but also a sociologist's personal story and a demonstration of the value of including explicit autobiography in the interpretation of social phenomena. Personal experiences inevitably shape our interests and the questions and answers that develop from them. Most of us, at some level, continue to search for meaning and to make and remake ourselves from whatever ideas and activities are available to us. That quest has led me through self-starvation and out the other side, because although I tried to deny it, the way to knowledge is always through our bodies. The same quest has taken me into another form of 'discipline': sociology. Social theory is not separate from experience or from storytelling and each of these has real, practical effects in the world.

Eating problems happen to women and men everywhere, though most often in cultures and sub-cultures where these behaviours have well-established meanings (where, for example, thinness is equated with self-control and therefore with beauty and moral purity). Other sociologists are beginning to write about eating problems among women and men from a variety of racial, ethnic and class backgrounds and from different sexualities. Since all these attributes can play a part in the genesis and the experience of eating problems, they are also important in the recovery process. Just as these differences shape the language people use about the problem, so they will shape their versions of its resolution. Those who spoke with me about their recovery and the meaning of its spiritual component were all white 'westerners', and most of them were women, but their stories invite comparisons outside the scope of this book.

Part I discusses the relationship between my narrative and those of participants in my research, between research methods and the knowledge to which they give rise, and between stories and healing; in the context of 'the study of society' in general and of recovery from eating disorders in particular. Part II argues that anorexia cannot be fully understood except from the perspective of recovery. It examines theories of anorexia and studies of recovery across many disciplines, evaluating them against the experiences and understandings of participants in my study, setting out participants' criteria for both anorexia and recovery and concluding with three stories that illustrate the variety and the commonalities among their experiences. The majority of these people (and many others whose accounts of recovery have been published) described their recovery as a 'spiritual' process. Part III discusses the meaning of spirituality in contemporary 'western' society, its continuities and discontinuities with religious beliefs and practices and its association with the ascetic rituals of eating disorders; especially with the rituals that are involved in recovery. The stories at the end of part III demonstrate what spirituality means for people in my study and its place in their recovery. Finally, part IV explores the meaning of embodied spirituality in the recovery process. It offers a new account of the importance of sexuality, language and food in the ongoing transformations that take place beyond anorexia.

All names and identifying details of participants in my study have been changed with their permission.

Acknowledgements

There are many people to thank for this book. The most important are the thirty-three anonymous participants in my research, all of whom shared with me hours of their time, acutely personal information about their lives and belief in the importance of my plans. I acknowledge here the ways they have reshaped my thinking and the potential of their stories to alter public ideas about anorexia and recovery. Adele Horin wrote the *Sydney Morning Herald* article through which I met them and I also thank her, Juanita Crowley and Geraldine Doogue of *ABC Radio National*'s 'City Extra' programme for their assistance in disseminating our joint ideas and Lynette Simons for helping me translate them for the mass media. For the very origins of the project and some of its literary form, I have to thank my teachers and mentors at Macquarie University in the 1980s; especially Carolyn Allport, Kerry Barlow, Mia Campioni, Tim Carrigan, Marie-Louise Claflin, Bob Connell, June Crawford, Mervyn Hartwig, Mark MacLeod, Carol O'Donnell, Kalpana Ram, Janet Ramsay, Sheila Shaver, Rachel Sharp and (at Sydney University) Liz Grosz; each of whom has contributed to and maintained a continuing interest in my work. At the University of NSW, Carolyn Quadrio warmly supported my research in its early stages and Liz Turnbull gave me intellectual stimulation and friendship. My greatest debts are to my PhD supervisors: Ann Daniel for her scholarship and wisdom and Andrew Metcalfe for his inspiring example as teacher, critic and writer.

Thanks go to all my colleagues at the University of Sydney, Nepean: in particular Helen Ledwidge, Alison Johnston, Tim Griffin and Jillian Maling who made the research and writing possible through imaginatively arranging various forms of leave betwen 1991 and 1996; Peter McGregor for telling me to write about what I knew best and Keith Bennett for reassuring me that I could. Deborah Chambers and Cate Poynton of the Women's Research Centre 'commissioned' some of the earlier papers which have contributed to this book; Deborah Lupton has made insightful and generous comments on a number of my manuscripts, encouraged me to publish and broadened my focus by introducing me (often in person) to other scholars. Meg Smith was not only a superb librarian and constant friend, but read every draft of every chapter of my thesis and shared all its ups and downs. John Bidewell and Clare Henessy in the Faculty of Health Studies contributed their technical and personal skills to its completion. My students, especially in the Eating Disorders seminars of 1993 and 1994, inspired me to refine and re-examine many of my assumptions.

For friendship, for their own work, for believing in the book and for their comments on a variety of its earlier forms, special thanks to Dorothy Broom, Morny Joy (Canada) and Joel Kovel (USA); also to Veronica Coopman-Dewis and Ros Downing, Lelia Green, Kath McPhillips, Ruth Parslow and Fiona Place. I learned a great deal from the NSW Department of School Education's Eating Disorders Project Committee with whom I worked in 1992–3 and I particularly appreciated the advice and friendship of Lee Bell, Jan Wright and Jan McCullough during that period. Members of The Australian Sociological Association (TASA) have provided encouragement, inspiration and opportunities over many years and among them I would especially like to thank Liz Eckermann, Jane Edwards, Jan Horsfall, Claudia Knapman, Alan Petersen, Kerreen Reiger, Toni Schofield, Jane Shoebridge, Stephanie Short, Charles Waddell, Yolande Wadsworth and Elizabeth Watson. From the European Council on Eating Disorders (ECED), Bridget Dolan (England) and Melanie Katzman (USA) have been lively and helpful contacts, as well as putting me in touch with Becky Thompson (USA), whose generous and enthusiastic suggestions helped me sharpen the manuscript. At Cambridge University Press, Phillipa McGuinness (Melbourne) and Catherine Max (Cambridge) shepherded the book respectively into and through its production. Many thanks to Catherine for her calm efficiency and crisp email instructions and Con Coroneos for his editorial suggestions. I would also like to thank those editors from other publishing houses who, though their companies could not take the book, took the time and trouble to give me detailed and valuable suggestions and contacts.

Earlier versions of some of the ideas and chapters in this book have been published in *Social Science and Medicine*, the *International Journal of Eating Disorders, Eating Disorders: The Journal of Prevention and Treatment, The Annual Review of Health Social Sciences, The Australian Journal of Guidance and Counselling* and *The Australian Journal of Communication*. I am grateful for the helpful comments of all the anonymous reviewers involved.

Personal thanks to Edith Adler and to Christine Long; each for her own kind of sustaining love. My daughter, Anna Johnson, shared this project from beginning to end with characteristic graciousness, intelligence and humour. My husband, Jeremy Nelson, has enriched it and me in ways I could never have imagined.

Glossary

Anorexia

Anorexia is the term I have used to refer to people's experience of eating problems, except where the differences between these problems are significant. In those cases, I have specified 'anorexia nervosa' (self-starvation), 'bulimia nervosa' (compulsive vomiting, with or without bingeing) or 'compulsive eating' (an addictive relationship with food). I have done this for several reasons. First, I use medical categories, despite their pathological connotations, because their invention has created them as real entities for sufferers and the general public (see 'discourse', below). In part II, however, I develop a detailed critique of their use, from the perspective of social theory. I have retained the word 'anorexia' because the term is now in popular use to mean 'self-starvation'. I want to recognize popular usage, but also broaden it to include other aspects of the problem; to show that many people experience episodes of starvation, compulsive eating, vomiting and laxative abuse in a variety of combinations and sequences. Secondly, I use 'anorexia' as a blanket term because existing psychiatric classifications (American Psychiatric Association 1987, World Health Organization 1992) are considered unsatisfactory by most psychiatrists themselves (e.g. Beumont 1992). The boundaries between different forms of harmful eating behaviour and their causes can be somewhat artificial and psychiatric classifications do not recognize the well-known and serious problem of compulsive eating. In addition, classifying food behaviours in detail has not proved very relevant to recovery. Thirdly, I have not avoided the psychiatric terminology altogether, because the diagnostic labels can be important when sufferers need financial support from government and other health funds for treatment. Finally, I have avoided using the term eating 'disorder' except in implied inverted commas, because the word 'problems' more clearly expresses their traumatic basis and their social causes (Thompson 1995: 6). The personal stories in this book will reveal the many subtle differences as well as the commonalities among these food-related difficulties. (I have used 'anorectic' as a noun and 'anorexic' as an adjective, a convention followed more often by British than American writers).

Autobiography

Autobiography, in this book, includes all its life stories; whether they are told in the first person or retold by a narrator. Although I have had more leisure than the other participants in my study to polish up the written version of my own story, although I have been unable to reproduce theirs (or mine) in their entirety, and although I have had the power to select extracts from theirs: the term still best describes the personal and narrative nature of the material, as opposed to data obtained in other studies by structured interview or questionnaire. I explain my use of the term in more detail in chapter 3.

Discourse

The term discourse is taken from Foucault (e.g. 1977: 49). A discourse is not only 'that which can be said' about something (an eating problem, for instance); but also the framework of power and knowledge which enables us to speak, or restricts us from speaking, about it. Discourses are not only words, but practices. They determine what gets counted as knowledge and as truth. They shape their objects, including people and the kinds of lives that are possible for them. As I show in chapter 4 (and Garrett 1994), there are now many discourses on anorexia, but all have been influenced by the powerful medicalized discourse of psychiatry. Consequently, people's perceptions and experiences of eating problems, in the second part of this century, have been formed largely within a medical paradigm. Discourses, however, are in constant competition with each other, offering us a range of different ways of being. This book shows the influence of the discourse of spirituality, for instance, on the recovery process. It also presents autobiographical discourses that challenge the dominant discourses and offer people a range of possiblities beyond the narrow 'subject position' of 'anorectic'.

Recovery

'Recovery' suggests a prior illness rather than the ongoing transformative process this book describes and analyses . It has also become associated with the 'recovery movement' and theories about 'co-dependency', many of which, individualistic and victim-blaming, fail to recognize the social basis of addictions and other self-destructive behaviours or the social resources which make it possible to abandon such behaviours. I have nevertheless retained the term in order to expand its meaning; using the associations of 'recovery' in the words of the participants in this study and exploring their stories for evidence of what 'recovery' means in practice.

Self

The 'self' to which this book refers is not the commonsense 'unitary' self, the modern individualized 'authentic' self, nor the postmodern 'fragmented' self. It comes closer to the idea of 'soul' which grows as 'ego' diminishes (Kovel 1991). Soul is something like the Hindu conception of 'Atman'; the greater Self in which we all participate, which is beyond intellect and beyond time (e.g. Iyengar 1993: 54). At the same time the self is made up of many facets linked together to form a whole, inseparable from its social matrix. Chapter 4 discusses the question of 'self' in greater detail.

Spirituality

'Spirituality' is an increasingly popular word that currently seems to include people's existential questions, their sense of the supernatural and their religious beliefs, if any; but this description does not do justice to the way it was used by participants in my study. For them, spirituality was a feeling of connection; with their natural surroundings, with other people and among the many parts of themselves including body, intellect and emotion. It was sometimes, but not necessarily, associated with religion. These people spoke of it as a power within and beyond themselves and almost always as something lost but regained in their transition from anorexia to recovery. Although our descriptions of this reality are always limited and shaped by the language and other symbolic systems available, and although it appears to belong outside the intellectual questions of sociology, it is a crucial underlying theme in recovery stories and it holds the key to the self-transformation this book explores. Chapter 7 develops the notion of spirituality in that context.

Stones

Participants in my study sometimes referred to 'stones' (colloquially used in the singular as in 'at my lowest weight I weighed four and a half stone'). These were the units in which weight was measured until the metric system was introduced to Australia in the 1970s. One stone = 14 pounds = about 6 kilogrammes.

Part I

Personal sociology

You must learn to use your life experience in your intellectual work:
continually to examine it and interpret it.   (C. Wright Mills 1959: 196)

1   Descent and return

1948–1954

In my earliest memories, my parents were godlike. Their words and their silences governed my actions and defined my world. As they held, warmed, bathed and fed me, love brightened their faces and their familiar scent; my father's sweat, my mother's hair and lap. Because theirs was my only love, theirs was also my only reality; but in their absence I had experiences they neither accepted nor explained. Alone in the dark, my fears defied their certainties. Sounds in the garden were robbers coming to harm me and I felt the pain of long sticks they poked through the window and under the sheets. When my four-year-old self found the courage to run to their bed for comfort, they were angry. They denied my experience and firmly took me back to my room and I knew it was better to put up with its terrors than risk the loss of their love. Life was also full of private joys. One summer day, a steamroller came to our street. My older brother, five, led me barefoot across the newly spread tar as we popped the membranes of its black bubbles. Control was intoxicating; the small explosion I created could change fragments of the world. 'Tar' and 'asphalt', my brother's words, rolled delightfully around my mouth. I was connected with him and with nature, an inheritor of technology and language. I was godlike too.

My body, however, was a problem from the start. If I failed to 'do a motion in the trainer' my mother would push a rubber tube up my anus and fill my bowels to bursting point with soapy water until I lost control. Her father, a doctor, prescribed daily cod liver oil. I had to eat everything on my plate, however much I gagged, or stay at the table for hours after everyone else had gone. Congealed uneaten vegetables accompanied me in jars to the homes of my friends. In our house, children earned dessert by enduring the first course and even that was withheld when, as punishment for bad table manners, we were sent to our rooms. Temper tantrums, the ultimate loss of control, were punished with smacks to our bare buttocks. It was the style of the times. Anger and shame lodged so deep inside me that I lost them. Instead, I stole sweet foods and gobbled them behind my hands, in dark corners.

My father was a Congregationalist minister, which defined my status and how I should behave. Religion held all the answers and religion meant Dad. He was the young and charismatic General Secretary of the Australian Council of Churches and although he was not attached to a parish, I often heard him preach. The first time I sat with my mother in the front pews, I stared up at the pulpit and frowned. My father wore a black robe and a forked white collar and joined his hands in dramatic prayer. He smiled down at me but I did not smile back. After the service I asked: 'Daddy, why were you wearing your dressing gown and a feeder?' Already, I had doubts about the ceremonies of the church. My father was clearly not God, since God always welcomed and forgave you, but his special relationship to God seemed to give greater authority to his truths and made it more difficult for me to believe in any others I might encounter or devise.

1954–1960

Our move to Europe when I was six took us to new cultures early enough for my brothers and me to learn the pleasures and the discomforts of diversity. Against the immigrant tide, we travelled for five weeks by ship to our new home in Geneva for my father to join the staff of the World Council of Churches. Our first European port of call was Naples, where my parents bought granitas at a sidewalk cafe and we were allowed a taste. My mother's was lemon slush – bliss on a burning day of strange new smells – but my father's was coffee and not for children, so coffee granitas joined all the other adults-only mysteries for which I longed. On our way back to the ship, we stepped into a vast basilica. There were candles burning under high vaults, people dipping their fingers in holy water and magical frosted-glass cases with coloured statues of the Madonna, lit from within. She shone like a fairy princess and I was filled with yearning. My parents, anxious not to miss the gangplank, shepherded us out of this sacred place into the dust, wind and glare of the piazza. As they struggled with my younger brother's stroller on the unfamiliar cobblestones, they exchanged private smiles and said 'Mmmm; very Italianate' and I knew they didn't approve of what we'd just seen. My religious impulse became immediately suspect. For years after this, when confronted with anything ornate, I would say decisively 'Mmmm; very Italianated' and not understand why my parents laughed.

They also laughed at my desire to be a missionary. This was confusing, because its source came from their own teaching. I knew almost by heart, through the books my father ordered from England, the lives of *Six Great Missionaries*. My brother and I would draw their portraits and perform their stories as plays. I planned to emulate Mary Slessor, go to Africa and be eaten by cannibals, or become a leper and identify with suffering like Father Damien. Alternatively, I could work in prisons like Elizabeth Fry in *Six Great Reformers* and, for a while, Quaker grey dresses with white collars were my ideal of feminine dress. Unfortunately, my heroes were all depicted as serene in their sufferings and serenity was not my strong point. I turned to the stories of *Ten Saints* – especially to those who tortured their bodies or destroyed their beauty in order to remain virgins. When I was eight, I went without chocolates and lollies for the forty days of Lent, hoarding any that came to me in a shoebox under my bed. I had discovered self-control.

On Good Friday that year, we walked the cloisters of the Abbey at Cluny, imagining ourselves as medieval monks. Before dawn on Easter Sunday, we drove to the ecumenical community of Taizé. We came into its thirteenth-century church, packed with villagers and visitors, in almost total darkness. The brothers entered in silent procession and prostrated themselves on the flagstones. As a single beam of light crept through a high window-slit, illuminating masses of daffodils and narcissis on the altar, they rose singing 'Il est ressuscité! Il est ressuscité!' 'He is risen! He is risen!' and at the conclusion of the service we gave our neighbours the kiss of peace. Then I remember a walk through fields of brilliant green wheat shoots, covered with dew and teeming with life, before sitting down at trestle tables with French farmers and church leaders from around the world, sharing platters of omelet and local sausages and breaking fresh, round loaves. The symbolism of death and rebirth with music, in nature and through community had entered me, but it was not until years later that I realized its significance.

Not long after this, I had a conversion experience. The art teacher at my school belonged to the Salvation Army and every Thursday, a day off for children in Geneva, she walked through the Old City in uniform to meetings at the Salvation Army Hall. Once, she invited interested students to meet Frère Pierre, who had just come back from missionary work in China. Brother Pierre was better than any of my Sunday School classes: he had lived his own adventure stories, he taught us to sing along with his guitar and he spoke to us as equals. He told us that God loved us whatever choices we made and that we were free to ignore or trust that love. When I came home, glowing with this revelation, to announce that I had been converted, my parents were amused as if children were incapable of spiritual awareness or commitment. Immediately, my joyful certainty was surrounded with rationalistic doubts.

In the two years when my mother was dying of Hodgkins' Disease, I would often climb into bed beside her after school to read and talk. Sometimes I would run to her room and find it empty because the ambulance had taken her back to hospital in pain. When this happened, energy and joy abruptly drained out of me. I hated the antiseptic smell of the hospital, not knowing how long she would have to stay there, waiting in the corridor while nurses modestly concealed the body she had never hidden from me. I took her gifts I'd made: drawings, embroidery and cupcakes. My tenth birthday fell in the last week of her life. Her presents for me expressed her hopes for my future; Dinu Lipatti's record of 'Jesu Joy of Man's Desiring' and a set of the best quality watercolours. J. S. Bach had always been my favourite composer and painting my most creative activity. 'Jesu Joy' eventually inspired my piano lessons and when I played it, people sometimes cried. This was the last time I saw her. When she was sedated, I chose not to go in case she did not recognize me.

We were told not to mourn. The funeral was for family alone and our grief was concentrated in the alien space of the hospital chapel. A few days later, there was a packed thanksgiving service. My older brother's teacher and mine brought both our entire classes. We gave thanks for my mother's life and her 'victory over death'. I had no idea what this meant, but I would not let people feel sorry for me. Immediately afterwards, we took a holiday beside Lake Locarno with both sets of grandparents and I broke only once, the night before our return. Three months later, my father fell in love with one of his colleagues (our favourite) and the following year they married. I was devoted to my step-mother, learning to play the piano, had joined the Swiss Girl Guides, met my kindred spirit Christine and started writing a diary. My adolescence had begun.

Christine's father was also a minister and she had spent the previous few years in Hong Kong. Our experiences of cultural relocation had made us unusually self-aware and we instantly recognized each other's sensitivity. Each of us felt that the other was a gift from God. Our parents were disturbed by our mutual obsession and their anxieties were fuel for a mild rebellion. We would take our bikes into the fields or forests and lie in each others' arms for hours, united with the world. We shared each other's beds and in the long twilight, dragged them to the window to gaze at the first stars and imagine my mother's spirit sanctifying our relationship. We listened to Beethoven and Brahms and read our diaries aloud. Then the friendship we believed would last forever was abruptly interrupted when Christine's family returned to the USA and, a few months later, mine took me back to Sydney. We dealt with the separation by distancing ourselves before it happened and lost touch for the next thirty years. In our early forties, I found where she lived, wrote and visited her and we reclaimed our connection – a model of spiritual relatedness which is once again central to our lives.

My diary was full of love for the land where I lived and gratitude for my friendships, often expressed in the sentimental language I met through my teachers and my reading. My internal experience mirrored the world:

Today, everything outside is beautiful. The trees with their new leaves, the pale blue sky, the spring daisies I see everyday coming home from school, the bright light, the little fleecy clouds . . . and I am happy; but my emotions are aroused by anything: the silver birches that make me think of how I am now, because of their fluttering leaves, and then the twinkling stars, that you sometimes see, sometimes don't and that seem uncertain whether to shine or not. . . . Each time I see this, it gives me a feeling of peace and joy so great that I think I may burst. . . . As Ramuz [the best known poet of Suisse Romande] says: 'there is a kind of voice that urges you to live, at this time of the year. It is in the singing bird, in the sunshine, in the swelling buds.' I love Switzerland more than I have ever loved it before. Switzerland is my real 'patrie' [homeland].

Growing up among the families of the World Council of Churches, at a school which took Christianity for granted, gave me religious words to explain my experiences, but they would have been no less spiritual had I not expressed them in those terms. After my mother's death, piano lessons were the high points of my week. When I stood in the tiled corridors of the Geneva Conservatoire, in the cross-currents of music which poured out of its rooms, I felt joined to its composers, living or dead, and to the music of the spheres. When my friends and I camped beside glaciers and lakes or rode down mountain passes with our hands off the handlebars or talked by torchlight in our tents about deaths, divorces and self-doubt; when we sang around the fire beneath the pinetrees and washed in rocky streams at sunrise, our feelings for each other and the land were replete with shared meaning. In losing Switzerland I lost, not French, but the reality of our common language. It was a long time before I found my way back.

At the same time, I began to rage against my father – my repressed grief no doubt encountering his. I rebelled at his failure to understand me, but I had internalized his value system and was beginning to use it against myself. After a particularly bitter row when I was twelve, I wrote:

I am feeling sick with misery. I don't know what to do to be liked again except to think of others, which I had been trying to do before Daddy told me I am getting worse and worse! I am going to sleep. Then I will forget all my troubles and I would like to sleep all my life, then they would be sorry! I hope I will be sick! I hope I will lose ten kilos! I want to look pathetically skinny and think of nothing but other people! Tomorrow I start a completely new life. Here is a list of my faults which I am going to abolish: Selfishness, Vanity, Rudeness, Dishonesty, Unpunctuality, Superiority. I will have to really slog to get all this out of my system!

Although there was perfectionism, pain and repression in my child-hood, it was never bleak. I was healthy, loved, and full of enthusiasm and hope.

1960–1965

On the aeroplane which brought us back to Australia, I was sexually abused in the cockpit by an aquaintance of my father's; an Australian judge. Heaving with nausea, I pulled my very pregnant stepmother into the cramped aircraft toilet and told her what had just happened. In the sixties, people did not talk about such things. At least she believed me. What he had done was wrong, she said, but some men were just like that; they could not help themselves and there was nothing to be done about it. I would have to put the experience behind me and get on with my new life in Australia. Only my parents knew what had happened and neither of them ever mentioned it again. After a few weeks, the nausea went; but the disgust with my body, the fear of its sexuality and of men were still there two years later when boys began to ask me out. In self-protection, I had separated myself from the source of my troubles – my body – and was frightened by its demands. Also, unknown to me, I was growing to look more like my mother and I could not understand why my father was pushing me away. I responded by rejecting what mattered most to him – his religion.

During my highschool years, my theological questioning was complic-ated. At school, I joined the Student Christian Movement which encour-aged critical inquiry into religion. I was also a Sunday School teacher at my grandparents' church, played the piano for its kindergarten and went to the weekly youth fellowship. In 1962 a new, evangelical, minister came to our congregation. Anxious about the dangers of 'juvenile delinquency', he zealously arranged for the entire youth group to spend a weekend at a Baptist campsite. The bait was horseriding, but all I remember is a stream of messages about hellfire and damnation. Most of the camp counsellors were converts fresh from the Billy Graham crusades, enthusiastic but unlearned. My older brother, a debater schooled in the history of the Reformation and horrified by the saccharine sentimentality of the music, stood aloof from the proceedings and provided a running critical com-mentary throughout the weekend. I was more susceptible to the emotional appeal of eternal salvation. I hoped that a 'decision for Christ' would save me from the doubts which had plagued me since I was twelve. I wanted to be reborn to escape my present suffering, so I went forward when the youth leader asked for 'decisions'. This time, my parents were angry at the distorted version of their faith which had been presented to me and this time, I agreed. I had been raised to seek intellectual justification for all my actions and when I found it missing from this latest experience I thought I had lost the possibility of any kind of faith forever. Shortly after this I declared that I was no longer a Christian and resigned from all my religious activities and my father, hurt and bewildered, ignored me as much as he could.

I still went to SCM school camps and conferences, because they nurtured my philosophical interests. Romantically and often painfully, I languished over two of the leaders (a man and a woman) and then found, to my amazement, that they reciprocated my feelings. Twenty years later, both had claimed a homosexual identity; but for us in the sixties, there were no stories, only tumultuous feelings. In my diary, I wrote: 'I don't know anything, think anything or express anything and everything seems unreal and very dark and desperate most of the time'. Although I longed to believe that God was in everything, I was told at an SCM 'science conference' that pantheism was a heresy of the early Church. Part of my tradition made me believe that what was intellectually unconvincing was wrong; but another part asserted that faith was a gift; one to which I was apparently not sufficiently receptive. During this period, encouraged by my school principal, another student and I composed a musical meditation on the Holy Spirit which was performed by a verse-speaking group, choir and orchestra. My contribution was wooden and uninspired and I never attempted to compose again. Struggling to make sense of the doctrine of the Trinity, I had no idea to what order of reality the events of Pentecost belonged. My own body was so obscure to me that I could not imagine the feelings of the Apostles in the story when they were filled with spiritual energy. At the youth group suppers after Church on Sunday evenings, I binged on cookies and cakes instead.

When I was fifteen years old, I decided to lose weight as a means of establishing to myself and to others that I was in control of my life. I had never heard the words anorexia nervosa, or that people could deliberately starve themselves to death or into a form of half life. I only knew that I was desperately unhappy and that I hated myself. I thought that if I carefully controlled what I ate, I could be transformed: there would be less of me to hate and an achievement to be proud of. I drew up written and mental lists of good and bad foods, good and bad times to eat and good and bad ways to eat. The lists and the practices they required were more and more elaborate and rigid. They became highly symbolic rituals and, for me, sacrosanct. Failing to observe them would bring about terrible retribution. Within a few months, I had lost over twenty kilos, I was terrified of eating, constantly shivering, weak but forcing myself to exercise and increasingly isolating myself in piano practice and study. My diary was full of suicidal thoughts. My buffer against despair was academic success and the pleasure of learning. When my final exam results were spectacular, I thought the examiners must have made a mistake.

During those and the next few years, I tried many times to gain weight; for the doctor anxious I wasn't menstruating, for my step-mother who cried when she saw the sharpness of my ribs, for my school friends worried by my shivering and hair loss and sometimes because I was afraid of dying; but I could not find the way out of the pit I had entered because I had not yet reached its bottom.

1966–1968

When I finished school, I broke with family tradition and left home to go to a university where I might not be identified with my father. I studied history and philosophy and seized on arguments about the illusory nature of the world. For a while, I was in love with a medical student in the college next door. Both of us were intense and repressed; a doomed combination, but safe. I was afraid of my sexual feelings because of a shame whose source I could not face. I alternated between weeks of contented sharing of college meals and bouts of food anxiety and restriction. I read Bernard of Clairvaux's letters on Caritas; the love which joins all humanity. I sought out moments of transcendence in the college choir, when we sang about mystical knowing and peace in anthems:

> Let all mortal flesh keep silence
> and in fear and trembling come
> Ponder nothing earthly minded
> for with healing in his wings
> Christ from sky to earth descended
> Our true homage to repay.

and in psalms:

> Thou wilt keep him in perfect peace
> whose mind is stayed on Thee.
> The darkness and the light are alike to thee.
> The night is as bright as the day.

I responded to the body/mind dualism of the anthem and did not read the rest of the psalm:

> Where could I go to escape from you?
> Where could I get away from your presence?
> If I went up to heaven, you would be there;
> If I lay down in the world of the dead, you would be there,

I wanted to be a better person and thought the way was through control, but I had created a pattern of living which cut me off from connection with my body, with others and with nature. It wasn't an illness, though it made me ill: I had fallen into a paradoxical form of spiritual suffering designed by my very attempt to escape from it. At the beginning of my third year at university, my parents and my three younger brothers went to live in Fiji and I spent my university vacation with them. Instead of the joyful reunion I had anticipated, I found a bewildered silence from my parents, shocked at my difficulties with food. The less I ate, the more they withdrew and the more they withdrew, the less I ate; until I was so weak I flew back to Melbourne where I went straight into hospital. Wanting to please the psychiatrist and the staff, who gave me the first sustained care I had had in years, and sedated to the point where I thought it didn't matter, I gained the weight they said I should.

I went back to university seven kilos heavier. I felt gross. I hated my new, more attractive body, and the loss of my anorexic identity. The barbiturates I was still prescribed made it impossible to think. When I tried to tell people about the escalating confusion and self-loathing in which I lived, they found it narcissistic or incomprehensible. Only the psychiatrist recognized some of the sources of my perfectionism, but my sessions with her had begun to touch feelings my anorexic behaviour had so successfully stifled and I was not ready to cope with their re-emergence. My despair ate up the world and myself with it. I was certain about two things only; that I was worth nothing and that I could not go on. A week after my twentieth birthday, close to the anniversary of my mother's death, I swallowed fistfuls of tranquillizers and lay down to die.

Twenty four hours later, a distraught fellow-student alerted the college principal and the lock on my door was broken. I remember going through darkness towards light and then being pulled into the world again by the energy of someone I loved. My older brother had flown straight from Sydney to the hospital where I lay unconscious and it was his hand, holding mine, which dragged me back, as I screamed with the pain of my return. This unsuccessful suicide was the turning point for my rebirth. It was nine months before the depression lifted and I could really see and feel my surroundings. I spent that time in Fiji with my family, at first staring at the floor all day, then starting to teach in a primary school, healing with the unquestioning love of my small half-brothers and my eight-year-old students and the warmth of the multiracial community in which we lived. Against my will, but because I didn't think I cared, I took anti-depressants for a while and they made a difference. One day, on the way home from work, I walked over the brow of the hill above our house and saw, as if for the first time, the aqua, green and ultramarine spectrum that stretched to the reef and the palms, frangipani and hibiscus on either side of the road. It was all so clear, so new, that I did not even know that it was a return. Soon after this experience, I decided to go back to Australia and become a real teacher.

1969–1981

Living happily ever after is not an ending. I now began to find what I had gradually lost since childhood. Recovery is a continual descent and return, rediscovery and remaking. Its source was at the same time inside and outside me; in my history and in the stories of others, in past experience and in new opportunities. The rigid barriers I had erected against anger, shame and loss had also shut off the awareness of connection that preceded my traumas. I had to find, and I am still finding, many ways to open and feel connected again. One way was through my vocation. Teaching made me responsible for others who trusted me and drew me out of introspection. It made me think again about knowledge and language. It made me tell stories.

In Jane Campion's film *The Piano*, there comes a moment in Ada's story when there seems no point in going on. As her piano falls over the edge of the canoe that is taking her away from the shambles her life seems to have become, she lets her foot catch in the rope that held the piano in place and is dragged towards the sea floor. It is only when she faces death that something inside her asserts her will to live. She kicks free and rises to the surface. It is the beginning of her new life and she slowly learns to speak again. The descent into anorexia and the turning point of my attempt to die were like the bardos of Tibetan Buddhism: chaos full of potential; part of the pattern of descent, crisis, discovery and return which is human experience. The crisis is different each time, but it always contains within it the discovery and return. We can't force the pace, but once we have chosen to live (or to die), we find the strength to do it.

1969 was my first year of real freedom. I shared a garage under a squash centre with an easy-going friend who took off for Italy half way through the year to study the relationship between Communism and the Church. Her friends, my brother's and my own from Teachers' College provided my social life. I was on a government scholarship and the course did not demand much study. I loved living alone. I had short but intense romances, cooked elaborate meals, ate out in Sydney's burgeoning restaurants, still panicked if I put on weight, but felt as if the future was opening and the past could never harm me again. Most of my friends were still virgins and we spent hours wondering how we would know when the 'right' man came along. When he did, by my second year of teaching, it was love at first sight. He worked as a clerk at the courthouse and studied law at night. Our desire to avoid convention in our relationship provided the safety for it to grow. He was gentle, intelligent and cared about social justice. He was younger than I was and still wounded by his parents' divorce. We did not think the differences in our backgrounds (his was working class and almost entirely secular) would matter and could not imagine anything that might separate us.

Where I had fled from sexuality during my years of acute self-starvation, I now embraced it with wonder. There were times when I still hated my body, but my husband's love made everything about me more acceptable. It also made me dependent on his constant reassurance. The most elaborate form of my perfectionism was in my attitude to food. Every meal was designed to deliver communion and ecstasy. I would go without food until late at night to intensify the pleasure and then be surprised when it did not always come. I collected and used almost a hundred cookbooks. Food, sex and the sacred were inseparable in my sleeping and my waking dreams.

I avoided religion, but I learned to practise Transcendental Meditation. It gave me time to begin exploring inner space without the unanswerable questions of my intellect and it taught me to relax. With my husband, I ate my way around Europe. On our return, almost as a penance, we became vegetarian; horrified to learn that every pound of animal protein we ate took nine pounds of plant food from the mouths of people in the Third World. TM and vegetarianism were less destructive paths than anorexia to the spirituality I still craved. On a second visit to Europe, this time alone, I visited Assisi on impulse and found myself in tears before the relics of Saint Clare; unable to say why I was so moved. My marriage, nurturing as it was, had failed to deliver the divine experience I had thought to find there and, although I denied it to myself and my husband, I was filled with a yearning I could not identify.

I had always wanted children, but when I stopped taking the pill, I did not conceive. We began a round of visits to gynaecologists. I had not yet encountered feminism (though I did read *The Female Eunuch* on my honeymoon and put it firmly aside for a few years) but the misogyny of these men was palpable. Most of them told me I had upset the balance of nature with my past anorexic behaviour, I had disrupted my hormones, I was not a real woman and I would never be fertile. I took my temperature every morning for two years, forgot about spontaneous sex and became a guinea-pig for triple doses of fertility drugs. At last, after seven years of marriage, I became pregnant. In spite of morning sickness lasting all day, I loved the changes in my body. I had an acceptable reason to eat, to gain weight, for my breasts to grow. I felt part of a timeless rhythm and a control beyond my own will.

My daughter was ten weeks premature. In the fortnight before her birth, my body ran riot with pre-eclampsia. Without eating or drinking (I was too sick), I swelled with fluid until my toes disappeared in my puffed feet, my skin began to crack and my lungs, nerves and brain threatened to burst. This time so close to death I only wanted to live – and most of all to save our child. She was delivered by emergency caesarian, weighing less than two pounds. For three months, she lay in a glass box, struggling for her life, until first her lungs, then her bowel, then her sucking reflex began to work. We sat beside her for hours, willing her to survive, and I used a breastpump until the day I put her to my breast and felt I had come home to the the place I found in sex, meditation and music. With motherhood, I took on a new identity, shared my body more generously and learned to recognize, then meet, my physical needs; eating and sleeping when I had to instead of when I'd planned. Time itself took on a different meaning and I felt a new solidarity with other women.

My marriage ended when my daughter was not quite three. Although my husband had welcomed my increasing self-assurance, he had also noticed my restlessness and the flatness that seemed to have come over us both; the differences in temperament, in education and in culture that had not mattered before began to strain the kind of marriage we had erected. We lost trust in it and, in some ways, in each other. Instead of expanding its boundaries and living up to its new challenges, we left it. The agony of our separation was terrible, but it allowed me to change in ways I had forbidden myself in the cocoon of our relationship.

On Christmas eve, three months after we separated, I went alone and in tears to a midnight service. I had not been to church for years, except when I visited my parents in Fiji. I had never taken Communion because when I could have been confirmed at twelve, I could not swallow the teachings of the Church from my father and later I literally forbade myself to eat or drink between meals. My deepest spiritual connection for nine years had been in marriage; the committed centre of my life which had given me a new sense of my body and my creative powers. Cut off from all these things, I desperately sought them in the Eucharist. I came away feeling nothing, but it was my first gesture towards understanding and reinterpreting my spiritual heritage and a recognition of the importance of ritual. I see now that the gesture preceded the realization.

1982–1988

Living on a supporting parent's pension, I returned to university study and joyfully reclaimed my intellect. I took lectures in a dozen subjects, from Chaucer to statistics, romantic literature to post-modern philosophy. While my daughter went to the childcare centre, I would spend the day in the library, reading about women's lives, Eastern mysticism, poetry and mythology. Through sociology, I discovered a new way of seeing myself and others; from the outside in. I began looking for social explanations of eating disorders in and beyond medical texts, across several academic disciplines and in conversation with other women, searching for the causes of the problem but still blind to the importance of its resolution. I transferred my leisure activities from cooking to running and swimming and in my thirties discovered for the first time the energy and glow of physical fitness.

During one long vacation I travelled to India. Among people who had no choice about starving, to eat was a daily privilege and food was a Grace. For those seven weeks, my remaining fears about eating disappeared and with them the rules I still used to contain them. A miraculous well-being replaced them. I did not tell myself that my journey was a spiritual search but from the moment of arrival I was plunged into the incense, chants, rites, language and inescapable spirituality of India. I felt it in the humour of beggars, in conversations with Indian travellers, in temples and in palaces. It overwhelmed me at Varanasi on the river at sunrise and again in the middle of the day when I came too close to one of the funeral ghats and, in the words of an Indian poet; 'faced reality on a different plane, where death vibrates behind a veil of fire'. I met it most fully when I was drawn into a puja ceremony at Pushkhar where a mountain peak rises like a child's drawing behind the lake on which the Lord Brahma and his consort once came to earth in a lotus leaf. As a brahmin priest placed a coconut shell and flowers on the surface of the lake for me, I was filled with the 'peace which passeth all understanding'.

1988–1997

After six years of study, I became a lecturer in sociology in a faculty of health studies, convinced that the education of nurses, teachers and community workers was where the integration of sociological and personal understandings could have most influence. I have worked there ever since. Over these years, I gradually began to reinterpret the myths of my life and my discipline. I faced them through psychotherapy and through research, using each to question the other. I tried to express what I knew in ways which would engage my students. In finding the words to do so, I found new meanings and began to act upon them; rediscovering creativity and physicality. On my fortieth birthday I cleared my desk of its computer and books and spent the weekend painting a large portrait of my house, surrounded by the strong, unkempt branches of its front yard eucalypt and the ferns I planted when I began studying for my PhD. The next year I joined a yoga class. I learned to breathe and to use muscles I had ignored; new names for body parts I'd hardly considered. As I stretched and opened I would sometimes be swept with gusts of unlocked memory. One morning, in my third year of yoga, our teacher made us do all the standing poses with pride: 'not being proud *about* your body', she said, 'but feeling the pride that is *in* your body'. She meant pride, the virtue, not the vice. It had taken over forty years for me to learn the difference.

My therapist was the first to read the diaries I had been afraid to open since I was twelve and fifteen. She drew my attention to the spiritual quest they described and whose early stages I had tried to forget. Through her acceptance I revisited and renamed some of my past. My doctoral work, including this chapter, took shape. When its first draft was complete, I decided to reward myself by going to a poetry reading in the Benedictine Monastery at Arcadia. The poet, whose work I did not yet know, sat very still and straight while his audience leafed through copies of the poems he was about to read; lyrical, crystalline visions of a world connected with God and humanity and shining with meanings. They were distilled from suffering and redemption. I took them with me and read them over and over. At the end of that year, I submitted my thesis on 'Myth and ritual in recovery from anorexia nervosa'. A few months later, I walked into a meeting and the poet was the first person I saw. When we talked it was as if we already knew each other. That Easter week, I went to his apartment for dinner and as I walked down the hallway to his door, the trumpets of a Bach Brandenburg Concerto came to meet me: music I'd heard in my mother's womb. Our first long conversation was about the meaning of the Resurrection.

The poet and I are married. I have altered this autobiographical sketch because different parts of my life have taken on new significance. It could be rewritten in many other ways. My life story has never been simply the story of my recovery from self-starvation, but they are so closely meshed that one cannot be told without the other. It is not a story of illness and cure, but of loss and rediscovery, trauma and healing. In the suffering was the beginning of its resolution. Pain teaches, but it is only when it is over that wisdom comes. Healing leaves scars but it also brings energy and hope. There is no recipe, personal or social, to eliminate suffering. Even recovery stories cannot spell out a method, proffer a single solution or bring about sudden reversals for others. My hope for this story and this book is that their words might lodge deep in some readers' consciousness and slowly become a small part of a greater transformation.

2 Researching recovery

Individual self-clarification occupies a position in a stream of self-clarification, the social source of which is a situation common to the different individuals. (Mannheim 1968: 44)

My thought must already have found what it seeks, otherwise it would not seek it. Unless thought itself had put into things what it subsequently finds in them, it would have no hold upon things, would not think of them, and would be an illusion of thought . . . All thought of something is at the same time self-consciousness, failing which it could have no object. (Merleau-Ponty 1962: 371)

Maybe, in the end, even the lies we tell define us. And better, some of them, than our most earnest attempts to tell the truth. (Malouf 1975: 170)

Introduction

The moving force of my research for this book was desire; mine and that of the people who chose to tell me their stories. Through the research process, we wanted to know and to change ourselves and certain aspects of our society. By telling our stories, exploring the knowledges they contain and putting both story and knowledge into the public sphere, we hoped to make a difference in the world. An eating disorder is itself an extreme form of desire; a spiritual craving expressed through the body.[1] This gives a special poignancy to the questions participants and I considered; theirs, mine and ours. Dealing with questions of research methodology and ethics, this chapter traces the trajectory of our longing – to know and to change – in the activities I've called 'writing down' and 'writing up' (Atkinson 1990). I use these terms to mean, respectively, collecting the 'data' (which included finding participants, formulating the questions, recording taped conversations and field notes) and writing the book (bringing this work together with theory into a coherent analysis). In both activities the imagination is active; noticing, interpreting and synthesizing; so this chapter considers the nature of the authorial imagination and its effects in my research. But although the book's arguments and conclusions are mine, they are never completely so, since they blend ideas from many other people who have experienced anorexia. This chapter, therefore, also examines the role of the other participants in my project: Who are they? How did they come to tell me their stories and in what ways did they tell them? What questions did they answer and ask? How did we influence each other and what kind of truth emerges from our interaction?

The research questions with which I began came from personal experience, but other people's recovery stories have suggested new problems and new solutions. I wrote my particular story to make clear the differences between us and to avoid projecting it, unexamined, onto their separate narratives. At the same time, knowing each other's stories has changed the way we tell our own. The similarities and differences were starting points for the analysis. My personal narrative is not the model against which all the others are measured, nor are our stories simply metaphors for recovery; instead, the trope that shapes them is metonymy: the 'I' in each story (or the 's/he' when I write them in the third person) does not 'stand for' all recovered people; instead, each of our stories makes up and comes from a broader story (or 'myth') – of descent and return – which we share. Since our experiences have been moulded by the society in which we live, our reflections reveal social processes; metonymy does not assume an identity among our various stories, but a relationship.

The relationship between researcher and researched has been of special interest in feminist methodology.[2] The attempt to theorize subjective experience has confronted feminism with the power relations involved when women interview women. Does academic research 'objectify' and 'disempower' women? Are academic women 'exploiting' their sisters or is their common experience as women sufficient to neutralize such dangers? (Oakley 1981; Finch 1984). Can the researcher herself be vulnerable (Walkerdine 1984; Cotterill 1992)? Although I consider each of these questions here (at least implicitly), I do so in relation to both women and men. My interaction with participants was determined more by our common experience of an eating disorder than by our sex (Garrett 1992). At the same time, I could not assume that our eating problems or their resolution had been identical. As with all desire, it was the differences between us that generated the new understandings this book provides.

'Writing it down'

Participants

I wanted to meet as many people as possible who would once have qualified for a psychiatric diagnosis of 'anorexia nervosa' and believed they had now recovered. I was particularly interested in people whose stories spanned several decades of recovery (which I already took to be a lengthy process) and who may not have used the term 'anorexia nervosa' for their behaviour when it was relatively unknown to the general public.[3] One way to reach them was through a newspaper with a wide circulation. I approached Adele Horin, a journalist from *The Sydney Morning Herald*, who wrote a regular column designed to appeal to people over forty; 'My Generation'. She suggested that my personal story would probably attract the most readers. It would also establish that my interest was not only academic. She came to my home and we spoke for several hours. Before publishing her article, Adele read it to me over the telephone. It was accurate, dramatic and sensitive and it explained my purpose exactly (Horin 1991).

Fifty people responded.[4] Some were journalists and publishers interested in my research. Others had questions about anorexic friends and family members or about recovery from other kinds of suffering. Some (like 'Lesley', a doctor) offered to speak to me anonymously because they believed that revealing their past would compromise their present lives. Others (like 'Meredith', a food writer who subsequently told her own recovery story to the press) were inspired by Adele's article to 'come out' publicly (Meredith's words). Some lived too far away for us to meet and a few did not respond to my letters after their initial contact. Of these potential participants, I eventually interviewed thirty. Three of these were men. In addition, three of my friends (Kate, Simone and Miranda) also agreed to participate. Counting myself, the stories of thirty four people were included in my research.

I did not reject anyone who wished to participate and the sample is in no way deliberately representative, since it selected itself. One of the criteria for self-selection was an affinity with my story (as told by Adele Horin). It touched people either because it had parallels with their own stories or because it seemed to hold answers to some of their questions; their desire is therefore inscribed in my text from its very origins. In spite of this, my 'sample' reflected many of the findings of quantitative research on anorexia and recovery. The proportion of men, for example, matched the figure of 6–10 per cent which is usually quoted in statistical studies[5] and the ratios of fully recovered, still affected and still seriously affected people were also remarkably similar to those of clinical recovery studies. These regularities do not necessarily confirm existing studies, however. One of the problems with those studies and with my own is that it has been easier to reach 'middle class' people with tertiary education than people from lower socio-economic groups who may also have suffered from anorexia nervosa. Almost half (16 out of 34) the participants in my study lived on

Sydney's affluent North Shore, including six, unknown to each other, within the same two-kilometer radius. Not all of these originally came from upper middle-class backgrounds (which used to be considered a factor in the onset of anorexia itself), but their current lifestyle may be thought to have an influence on the way in which they interpret their recovery. Unfortunately, even this would be a false assumption since, of these sixteen participants, six were still struggling with anorexia. Their ongoing suffering, rather than their experience of overcoming it, determined their definitions of 'recovery' and this enabled me to show how the concept changes as recovery progresses.

Participants' ages ranged from twenty-six (Lesley) to sixty (Marjorie). Their average age was 37.6. I had made clear that I wanted to meet people with a longer period of recovery in order to gain insights usually only available from longitudinal clinical studies (like Theander 1983). I also tried to attract people who believed they had completely recovered and who had their own definitions of what this meant. Given the 'revolving door syndrome' (the high rate of recidivism for people with eating disorders) I thought that this older population would reveal more accurate patterns than one made up of younger people whose recovery was less established and who might still be measuring it within psychiatric paradigms acquired during treatment programmes. Their educational level was high: thirty had a first tertiary degree; of whom seven had completed, or were engaged in study for, higher degrees (Masters and PhDs) and the remaining three had other forms of professional qualification. Although *Sydney Morning Herald* readership was a factor in this apparently skewed educational level, it also reflects the ubiquitous comments in the literature on anorexia about the intelligence and thirst for educational 'achievement' amongst people who become anorexic (e.g. Lawrence 1987b).

As in the clinical recovery studies, participants' occupations included many of the 'helping professions' (nursing, social work, medicine, physiotherapy, psychotherapy, relationship counselling) but several worked in creative fields (as musicians, writers and artists and in film and radio production), several were teaching (in schools and universities) and several worked in business (advertising, fashion marketing, management consulting) or government bureaucracies. A few (like Rosalie and Miranda) who had young children were having time away from their working careers. One had recently been made redundant from her job and was in crisis about her future directions and identity. Unsurprisingly, given the anorexic obsession with food, several had also worked in 'food related' jobs (like food journalism, catering and hotel management) and a few still do.

I am often asked about the class and ethnicity of these participants. Hoping to meet recovered people from a broader range of socio-economic and cultural backgrounds, I tried to reach newspapers read by a less elite and homogeneous population, but though journalists were willing to help, editors were not. Eating disorders certainly affect people across a wide class spectrum (Beumont 1992). Nurses in eating disorders units of the large public hospitals, for example, have noticed an increase in patient admissions from lower socio-economic areas of Sydney during the last few years, partly because more affluent patients are referred to private clinics. These nurses have also noticed differences in the reasons patients give for their behaviour and in the ways in which they recover,[6] but many questions remain: Are eating disorders increasing amongst social groups where they were previously unknown, or have they merely assumed a character which is more recognizable within current discourses on anorexia? If I had been able to meet 'former anorectics' across a greater social range, would they also have seen their recovery in existential or spiritual terms; or would they attribute anorexia to the pressures of fashion and the media[7] and explain recovery simply as normal maturation? Some of the answers to these questions are in fact present in my data; for although all participants have now become 'middle class', many came from working class or rural backgrounds.

The group's ethnic backgrounds were also similar. All were Caucasian, and of those not born in Australia, only one (Ilse) came from a non-English speaking background, but several were born or had parents born overseas and their life experience reflected this (Susanna's father, for instance, was a Polish holocaust survivor; Zoe's was an Austrian aristocrat). Five were English, one was from New Zealand and two were from the United States, but the resulting differences in their experiences (discussed in the relevant chapters) do not affect my overall arguments. Studies are now available of anorexia in Japan (Takaoka et al. 1990) and among African-American and Latina women in the United States (Thompson 1992, 1994). They demonstrate that poverty, racism, cultural dislocation and homophobia are often responsible for the traumas which generate eating problems. In these studies, self-destructive eating is correctly understood as a logical response to insoluble social problems; often a protection against the source of the trauma itself. I have met a young woman in an Indian slum who refused to eat when confronted with a conflict between her father's Hindu beliefs and her recent conversion to Christianity and I have anecdotal evidence of anorexia among Aboriginal women in Australian cities and country towns; but the majority of those affected in the age group I am considering seem to have been white, middle-class women in western industrialized societies.[8] A comparative study involving a different group of participants might reveal significant differences in the ways people conceptualize their recovery, but I still believe that underlying whatever reasons are given (whether they are drawn from media commentary, peer group or medical discourse) lies a fundamental desire for 'being'. If the people in my study articulated it as clearly as they did, it is because their educational and other opportunities have given them the words to do so and not because their existential or spiritual aspirations were unique.

To return to the issue of desire; these people chose to participate in part for their own benefit; they saw participation as an opportunity to discover, develop and create deeper understanding of their lives, outside a clinical setting; many of them made copious notes, re-read diaries and brought out photographs in the weeks leading up to my visit, looking forward to reassessing 'what it had all been about'. Above all, however, they wanted their stories to be of value to others.[9] In telling them, they hoped to correct some of the misconceptions about anorexia and recovery they had encountered in media reports and among the general public. As a result, the knowledge that emerges from this study, although it is imprinted with my own understanding, was also jointly created. As in most research (even when this is not acknowledged), my questions helped shape participants' answers and their responses altered my perceptions. 'How did I recover?' became 'how did *we* recover?' as participants put the question to me in this very form. The epigraph from Mannheim which heads this chapter refers to a vital part of the sociology of knowledge; 'individual self-clarification'. This is not a selfish desire, but a longing to apprehend the ties between members of a society; ties that exist because of what we already have in common. The 'stream of self-clarification' is the ongoing human quest for understanding. To find its 'common social source' is the goal – the desire – of sociology.

Conversations

Participants first reached me by letter or telephone. These initial contacts were often very moving and raised new issues to add to the research questions I already had. We arranged mutually convenient dates for our conversations. These lasted for about two hours and were tape-recorded, usually in the participant's home; although I met Pip in an outdoor mountain setting, Michael in a café and Aleisha told me her story sitting on the end of my bed. As Lelia Green (1991) points out, the setting of interviews does affect the data: Pip drew her metaphors for growth from the botanical gardens where we spoke and her mother's presence determined some of the content of the interview; Michael took me to a park so that he could take off his shirt and expose his emaciated torso; Aleisha made direct reference to the paintings on my walls to speak of changes in herself. Partners, parents, or children were sometimes in the house and a variety of domestic dramas had to be negotiated before or during our conversations. All of these form part of the fabric of the research.

When we met, participants often launched straight into their story or asked 'where do you want me to start?' I mentioned two of the three areas that interested me: their story and how they would now define 'recovery'. I only later introduced the third area, spirituality, if they did not refer to it themselves. Most gave at least some background description of how their eating problems began. I simply requested that they concentrate on how they 'got better'. I questioned them about the length of the recovery period and its stages and turning points. If they said they had not yet recovered, I asked whether they believed that recovery was possible and how they would know when they were there. I asked why they needed, and why they no longer need, their 'eating disorder'; whether they had treatment, what it was like and about its effects and what had most strongly influenced their recovery.[10]

We often discussed the (ethical) problems of objectification, disempowerment and exploitation that can occur in this kind of research. Some of these were already reduced by the fact that, having read 'my story', these people already knew a lot about me before they chose to participate. Several were eager to read what I had written about them and offered comments which were then incorporated into my writing. This acted as a corrective to any potential megalomania on my part. I have not made any claims with which participants would strongly disagree, but nor did they accept all of my interpretations. The ethical point here is that participants do not consider themselves to have been 'used' for the researcher's purposes (Watson & Mears 1991). Instead, they too feel that they have gained from the research process and had some measure of power within it. Ann Oakley (1981) and Janet Finch (1984) have written of the special difficulties which arise in feminist research because the model assumed in these interactions is often that of friendship. They worry that participants may feel betrayed by the lack of follow-up. I tried to minimize this problem by raising it with participants and remaining in touch with them by letter during the two years of data collection and writing up. With several participants a closer ongoing relationship has developed, initiated by them and based on mutual interests other than the research.

A different ethical question is whether I may be usurping the participants' stories by telling them in my own way, even when I use their words; assimilating their personal accounts to my own experience or my own theories. This can happen either during the conversation or in its 'writing up' and I will give examples of each of these situations. In the first example, my interaction with Miranda illustrates how my own concerns might at first appear to be swallowing hers. When we recorded our first conversation about her recovery, she did not see her bulimia as having had any spiritual meaning. She was emphatic about this, although apologetic about not fitting in with my developing argument (about which she had enquired). Her apology was unnecessary, since the 'spiritual' link could have been unconscious anyway. A year later, however, she told me that her point of view had shifted considerably. She had been engaged in what she named a spiritual search for several years, but had never connected this search with her bulimia. Now, she said, she had made that connection. This change took place, she stressed, not as a result of my persuasive powers, but because of other opportunities for self-reflection in her life since then. If the researcher is a catalyst in the lives of the researched, the elements of the reaction must have been present before the catalyst could take effect. Those elements, as my interpretation of Mannheim makes clear, are made up of our common life experiences and our common social location; Miranda and I have several similar major life events and acquaintances in common and read many of the same books and it is not surprising that we should independently reach similar conclusions. With Miranda, the intervention which might be considered methodologically problematic[11] occurred in our initial *conversation*. She had no criticisms of the way in which I *wrote* about her story, and was delighted with the place it occupies in this book. In contrast, Naomi's challenge to my reconstruction of her story came after I had written it which is why I will discuss it under the heading of 'writing it up', below.

What kind of knowledge comes out of this way of proceeding? Was I, as can happen to biographers, being 'seduced by the interviewees'? Introjecting their desire? Projecting mine onto them?[12] Were participants, in a sense, inventing the stories they wanted to tell or, worse still, the stories I wanted to hear? Most participants were well aware of these possibilities. As Kate said, almost as an aside; 'Maybe I'm lying, but –'. Kate was referring to the possibility that the perspective she gave me today might not be the same one she would offer tomorrow; that she might decide her first interpretation had been wrong. Participants' stories, including events and explanations, are constructions about the past made in the light of the present but, as I have already shown, not only the time but also the place, my presence and a host of other circumstances affected the responses of participants. It is Kate's 'but' which is most significant here; it refers to the inevitably incomplete, particular, circumstantial nature of qualitative material. This is, in fact, the strength of such material. In my analysis of what participants tell me, I can take account of some of the details which surround it to demonstrate how knowledge is constantly being created and recreated. One such detail here is the fact that, at the time of the conversation, Kate and I had been friends for five years and had many discussions about our very different interpretations of the anorexic experience; shifting her thinking and mine. To pretend that this did not affect our interaction in the research would be to obscure an important dimension of my arguments about recovery itself; the sense in which its meaning is not only re-created, but also co-created.

Autobiography has been described as a form of anxiety or melancholia (Woodward 1988: 105–9), but our reciprocal storytelling was about discovery, not loss; which is why I place it firmly under the sign of desire. What was taking place in our exchange was something akin to psychoanalytic transference. For Freud, transference and countertransference were the mainspring of the joint work of analysis. In the research process, it is only through this mutual desire that communication and the joint creation of meaning become possible. If autobiography is a dialogue with the self, itself motivated by desire for greater self knowledge; when the dialogue is with someone else, this desire is also projected onto the other. I found these people's lives fascinating for what they reveal about recovery and most of them were in turn fascinated with mine. Each of us asked the other: 'How did you recover? What do you think recovery really means? What can we learn from each other?'. While they sometimes felt challenged by my questions, like: 'How would you feel if you put on another stone [stones were the measure most of us used when we were anorexic]?', they faced me with equal challenges, like: 'Why are you still thin? How did you climb out of this prison? What's the story of your life?' and the answers were important to us both.

The way participants perceived me was also an essential part of the research, determining what they chose to tell and to hide. Many of them alluded to this, mentioning their identification with me, their approval of my appearance or my manner with them as keys which unlocked intimate disclosures. Joanne told me she had really enjoyed our conversation 'because you let people be who they are'. Freda, who did not believe she would ever stop binge eating or return to a comfortable weight, asked 'how did you do it?' She thought I had 'turned out quite nicely' and said 'You don't look emaciated at all!'. Jodie, well into recovery, said she had never talked to anybody else who had been anorexic and was unsure whether her own recovery story would be helpful to anyone else. She said: 'They might look at me and think "I don't want to be like her", because I'm not thin – I'm overweight, from an anorectic's point of view'. She went on: 'You're not. You opened the door and I thought: "she's thin" – I mean amongst other things.' After a moment she added: 'Do you think some people might think you hadn't recovered?'

As Jodie so candidly indicates, the very bodies of researchers and participants always affect the communication which takes place in face to face interviews. In research on eating disorders, mutual physical appraisals are particularly important. It would be too simple to say that recovered participants accepted a wide range of body types while those still anorexic or recovering did not. When 'unrecovered' 'large' participants met me, they were more likely to trust me because I 'look recovered' (Freda) than to be suspicious because I 'look too thin'. When they were still seriously underweight, they were as likely to be reassured by my small size that recovery does not necessitate great weight gains as they were to be alarmed if I was larger than they were. The two most dramatic physical responses to our interaction came from the two thinnest participants. Michael said goodbye with a spontaneous hug which surprised even him, while Jacqueline took up a position as far away from me as possible on her long sofa, saying 'Until recently, I would not have felt comfortable sitting so close to someone'. For her, this was a measure of how far she had already come. Although it is impossible to draw out common patterns of physical response, each different response indicated something important about that person's recovery.

The relationship between us often became a topic of conversation. Zoe, for instance, asked me 'Do you think I'm intense?' and I had to say she was, in a way which complemented my own intensity and made our communication flow more freely. Zoe unconsciously acknowledged this in her reply, saying: 'I wouldn't recognize *your* intensity, because I appreciate so much the opportunity to speak to you on whatever level. To me that's what I see in a person; the lack of barriers.' Emotions also entered the research process on both sides when our ideas clashed. Since I did not approach participants as a neutral observer (blank screen or mirror), there were moments when we disagreed quite strongly about the nature of recovery. A section of my conversation with Lauren provides an illustration. Lauren did not think she had fully recovered, but she had recently put on a lot of weight in a short period and was very distressed. She considered herself overweight, although she acknowledged that she was in the 'upper range of normal' on insurance company charts for women of her height. When I pointed out that this is still not 'overweight', her voice began to rise:

LAUREN: Of course normal is overweight! Well, normal in Australia is overweight.
CATHERINE: By whose standards?
LAUREN: Most people's standards!

CATHERINE (only hearing the irrationality, instead of the emotional truth of Lauren's statement, voice also rising): That's ridiculous!
LAUREN: But that's the culture we live in!
CATHERINE: Yes, but it doesn't mean that we have to subscribe to its values!
LAUREN: No, if you are strong enough not to be influenced by other people, which I'm not!!

On her own premises, Lauren was correct. One of the reasons recovery is made so difficult for her is that putting on weight does not attract social approval. In this part of the conversation, by suggesting that we need to place ourselves outside the norm in order to recover, I was not being sufficiently sensitive to Lauren's predicament, even though participants who had fully recovered made precisely this point ('You've got to step outside the social norms', said Vivienne). I am not defending my unconsidered response to Lauren, made in the heat of the moment, but the differences it uncovered did provide me with another important understanding of recovery. I was subsequently able to trace a pattern of 'Lauren-like' and 'Vivienne-like' responses which correspond to 'not recovered' and 'recovered' stances. Without the strong emotions generated on both sides, I may not have acquired this insight. Because our interaction was understood as an argument between equals rather than between patient and therapist, or with a dispassionate, objective interviewer, it was possible for each of us to state our own positions quite strongly and be forced to reconsider them.

It was, in any case, impossible to leave out the personal element in situations where participants were eager to make comparisons between their recovery and mine. They frequently asked for details of my life and my way of carrying out the research, for example:

Do you find it painful sitting and talking to people about this? Is it too close to home? Do you worry about your daughter and anorexia? (Jodie) You don't ever get big, do you? Do you think it might be fairly hereditary anyway? (Victoria) Oh dear! you need [me to agree with] this for your thesis, don't you? (Miranda)

Being involved in my research helped them in formulating their own theories. Naomi (long recovered from her problems with food, but still coping with memories of sexual abuse) explained that talking to me was 'consolidation'. 'After all', she said, 'I'm only just getting up courage to talk about this stuff to my best friend! But it's getting all tangled up, whereas when I first rang you it was relatively neat, this stuff I'm resolving, and all my theories have gone by the board. I'll have to work out some more!' Lesley (who saw herself at the beginning of recovery) said it was helpful to put into words feelings she had bottled up for a long time and to order her thoughts into a concrete framework; it gave her a valuable measure of her own recovery. Rosalie told me she had no remaining interest in something that had been resolved so long ago, but she did want other people to know you could recover. Only Freda, who had written me a detailed letter about her life, could not say why she had done so and denied that our conversation would have any effect on her at all. The active choice to participate, whatever its motives, was still a force of desire behind their contributions and the reason for the emotional power of their self-revelation. This increased my responsibility as the bearer of their stories.

'Writing it up'

'Writing up' included two interwoven processes, analysis and shaping into text, which I now discuss in an appropriately overlapping fashion. Analysis of these conversations involved note-making, transcribing, coding and grouping. After each conversation, often as I sat in my car, I made notes about my strongest impressions of the experience, especially its non-verbal aspects which would not be available to me when I listened to the taped versions. These notes also included preliminary links with other interviews, with my reading and with my developing ideas. I transcribed all the conversations myself, usually within a week of the interview. This allowed me to 'see' as well as hear them. I then spent two weeks coding extracts from the transcriptions into approximately fifty computer files.[13] These included codes arising from my original questions (like Recovery, Spirituality, Body, Relationships, Stages and Turning points), from additional recurring themes in the data (like Travel, Achievement, Control, Identity), from existing theories about anorexia and recovery (like Mourning, Metaphors, Ritual) and from methodological concerns (Methodology, Immediacy, Catherine). Some were dozens of pages long, others contained only a few chunks of text. I played with the connections within and among them, looking for similarities and differences, gaps, contradictions and clichés.[14] Another way I made sense of the data was by arranging the contents of each code file into three groups, according to how participants chose to define themselves: not recovered, recovering and recovered. I usually agreed with the self-classification of people in the first and last groups, but not always with that of participants in the middle group. Some of those who regarded themselves as 'recovering' seemed to me as 'recovered' as members of the third group, while others seemed more like those in the first. As I wrote, however, I understood why they had positioned themselves as they had. Since the labels they chose reflected their subjective experience, they indicated recovery more accurately than my external impressions.

This analysis rarely felt 'merely' mechanical because the imagination was constantly sifting and rearranging the data; generating patterns, questions and insights. The three vital elements of this process were time, the computer and the unconscious. Time was essential for the gestation of ideas. The period between transcription and analysis (almost a year, during which I was engaged in teaching and other research projects) allowed me to think about what I had learned and how I might use it. Most of this thinking took place in the interstices of daily life; in the shower, driving to work, listening to music, gardening, reading apparently unrelated texts and talking to other people. Time was a gift to the unconscious, the ultimate organizer in the research process; that which the computer does not possess. The computer, however, was essential. As super-brain it was the ultimate back-up system; holding in concrete form most of the ideas I hoped were also in my head and enabling me to set out on the screen the connections and the contrasts I needed to make. As super-scissors and super-paste it made it possible to juggle ideas and evidence. Finally, as super-pen, the computer gave me new writing confidence, knowing that I could change or erase ideas *ad infinitum*. The computer has been far more than a tool of my intellect. It has provided me with metaphors for the way my mind works, including the way files may be lost and retrieved, or sometimes vanish forever.

But (to return to another dimension of a problem I've already mentioned) was my writing itself usurping participants' stories? This question arose when Naomi read my first draft of 'her' story and wrote me a long letter in reply. Some of the changes I had made she did not consider important (like locations, usually deliberately altered to conceal her identity), but others (like my inadvertent rearrangement of her life's chronology) obscured essential patterns which she patiently explained to me. I made the necessary modifications until we were both satisfied – and learned a great deal in the process. Her final comment was the most interesting in her letter. She wrote: 'I was a bit overwhelmed. This all sounds a bit too elegant as a description of me!! I tend to see what I'm doing as me stumbling along, keeping myself together most of the time and occasionally not managing it'. To Naomi, my account of her rituals of self-transformation seems too neat because she is still in their midst.[15] Nevertheless, my perspective on her life, whether or not she fully accepts it, is one facet of its truth and the best I can give her.

Although methodology textbooks rarely discuss the place of writing in research, it is really the primary site (even more than conversations) for the creation of new understandings. It is in writing that I have been able to link autobiography, biography and theory; in writing that I have decided what will and will not be significant; in writing that I have connected ideas to make arguments. I have alluded to the way writing comes from my body, from spaces in time and from communion with the computer as much as it does from conversations, reading and logical analysis. I can now give a more complete description of the authorial imagination which I mentioned in the introduction to this chapter. The sociological imagination is not only a personal imagination. It also depends on the unconscious and the ways it has been shaped by the culture of authors and research participants. If the unconscious is the site of repressed elements in personal life, it is equally the site of repressed social experience. It erupts in sociological as much as any other texts. In acknowledging its eruption, I am not only recognizing the personal sources of writing itself, but also its social origins.

3   Autobiography, narrative and healing

> We have, each of us, a life-story, an inner narrative – whose
> continuity, whose sense, *is* our lives. It might be said that each of us
> constructs and lives a 'narrative', and that this narrative *is* us, our
> identities.
> (Sacks 1985: 105)

> Sociology's truths are not found but imaginatively fabricated with
> specific tools . . . While the facts of scientists and the fictions of
> novelists are created under significantly different disciplinary
> constraints, both try to simulate and tell truths about a world to
> which neither has unmediated access. Academic knowledge's
> commitment to truth is not belittled by my claim that it necessarily
> relies on storytelling.
> (Game and Metcalfe 1996: 63–6)

> The recurrent effect of narrative on physiology, and of pathology on
> story, is the source of the shape and weight of lived experience.
> (Kleinman 1988: 55)

Introduction

Sociologists using personal narrative are sometimes criticized by their
peers for being self-centred and apolitical in a world which cries out for
new stories about broad social events and social relations. In this chapter, I
explain my use of autobiography and of narrative more generally. Since
both autobiography and sociology are unavoidably narrative in form, both
kinds of writing can be made the subject of analysis and doing so results in
richer sociological texts and understandings. This approach is not without
its dangers, including the slipperiness of memory and the political nature
of writing itself, both of which I address. But narrative is so powerful that
not only is it the tool for revealing ourselves to ourselves as social beings
(sociology), but it is also able to effect healing (recovery). This chapter
describes how the healing power of narrative derives from its 'sacredness'
and why stories of recovery are therefore inevitably 'spiritual' stories.

Autobiography and sociology

First, a warning about my use of the word autobiography. There are obvious differences between my story and the stories I have made from my conversations with others: it is longer than theirs, it was written whereas theirs were originally spoken, I began by answering my own questions whereas they were answering mine (though I have ended up addressing some of theirs too) and I have had the final say in the construction of my own story whereas they have allowed me to shape theirs. But more important similarities justify my use of the term 'autobiography' to describe all first-person accounts in this book, including those I've deliberately rendered in the third person to signal my part in their construction. As the previous chapter explained, each was a co-creation, an attempt at self-clarification and an effort (from experiential perspectives) to supply omissions and correct misinterpretations and misrepresentations in public discourses on anorexia and recovery.

What difference does the inclusion of my personal story make to a sociological understanding of recovery? Does it, for example, make my theories more believable? Anthropologists have long asked similar questions about their fieldwork. Once, their overt presence in their writing used to be a way of showing that they had 'been there' and had really witnessed the strangeness of the other cultures they described; 'being there', using 'I' and including emotion in an academic text lent credibility to their assertions and theories. Today, anthropologists are more analytical of their own authorial position (Bruner and Turner 1986; Clifford and Marcus 1986; Geertz 1988). Sociologists, on the other hand, although they cannot avoid translating personal observations into theory either, and although many of them also believe that 'participant observation' and 'ethnographic methods' make their messages more authoritative, have usually been primarily concerned with the ethical aspect of these methods; the problem of 'using' others in gathering their data. They have rarely looked at the place they and their informants occupy in the stories through which they present their arguments.[1]

Among sociologists and other academic writers, feminists in particular have defended the inclusion of subjectivity as a focus of research; arguing that all knowledge is already 'biased' by the knower's standpoint (Harding, 1986: 191)[2] but that this is more of an advantage than a problem, since stories of personal experience can be deconstructed to reveal social influences in our lives (Haug 1985, 1987; Crawford et al., 1992; Lupton 1996).[3] Subjectivity has therefore been claimed as a strength, not a weakness, of feminist scholarship. These influences from feminism and anthropology increasingly compel sociologists to do more than simply reveal the *sources* of their information (leaving readers to decide how much to believe); in addition, sociologists must now examine the links between personal and social in their own *writing*. To answer my original question: the fact that I have 'been anorexic' and have 'recovered' is not an automatic guarantee that what I have to say is believable or even useful. It is not just 'having been there' which gives authority to a sociological analysis, nor does having studied an academic discipline make for 'expert' accounts. Rather, it is the combination of personal experience, attention to the experience of others, consideration of social theory and a critical appraisal of them all in the light of each other which give readers the broadest information from which to make up their own minds. Subjectivity is a valuable aspect of research when its own part in the story is analysed like any other part.

But why use autobiographical data to understand *society* (the social sources of recovery, for instance)? Autobiography has been hailed as an essential ingredient in the modern sensibility, that is, the concern with how we become individuals with separate, yet socially formed, identities (Giddens 1991); but the use of autobiographical data to understand social processes also has a venerable history, Vico's 1744 Autobiography (1963) being one of the earliest examples. Most recently, however, postmodernism has thrown all these issues into question by asking whether there is any such thing as an authentic, unitary self (Lacan), or even an authorial voice (Foucault, Barthes). At its extremes, the postmodern stance leads to nihilism. If there is no self, no author and no 'society', but only competing discourses, why bother with the process I'm using in this book; writing about a personal and intellectual journey of discovery and giving voice to the similar journeys of others? Despite postmodern anxieties, there are good reasons for autobiography and good reasons to use it in sociological writing.[4]

First, autobiography is one of the strategies human beings have developed to make life matter; to ratify the form one has given to one's life and to create its *meaning* (Mandel 1980: 64). The writing of journals, for example, is often a way of making meaning out of the complexity of daily experience, as it has been for many of the participants in my study, who read or lent me accounts of anorexia and recovery they had produced at each of these stages in an attempt to organize their thinking. These autobiographies are not simply descriptive; they are frequently the place where ideas are refined and theory begins to be created (Olney 1966: 26). Even as participants told me the stories of their lives, they were explaining them; theorizing *in situ*. The development of theory (another strategy to make life matter) has therefore always relied on autobiographical material. Nietzsche once stated that 'every great philosophy has been the confession of its maker, as it were his involuntary and unconscious autobiography' (Olney 1980: 3). Sartre's existential philosophy, for example, tells us a great deal about Sartre, and Freud used his own experience and that of his patients to develop the great theoretical 'myth' (Kirsner 1995) of psychoanalysis.[5]

Secondly, autobiography can demonstrate links between individuals and culture which are at the very heart of sociological concerns. It does this best when the experiential and the critical voices in the writing are used to reflect upon each other, without giving priority to either. For example; the form of my first chapter (a spiritual autobiography) already reveals the influence of a Christian upbringing on my thought and writing. Its content describes both negative and positive effects of particular forms of Christianity in my life. In the more theoretical chapters, it is also my voice that critically explores the meaning of spiritual phenomena in my own and other stories of anorexia and recovery. To give another example; Vivienne told me her story in a framework of ideas shaped by her encounters with Buddhism, the writings of Carl Jung and her membership of Alcoholics Anonymous; but she accompanied her narrative with a critical evaluation of these philosophies. The publication of experiential material and its creators' reflections upon it also invites readers to participate in their own construction and critique of social theory. It can be an attempt 'to pry open the process of subject formation, to rehearse it with the reader' (Sommer 1988: 109). In Vivienne's story, for instance, readers are able to trace the social influences in what she says and reach their own conclusions which may be different from mine.

Thirdly, the form as much as the content of personal narrative is an invaluable source for understanding the connection between individual lives and their social context. 'The truth of the life is not different in kind from the truth of the work' so that there can be classical, baroque, romantic, decadent, and existential lifestyles, each, presumably, linked with a particular historical and cultural consciousness (Gusdorf 1980: 47).[6] The majority of participants gave me spiritual autobiographies, whereas thirty years ago their narratives might instead have taken an existential form.[7] Autobiographical data are therefore especially relevant to the theme of this book because participants' stories offer insights into the social construction of spirituality in the late twentieth century and enable comparisons to be made with earlier historical periods. They provide evidence for the existence, processes and importance of 'spirituality' in a world that is supposed to be increasingly secular (P. Berger 1969; B. Turner 1983).[8] They are part of a long tradition of spiritual autobiography, going back to Saint Augustine's *Confessions*, which has been largely neglected in social theory.[9]

The 'spiritual autobiography' is important to sociology because it reveals the way in which people come to know themselves in relation to an imagined (social) ideal and the way they attempt to change themselves in the directions suggested by this ideal. The task of autobiography is, of course, first of all 'a task of personal salvation': It is a matter of concluding a peace treaty and a new alliance with oneself; but it also includes making a new alliance with the world. 'In becoming conscious of the past, one alters the present' (Gusdorf 1980: 47) and I am optimistic that such alterations go beyond the personal and make some difference to the world as well. For example, one person's recovery story is often the catalyst for the creation of another's because it makes visible the process of re-storying and the ideal towards which the story is directed. Alcoholics Anonymous, Al Anon and Eating Disorders Anonymous certainly work on this principle, with considerable success (Turnbull 1997). Spiritual autobiography is also important because it includes moments of 'confession': the admission of one's past errors seems to be necessary in order to move forward into the ideal future.[10] The stories in this book, however, do not speak of guilt. Instead, they recognize eating problems as painful but necessary steps towards a fuller life. Eating disorders are like the 'dark night of the soul' that often precedes a spiritual awakening. Sociology itself is a form of 'recovery' story; using the data of social experience to create new frameworks for understanding and for living. Even sociology relies on the confession of its own inadequacies to allow its theoreticians to make fresh starts. In being explicit about the autobiographical component of my text and its spiritual nature, I am highlighting the subtext of most forms of writing to examine what is usually unacknowledged: the sacred dimension of narrative which I discuss below.

The dangers of autobiography

Using autobiographical data, however, is not without dangers. Writers often become Godlike figures; creating reality in their own image.[11] One answer to this problem can be drawn from Durkheim's (1976) account of religion in society and a better one, I think, from Kovel (1991) (both thinkers are further discussed in chapter 7). Durkheim argued that what is sacred (another sense of Godlike) is only sacred because a society makes it so; for him, society is religion and religion is society. Following this line of argument, writers become messengers of the Divine to the extent that they apprehend, transmit and change social reality. There is a lurking relativism and a circularity to this argument in which nothing seems to exist outside the social. For Kovel, however, 'ego' in the writer (as in all humans) diminishes in proportion to the growth of 'soul'; and spirit exists beyond the social. From this perspective, texts are truthful to the extent that 'spirit' speaks through them to reveal and transform society.

Another danger of autobiography is that it may always include errors of fact, especially given the unreliability of memory which I am about to discuss. What, then, is the truth value of personal narrative? Autobiography is the attempt to elucidate the present, not the past, and this makes it particularly suitable as a vehicle for understanding recovery, since recovery concerns the present (and future) life of the subject. The facts of each person's life are less important than the way that person selects certain facts over others and interprets them in constructing his or her story. As well, some of these facts have been modified in my retelling to protect participants' privacy. This book is concerned with the truth being produced through narrative. Its autobiographies offer an imaginative truth as valid as the truth of literature; a poetic, if not an empirical truth (though much of the book is 'factual' too because the events in it really did take place).[12]

The 'truth' of autobiography is also safeguarded, to some extent, by a series of 'autobiographical pacts'; with participants, readers and oneself. My pact with the participants in my research was to put forward a truth they would recognize, even if the details have been changed and their reframing creates a distancing effect for them as readers. In return, they would tell me their truth as they understood it at the time. In its pact with the reader, too, autobiography promises intimate revelation and sincerity (writers engage to deliver personal insights and readers to accept them in the spirit in which they are given). It offers the kind of 'truth' which is embodied when the reader 'seeks confirmation of his or her own perceptions of reality in terms of those experienced by another mortal' (Mandel 1980: 55). This book invites readers to compare their own experiences of self-transformation with the stories it offers about recovery from anorexia and to discover the truths they all share. My pact with myself has been to examine my own life with at least as much rigour as those of participants and with the same hope; to acknowledge as much of the past as possible so that it might not unconsciously distort the present. To summarize: just as I've accepted as true the stories people told me for this book and they've taken my story in the same spirit, so you the reader are invited to share the account of recovery which I elaborate from theirs and mine. In short, the knowledge I am producing here is an imaginative knowledge. It is also provisional, subject to change through reading as much as through writing, and inevitably coloured by memory. I now address each of these issues (the mobility of the text and the problem of memory) in turn.

The politics of writing

'Political' also means 'mobile', subject to change, open to possibility, open to other powers of meaning. Every text is subject to political interpretations and each autobiography and its accompanying explanation can be written in such a way as to foreclose particular readings (Cottom 1989: 10, 21). For example, this book could be written within a poststructuralist framework which argued that the self is always irretrievably split, that spirit is a creation of discourse and that recovery is the illusion of a 'unified' self produced through narrative; in other words, that recovery is purely an effect of language. This would foreclose a commonsense reading of participants' stories that suggests people do have a 'self', that spirit is a real, material force in their lives and that recovery comes through bodily action as much as through thought. It would make recovery an effect of false consciousness. To solve this dilemma, I have tried to leave open a variety of readings, commonsense and theoretical, using them to question each other and so reveal new possibilities.

This book is also political because it creates a medium of resistance and counterdiscourse to the hegemony of clinical psychiatry and psychology. Autobiography is 'the legitimate space for producing that excess which throws doubt on the coherence and power' (Sommer 1988: 111) of dominant stories about recovery. Several people joined my study because they wanted their own, very different, accounts of eating disorders and recovery to challenge those of the 'professionals' whose words have shaped public understanding. It is this political purpose which gives my project its authority for, as Carolyn Heilbrun has said of women's autobiographies: 'power is the ability to take one's place in whatever discourse is essential to action and the right to have one's part matter' (1988: 18).

Memory

From the perspective of a 'scientific' psychology, my use of people's stories has little value because all the memories I recount (including my own) are 'contaminated' by our subsequent experience,[13] including encounters with each other's stories and sometimes with the discourses of psychotherapy and counselling (either directly, or indirectly through books and articles on our 'condition'). But the present *inevitably* 'contaminates' the past, for it is only possible to speak about the past from the present. Without memory, experience would have no coherence at all. As St Augustine observed, consciousness presupposes memory; it 'anticipates and attends and remembers, so that what it anticipates passes through what it attends into what it remembers' (translated in Crites 1989: 73). Recovery itself is a process of contamination. For recovery to take place, the meaning of an eating disorder *must* be 'contaminated' by new ideas and experiences.

My study has been called retrospective in contrast with the prospective studies which I'm told are more reliable; but recovery, like autobiography, cannot be properly understood *except* in hindsight. A prospective study might take a group of people in the throes of an eating disorder and record their gradual emergence (or continuing problems). This has been done, for example, by Bruch and Palazzoli (see chapter 6) who worked from notes charting the changes in their patients across months and years of conversations and in a Swedish longitudinal study (Theander 1983) combining interviews and questionnaires. There is nothing particularly 'pure' about these accounts. Like mine, they rely on careful selection of what clinicians considered to be the important features of the recovery process and they, too, show the effects of the therapist's ideas on the patient's. There is nothing 'complete' about them either, since their authors' recovered patients were reinterpreting their own experience even as their therapists or research assistants tried to set it down in writing. Like life and like a work of art, recovery is not properly over until you die, because it is always subject to reinterpretation.

Three theories can be used to explain what was happening when participants spoke of recovery as 're-discovering' something they had lost – a kind of remembering. First, they may have experienced a 'return of the repressed' (of an unconscious or semi-conscious memory). Second, they could have been superimposing present beliefs and experiences upon the past. A psychoanalytic perspective might suggest the former and a social constructionist view the latter. I favour a third position, similar to that of 'memory work' (Haug 1985, 1987; Kippax et al. 1988; Crawford et al. 1992) which includes the other two possibilities. These authors stress that 'each memory refers to some real event in time, but the memory is a construction of that event ... which changes with reflection and over time'. It is the construction they are interested in, not the event, because the construction relates to the social; 'the *meaning* of the episode for each individual is what is crucial' (Crawford et al. 1992: 8, my italics). Understanding this meaning helps us understand the context that shaped it.

The experience of 'spiritual reconnection' which I describe and analyse in this book is the return of a repressed memory, even if it is coloured with desire in the present and nostalgia for the past. It is socially constructed, in the sense that it can only become available in a present which offers a spiritual language of some sort within which it can be articulated. Of course the language used changes the perception of the earlier experience, but this does not mean that the experience never took place; only that it has become available in a different form in the present. The stories through which people tell of their recovery are healing to themselves and potentially healing to others. They draw upon the great myths through which humans make sense of things they can never fully know. One of these is the miracle of healing.

Narrative and healing

There is already a story of recovery in the viscera, muscles, nerves and brains of those who have recovered; the stories these people articulate about recovery are superimposed on the image-stream of the original chronicle. My role has been to look for the common narrative underlying each of those I've been told. I measure the extent of my success by the chords these stories and my master narrative about them strike in my readers and listeners. 'My' stories seem to resonate with the memory of my audience; the deeper story embedded in their own bodies; a sacred story they too experience as if it had been rediscovered. By 'sacred' I mean 'other', apart and therefore to some degree always unknown, yet at the same time able to be represented by a potentially inexhaustible number of metaphors.

This book provides, as well as extracts from people's narratives, several of their stories in narrative form. The stories are indeed artfully constructed, but not in an arbitrary or misleading way. They are here to reveal some of the deeper narrative patterns (like the quest motif, the theme of descent and return) on which participants' accounts of their recovery are founded. The form of the narrative is crucial to recovery itself; for it seems that the more coherent the recovery story, the more likely it is that recovery has actually taken place. The stories are also here because only narrative can contain the past, the present and the future, which is why our very experience is understood in our storytelling. Narrative is so powerful that without our own life stories, we lose our sense of self.[14] This is because memory takes the form of a chronicle, linking past, present and future into a continuous whole. But memory is an ongoing chronicle; its content is constantly being revised in relation to events and perceptions in the present. My use of personal narratives in this book confirms both the form of human experience and its ongoing/never fully resolved or understoood nature. This lack of explanatory closure is both deliberate and inevitable. Participants often stressed that recovery and its interpretation are continuing processes. Finally, I've included stories because they reveal to people the kind of drama in which they are engaged and perhaps its larger meaning (Crites 1989: 81); they offer those who read them a variety of models for the creation of their own stories.

Narrative is also the main tool of sociology and the particular power of sociology comes from its association with sacred narratives (Game and Metcalfe 1996). The 'myths' of sociology draw on authorless stories so deeply embedded in the consciousness of a society that they can only be told indirectly. They convey the deeper story of human reality; of our connections with each other, with our environment and with our unconscious selves. These deeper stories live in our bodies, which is why we respond to the rhythm of narratives that ring true for us and why they are often mimed in acting and dance. Sociology takes the form of a quest, as at least one of its introductory texts makes clear (Willis 1995). The quest is to understand the (social) world we live in and to find and tell stories about our human connections; stories which (like personal narratives) are continually being remade. The quest is also sacred and all narratives are, in some senses, spiritual creations.

Within each society, people's experience is structured by symbolic forms; the linguistic, visual and performative ways each culture uses to represent reality. Of all these symbolic systems, prevailing narrative forms are among the most important. Each society, in its different historical periods, gives rise to certain 'master narratives' which determine people's perceptions of reality. Master narratives about self-starvation are a good example. Joan Brumberg's (1988) history of 'prodigious fasting' shows how, in different contexts, fasting girls and those who observed them selected their interpretation of this behaviour from a pool of culturally and historically specific meanings. In medieval Europe, the dominant narratives were Christian and many of these fasting women were 'saints'. By the end of the nineteenth century, the dominant narrative about the body was medical and the same behaviour was understood as illness. As we approach the twenty-first century, other stories are becoming available. Some of these (concerning the 'New Age', 'therapy' and the 'recovery' movement, critically explored later in the book) will perhaps provide different story-lines which enable the anorexic quest to end in discovery and recovery.

Narratives have the power to heal. In *The Illness Narratives* (1988), Arthur Kleinman begins to make the case for the healing power of stories. He starts from the premise that 'witnessing and ordering the experience of illness can be of therapeutic value'. The ordering inevitably takes place through the stories each culture constructs about illness; stories which ascribe cultural meanings to various forms of suffering. Through stories and their accompanying practices, 'cultural symbols provide both the theoretical framework of myth and the established script for ritual behaviour that transform an individual's affliction into a sanctioned symbolic form for the group' (Kleinman 1988: 26). The suffering we call anorexia has certainly been incorporated into a variety of stories across the centuries (Brumberg 1988) which have often given it a religious or miraculous rationale; but these 'group sanctioned' stories have not included recovery as the usual dénouement. The narratives in Kleinman's book are about *chronic* illness and how to cope with it by transforming its meaning when there is no other way out; but there *are* ways out of anorexia and they include reshaping stories about it; both on the individual and the social level.

Some therapists have incorporated 're-storying' into their practice and called it narrative therapy. The framework for narrative therapy comes from post-structuralist ideas about the power of the text. 'Meaning', write Epston and White (1989), 'is derived through the structuring of experience into stories, and it is the performance of these stories that is constitutive of lives and relationships.' The problems which require therapy occur 'when the narratives in which [people] are storying their experience, and/or in which they are having their experience storied by others, do not sufficiently represent their lived experience'. One of the dominant narratives about humanity in twentieth-century western culture is told through medical (including psychiatric) discourse; the story that turns the 'unusual' into the 'sick'; changing spiritual pain into psychological misfunction. For Epston and White, restorying is a form of resistance to these dominant narratives. They see recovery as reclaiming a life lost to the 'problem' of anorexia. One of their solutions is to install in the person's narrative a device which can turn it towards a problem-free future. In one example, they do this through a letter:

> Dear Molly,
> Anorexia nervosa had claimed 99% of your life. You only held 1% of your own territory. You have said that you now hold 25% of your own territory. This means that you have reclaimed 24% of yourself from anorexia nervosa, and you achieved this over the last eight months. And yet, you despair for all those lost years, for the two-thirds of your life under its influence.
>
> Tell me, if you were to pick up another 24% over the next eight months, and then 24% over the next eight months and so on, how long would it take you to reach 200% and be experiencing double value in your life? (Epston and White, 1989:77)

Here the metaphor of regained territory is inserted into a personal narrative to encourage its forward movement. We meet 'Molly' when she is at least a quarter of her way to recovery. There must have been an earlier intervention into her story, perhaps reifying and externalizing 'anorexia' to separate it from Molly's identity; which is another way these therapists work. Techniques such as these are increasingly popular in counselling and therapy.

Meanwhile, 'recovery stories' have become a well-established genre in publishing and journalism.[15] They form part of the 'recovery' movement associated with the New Age, popular psychology and therapy.[16] The 'recovery' shelves of bookshops are overflowing with autobiographical accounts of eating disorders and new versions appear every year. They almost all deal with only half the narrative – descent and crisis – without explaining how their protagonists came to 'live happily ever after.' A stage example is typical: the play *What's the Matter with Mary Jane* (Harmer and Robinson 1994) is based on its performer's personal experience of anorexia and bulimia. Because suffering and disruption can be displayed more concretely than their opposites, the drama is prematurely resolved in its last five minutes as the audience is told, not shown how, a 'specialist' held the cure. To tell the full story artistically requires a different narrative form; perhaps on the model of the detective novel, in which the crisis occurs at the beginning and the necessary tension is sustained by offering clues to a mystery solved in the last few pages. Another reason recovery stories evade the difficult 'how' is that it is often hard to say which particular events in the story were crucial to recovery.

Recovery, like all rituals, has a basic pattern with an infinite number of variations and so it is with recovery stories too. Recovery is rarely recorded step by step. Even when it is, its fine details are different for each person and, in the end, it is difficult to establish which of them have been essential. Only a few authors have attempted a full account of the recovery process using personal narratives. Karen Way's *Anorexia and Recovery* (1993) traces themes in the lives of recovered anorectics from crisis to recovery, but despite its title, the major emphasis of the book is still on the crisis and its genesis. Only Lindsey Hall's *Full Lives* (1993) acknowledges the difficulty involved in telling recovery stories. Instead of telling people 'how' to recover, her contributors' brief is to show *why* it is worth recovering. Ultimately, as Hall's book recognizes, each person must construct his or her own story. At the time the journey to recovery begins, the traveller is barely conscious of what is involved. Novelists – whose art is narrative – know how hard it is for words to make sense of this chaos. As Margaret Atwood has one of her characters say:

When you are in the middle of a story it isn't a story at all, but only a confusion; a dark roaring, a blindness, a wreckage of shattered glass and splintered wood; like a house in a whirlwind, or else a boat crushed by the icebergs or swept over the rapids, and all aboard powerless to stop it. It's only afterwards that it becomes anything like a story at all. When you are telling it, to yourself or to someone else. (Atwood 1996: 298)

Part II

Anorexia and recovery

Strictly speaking, the question is not how to get cured, but how to live.
Conrad, *Lord Jim*, cited in Szasz 1979

4   Reinterpreting 'anorexia'

Introduction

A life story, coherently conceived, is a connected whole to which each part gives meaning. In retrospect, the stories of 'recovery' and 'anorexia' are inseparable: descent and return amplify each other. But this is not the way they have been described in the medical literature or even by its feminist and sociological critics, who all share a blindness to the importance of the recovery period. In this chapter, I discuss clinical, theoretical and experiential accounts of the descent into anorexia, somewhat artificially separated from the return to recovery. My critical evaluation of all these accounts, from the perspective of recovery, points to some of the inadequacies of existing classifications, theories and treatments of so-called 'eating disorders'.

Clinical definitions

When most participants in this study began starving, bingeing and/or purging, the psychiatric classifications 'eating disorders', 'anorexia nervosa' and 'bulimia nervosa' and the criteria used to define them were not part of popular consciousness.[1] Most, myself included, first became aware that our behaviour fitted a known pattern when we met someone else doing the same thing; only later did we hear or read the label for it. When we did, we found the medical descriptions inadequate to describe our experience and its rationale. These inadequacies can be better understood when we consider how the clinical terms arose.

Although self-starvation is an ascetic practice dating back thousands of years in many cultures, the term 'anorexia nervosa' has only been in existence since 1874.[2] The name was coined by William Gull, physician to Queen Victoria,[3] 'as a way of making meaningful to the medical profession – not the starver – a set of symptoms and patterns of behaviour which were unreasonable and inexplicable' (Robertson 1992: xiv). Classifying and naming confers power, and the labelling and definition of 'anorexia nervosa' at the end of the nineteenth century was part of a strategy by the newly created medical profession to control knowledge of the body and the mind, in a period of increasing freedom and political influence for women.[4] The strategy was so successful that medical discourse has held pre-eminent authority to pronounce on the human condition for most of this century in western society[5] and to define the problems, and speak on behalf, of fasting girls.[6]

Medical discourse rests on the scientific view that a problem must always be traced to its causes and most of the problems in defining 'anorexia nervosa' arise from this over-emphasis on origins. Each of the three main explanatory models for the condition; biomedical, psychological and cultural (Brumberg 1988: 24–40), assume that discovering the cause or causes of anorexia nervosa will suggest means of treatment and possibly of prevention. Evidence from the extended recovery period is largely neglected. While this assumption is strongest in the disciplines which take a positivist view of science, it has also informed the more hermeneutical approaches of social psychology and sociology and is very much alive in popular conceptions of 'anorexia nervosa'. Although it is now usually accepted in psychiatry and clinical psychology that eating disorders are 'multi-determined' (Garner and Garfinkel 1982) and 'bio-psycho-social', the emphasis remains on aetiology (causes of the problem), not recovery (understanding the solution).

Another difficulty with the term anorexia nervosa is that it fails to cover the range of experience encompassed by self-starving behaviour. For those who have experienced it, the definition of anorexia nervosa is quite elastic, since they often swing violently between the extremes of starving and bingeing and may accompany either with the purging techniques of vomiting and laxative abuse. Since many people in my study had experienced all three 'eating disorders', sometimes in short episodes and sometimes for years on end, the connections among them cannot be denied.[7] Yet compulsive eating, a pattern which is abundantly documented in the non-medical literature, receives no recognition in the official psychiatric classification of mental disorders[8] and 'bulimia nervosa' has been placed in a separate category from 'anorexia nervosa', though DSM IIIR (American Psychiatric Association 1987: 413) recognizes that the two 'disorders' are closely related. Membership in the categories 'anorexia nervosa' and 'bulimia nervosa' is determined by the very definite criteria of two classificatory systems: the *Diagnostic and Statistical Manual of Mental Disorders* of the American Psychiatric Association or the British ICD.[9] Many 'recovered' participants have never met all of these criteria. For example, some continued to menstruate and two conceived and gave birth while seriously underweight; an impossibility according to psychiatric criteria. Several of those who say they have not recovered do not meet the required criteria for the condition they say they have. These problems of categorization highlight a subject of constant debate in psychiatry: the inconsistencies in the system of classification itself. They also restrict the availability of medical benefits for those who seek treatment.

Theoretical voices

Theories about eating disorders have now been conceived in many academic disciplines and outside them. 'Discourses' which have addressed and influenced the problem include psychiatry, psychology, sociology, anthropology, philosophy, history, literary theory, autobiography, biography, fiction and feminist theory in each of these (Garrett 1994). These 'expert accounts' shape public awareness of anorexia. But even when they are critical of the medical model, most theories of eating disorders unconsciously rely on psychiatric definitions and assumptions. Some of the books (if not the articles) I am about to discuss do, of course, provide examples of recovery and its trajectory; but even those that claim to be about recovery (e.g. Way 1993) devote almost twice as much space to the aetiology and description of anorexia itself. Few of them offer sustained description, much less analysis, of how recovery takes place.[10] For this reason, they unintentionally fail to offer the hope which is an essential imaginative ingredient in overcoming anorexia. For the same reason, they must be regarded as intellectually unconvincing. At the same time, they are the basis on which stronger, more inclusive theories must build and many of them contain valuable material for that purpose.

The continuum

Most theories about anorexia see it as the endpoint of a continuum that begins with 'normal dieting' and argue that all women in contemporary westernized societies suffer to some extent from dissatisfaction with their bodies. By suggesting that women's response to social pressures to be slim is only a matter of degree, they implicitly accept the inevitability of this dissatisfaction and condone dieting. Anorexic behaviour is not always (or even often) a result of 'normal dieting' which slides to the other end of a continuum. Some sufferers had never heard of 'dieting' as a normative practice when they began their own fasts. Many other factors are involved. Even as a metaphor, a continuum is not a very useful theoretical prop. It relies on the false premise that everyone can be placed somewhere along its length. When it is used in the attempt to explain anorexia, it cannot account for anorexia in men or for those women who are not dissatisfied with their bodies; either because they never were or because they have found ways not to be. Nor can it explain why some women and not others become anorexic.

Some research in psychology has tried to make a qualitative distinction between 'dieting' and anorexia. Garner, Olmstead & Garfinkel (1983) for example, carefully separate 'pathological' dietary restriction from 'extreme dieting'. They argue that anorexia supplies primary gratification; that it is almost an end in itself; whereas the chronic dieter suffers reluctantly to achieve greater attractiveness. In contrast, a South Australian study (Ben-Tovim & Morton 1989) found that almost half the women in the 'age group at risk' displayed some 'anorexic and bulimic tendencies' (although no more than 1 in a 1,000 meets the full set of criteria for 'anorexia nervosa' and 2 in a 1,000 for 'bulimia nervosa'). Women are clearly suffering, but the continuum model is not very useful in explaining why. It cannot account for factors other than 'body image' in the genesis of eating disorders and it cannot adequately explain recovery. Wherever 'normal' behaviour is located on such a continuum, 'normal' women will always retain some anxiety about weight and appearance.

Body image

Academic and popular psychology have often assumed that anorexia is 'a cognitive disturbance in body image'[11] portrayed at its most simplistic in the cartoon of the anorexic girl looking at herself in the mirror and seeing an obese figure. Psychologists have used an adaptable video screen image to assess the extent of women's distorted picture of themselves, by inviting them to manipulate the image to show first how they perceive their bodies and then how they would like them to be. The responses are used to demonstrate that women with eating disorders have significantly distorted self-images because they see themselves as fatter than they 'in fact' are.[12] But when I was anorexic, I knew very well that I was thin; this did not stop me from *feeling* fat – in relation to my ideal, not to objective visual reality.

Where do these distorted images come from? In *The Beauty Myth* (1991), Naomi Wolf argues that media images, dieting and cosmetic surgery impose upon women 'weak body boundaries' similar to those of people with mental illnesses like schizophrenia. Splitting women's bodies into separate parts, they present women with pornographic versions of their bodies. The solution to this problem, for Wolf, is for women to work individually and collectively against the beauty myth and to redefine ideals of feminine beauty. While this in itself is a worthy endeavour, I doubt that it would make much difference to the prevalence of eating disorders. Public portrayals of women and women's internalized negative images of themselves arise from the same social roots as eating disorders (from splits between body and self, masculine and feminine, secular and spiritual), but they are not per se the causes of the problem. Anorectics are not hallucinating; their insecurities about their bodies are their insecurities about themselves; socially induced, but in different ways for each person.

The concept of 'body image disturbance' can, therefore, be useful in understanding eating disorders when it is not posited as their 'cause' but read as a symptom. Physically, having body boundaries is about knowing one's bodily needs and finding ways to take in what is nourishing and to reject that which is not – issues of great relevance in eating disorders. Psychically, bodily boundaries are also about the self; knowing the difference between 'me' and 'not me'; acknowledging the difference between 'shared reality' and 'inner reality'. The disturbed body boundaries of anorexia, bulimia and compulsive eating can therefore be interpreted symbolically, as Mira Dana (1987) simply and brilliantly explains. The anorectic, she suggests, is refusing to take in (to accept) other people's versions of who she ought to be. The bulimic symbolically spews out the intrusions of others. The compulsive eater attempts to control the world by taking it into herself. Body boundaries therefore act as metaphors for social relations. The way we allow people into our 'space' is a crucial identifying factor in the anorexic period, while the changes which occur in this area are an equally important part of recovery. Body image is one aspect of the self which changes during the emergence from an eating disorder but the change is a metaphor for a much more profound transformation.

Addiction

To speak of eating disorders as addictions is also to make a metaphorical connection; they certainly are *like* addictions. Several treatment models (notably that of Overeaters Anonymous) assume that they are. There are many parallels: addictions are means of dealing with psychic pain; they include a physical dimension as well as a psychological one; they involve habitual behaviour which alters the individual's psychological and physical state; they may be initially unpleasant, but eventually come to feel 'right' and they are characteristically denied by those who suffer from them (Abrahams 1982; Brumberg 1988:31). Their recovery patterns are similar too: just as addicts must confront the problems that led to their addiction, so the anorectic is recovering from the pain the eating disorder served to mask. Both addicts and people with eating disorders have lost trust in themselves and their lives and must find (and continue to nurture) the realization that they are meaningful parts of a meaningful universe (Woodman 1988: 52).

A few participants in my study found it helpful to refer to anorexia *as* an addiction. Rosalie was treated fifteen years ago in a drug and alcohol unit and, using the language she learned there, she speaks of her treatment as 'drying out'. Freda recognizes that anorexia was only one way of blotting out her memories in order to survive their pain. She described herself as switching from addiction to addiction; from 'the highs' of anorexia to those of alcohol, AA, compulsive falling in love, madness, work and junk food. Miranda referred to her bulimia as a 'dependency'; ritual vomiting helped structure time which she otherwise experienced as meaningless, and her obsession with the ritual, together with the physical exhaustion it induced, prevented her from confronting her feelings of rejection and worthlessness and, she says, protected a vulnerable inner self.

The search for self

The theories of 'false' body image and of addiction-as-mask both suggest that behind the 'front' lies a true self to be discovered. This 'search for self' is used in a variety of ways in relation to anorexia. First, anorexia may be described as a watershed in the development of identity: since it has most often (though not invariably) manifested itself in adolescence, it is often interpreted as part of the individual's struggle for autonomy from parents. To the extent that we continue throughout our lives to define ourselves as different from our families of origin, this can be a useful approach. It can even be used to explain eating disorders in older women (and men) as attempts to resolve psychological conflicts left over from the chronological age when they are usually addressed. Whether the parents are alive or dead, the eating disorder may be still (or even more) relevant in this process of self-formation.

A second variation, widely used in feminist and psychoanalytic theory, comes from the object-relations school.[13] This theory (also 'developmental') asserts that when the child's earliest needs are not appropriately met by the caregiver (almost invariably the mother), the child constructs an internal world in which the caretaker becomes both a 'good object' (the object of desire) and a 'bad object' (the rejecting object). The withdrawal into a fantasy life which accompanies these operations also creates a 'false self'; a self without needs (since these cannot be met) and who attempts to meet the projections of others. The 'real self' is thereby split off and rejected. In some versions of object relations theory (Orbach 1986: 88–90), the anorexic takes on a false body; a body malleable along approved lines, as a defence against the unaccepted real body which has become a 'bad object' for her because it represents negative aspects of the mother. Another object-relations theorist, Catherine Steiner-Adair (1990, 1991) argues that anorexia results from a failure to admit the necessity of relationships in the formation of feminine identity (p.164). Because their bodies resemble those of their mothers, girls achieve identity through connection and relationality, not through the separation and autonomy required of boys. Girls, she says, are more prone to eating disorders because they are socialized to rely heavily on external acceptance and feedback to inform their identity. Their 'authentic self' is not 'autonomous', but 'connected'. One problem associated with feminist object relations theory is its mother-blaming aspect and another is that the nature of the 'authentic' self is never fully specified, but it does highlight the importance of human connection and reconnection in recovery which was mentioned by most participants in my study.[14]

A third account of the self in anorexia and recovery is derived from poststructuralist psychoanalytic theories which posit a fundamentally and irretrievably split self; almost the opposite of the self in object relations theory. In Lacan's influential 'The Mirror Stage' ((1949); 1977), for example, the 'unified self' is based on a false image of wholeness given in the mirror. In Lacan's terms, the individual's destiny is to be permanently alienated from any 'real' self, since the only self-knowledge must come from others, and therefore offers merely an illusion of autonomy. Feminist poststructuralism suggests that women, especially, experience a split between their imaginary body experienced in the pre-Oedipal period ('active and uncastrated, total and traversed by polymorphous impulses, desires and satisfactions') and the symbolic body ('constructed as compliant to men's needs and desires') (Celermajer 1987). In this account, too, anorexia is seen as a rebellion against a phallocentric symbolic order – the masculine construction of the system of symbols through which we describe and come to understand ourselves in the world.

It is true (as I argue later in this chapter) that anorexia is an *attempt* to return to an experience before language and the symbolic, but it is also true that only in recovery is the symbolic consciously integrated into the self. Beyond anorexia, the self is experienced as 'real', 'whole' and 'autonomous': recovered participants in my study consistently referred to a sense of 'inner connection'. In order to understand 'recovery', the self must be understood as made up of many interconnected parts and recovery must be conceptualized as a transcendence, not of self, but of ego. The self in this book is made up of many different aspects engaged in an ongoing process of transformation. Recovery is the movement towards their connection, so that they are experienced as parts of a whole. Indeed, in recovering, the illusion of a single 'anorexic' identity gives way to the creation of a variety of selves, each experienced as part of the same person. In this sense, the self is 'dynamic and multiple, always positioned in relation to particular discourses and practices and produced by these' (Henriques et al. 1984: 3).[15]

Fourthly, existentialist theories[16] explore the possibility that anorexic symptoms are forms of self-realization; a means of coming to terms with the world and one's own existence in it – a manifestation of the human existential quest. An existentialist approach to therapy treats anorexia nervosa as 'a voice calling for an answer'. For existentialism, the 'authentic' self is the self which does not shrink from the quest but finds (by continuing to create) its own 'being-in-the-world'. The aim of existential therapy is to help us accept the human condition for what it is; to have the courage to mature to the full and learn to come to terms with our own death (Palazzoli 1963: 136, MacLeod 1981:139). Questions of life and death are central to the argument I present later in this book, but my answers move beyond existentialism to 'transpersonal' explanations.

Transpersonal psychology, a fifth variation of the search for self, introduces a spiritual element to the existential quest.[17] Emanating from humanistic psychology, it includes mystical states in its definition of the self. In common with the world's 'great religions' it holds that the ego or individualized self is not the ground of human awareness but, instead, one reflection-manifestation of a Self 'beyond the personal', a pure conscious-ness without subject or object (Valle & Halling 1989: 261). This idea of self comes closest to the experience described by the recovered people in my study who constantly transform themselves in interaction with, but not at the mercy of, the society in which they live. The ideal towards which this transformation takes place is elaborated in humanistic discourses on human freedom (Ditmar & Bates 1987) and in discourses concerning human spirituality. These ideals are always socially created but they are also dependent upon a notion of spiritual energy which precedes, though it is shaped by, the social. The precise relation between the individual self and the society of which it is a part is the subject of the next set of theories I consider.

Anorexia as metaphor[18]

As Sontag's *Illness as a Metaphor* reminds us, it is impossible to avoid thinking metaphorically, but some metaphors are more useful than others (Sontag 1988: 5). Sontag argues that infections like leprosy, cancer and AIDS have been used innapropriately as vehicles for social anxieties when they are really nothing more than forms of biological contamination. Her arguments are not strictly applicable to anorexia because, despite attempts to link it to genetic factors or to biological factors like brain dysfunction,[19] even most medical opinion now recognizes that it does have social roots. What is not usually recognized is that medical definitions of anorexia are themselves metaphors, since they describe anorexia 'as if' it were a physical or mental pathology like an infection. Medical anthropology and sociology, on the other hand, make a useful distinction between illness and disease: illness is the phenomenological experience of human suffering, while disease is an epidemiological occurence; 'it' – the diagnostic entity. (Kleinman 1988: 5, B. Turner 1987). Thought of metaphorically, the concepts of 'illness' and 'disease' can provide real insights. For example, as I explain below, the relation between 'anorexia as illness' and 'anorexia as disease' parallels the relation between the individual and society. Dangers arise, however, when the metaphorical dimension is lost and anorexia is 'reified' as illness so that individual pain is seen as an inevitable by-product of collective social problems. Dangers also arise when anorexia is understood literally as a disease and treated as an entity that can be 'caught' and 'cured'; people are tested and labelled 'at risk', made responsible for their own suffering and given often inappropriate medical treatment.

The anorexic body is sometimes deciphered like a text, using the techniques of literary criticism (themselves influenced by psychoanalytic method). Sheila MacLeod (1981) has read her own anorexic body in this way, seeing the bodily states of anorexia as substitutes for personal problems. Where anorexia appears to be a kind of vanity in the body, she reads its subtext as pride in achievement. Where anorexia seems to be choosing death, she reads it as a paradox; a simultaneous bid for life. When Freud used this technique to read the unconscious meanings of bodily symptoms in his studies of hysteria,[20] it often led to an 'abreaction' of the symptoms themselves (a 'release of affect' and their subsequent disappearance). As I have shown in my discussion of participants' reaction to my own 'recovered' body, such interpretations should be approached with caution. It is one thing for people to analyse the meanings of their own bodily states as keys to their unconscious minds, but quite another for external observers to jump to conclusions about the state of a person's psyche from his or her external appearance: scars, for example, are reminders but not active wounds.

In sociology, anorexia is often read as a metaphor for social problems or, more accurately, as synechdoche, in which individual anorexic practices stand for processes of control in the society as a whole. The sub-title of Orbach's *Hunger Strike* (1988) – 'the anorectic's struggle as a metaphor for our age' – encapsulates this approach. If all illness is social illness, the argument goes, then anorexia must be read as a disorder of society.[21] As such, it is inseparable from the patriarchal control of women's bodies; a subtle contemporary refinement of the more direct means of control of earlier times, like the wearing of corsets. In *The Body in Society*, Turner (1984) argues that anorexia nervosa 'reflects' patriarchal anxieties about women's bodies and 'expresses' the modern view of beauty as thinness. What it also does (and Turner does not directly address this) is to 'construct' a way of living for the anorexic woman and, possibly, a model way of life for other women. This is why metaphors for *recovery* are so important.

If psychoanalysis, literary theory and sociology have given us metaphorical ways of reading anorexia nervosa itself, they should also be used to decode and disseminate the meanings of recovery. Using synechdoche as a means of interpretation leads to the conclusion that anorexia is a part of a society in spiritual crisis. At the same time, the lives of those who have recovered are also 'synechdochally' related to the society in which recovery is possible. The experience of recovery may therefore offer some insight into what might be necessary for the spiritual healing of the society as a whole.

Control or rebellion?

In recent poststructuralist social theories of anorexia, which rely heavily on the ideas of Foucault, individual anorexic behaviour is often read as a capitulation to social control[22] and also, paradoxically, as a rebellion against it. Foucault's notions of 'governmentality' and 'power' are invoked to describe the development of the category 'anorexia nervosa' as part of the wider targeting of the health of entire populations. According to this interpretation, anorexia is one of the very practices by which the self is formed in today's society; constructed by the 'psy' disciplines (psychology, psychiatry, psychoanalysis) which have replaced more obvious systems of social control (Tait 1993). Convincing as this may sound as an explanation for the rise of the category 'anorexia', it cannot account for recovery.

As rebellion, anorexia is described as a protest against consumerism and against patriarchal control over women's bodies; both a symbolic struggle against forms of authority and an attempt to resolve the contradictions of the female self, fractured by the dichotomies of reason and desire, public and private, body and self, nature and culture.[23] This kind of analysis does not point out that the rebellion is ultimately ineffective, or ask how the dichotomies might be resolved.[24] It fails to see that the real alternatives to capitulation are found among people who are not anorexic because they are seeking other ways to resolve these contemporary social dilemmas in their personal lives. If, as Foucault (1979) himself puts it, the truth of a discourse lies in the strategies which it brings into play, not simply in what it says, then theories which are not concerned with or directed towards recovery may themselves be part of the ongoing problem of anorexia.

Anorexia as personal and social ritual

So far, I have been showing how sociological theories about anorexia rely on rhetorical tropes (especially synechdoche) and on a particular understanding of the meaning of 'self' – the self as an active, embodied subject that is nevertheless constructed by social processes. In spite of its best efforts, this kind of sociology still manages to separate body from self, making the (unconscious) body speak for the self from which it is irretrievably split and making it difficult to talk about the multiple connections among body, self, society and the cosmos. I now want to suggest that the 'search for self' which began a few pages ago can be more satisfyingly concluded by taking a less western view of the relations between self and society, as Kleinman (from an anthropological perspective) invites us to do:

> For members of many non-Western societies, the body is an open system linking social relations to the self, a vital balance between interrelated elements in a holistic cosmos. Emotion and cognition are integrated into bodily processes. The body-self is not a secularized private domain of the individual person but an organic part of a sacred, sociocentric world, a communication system involving exchanges with others (including the divine) . . . in symbolic resonance with the social and even the planetary microcosm (rather than reflecting it). (1988:11)

This model of self and social relationships is more conducive to theories of recovery as spiritual transformation in both individuals and their societies than the familiar medical model or the more recent sociological metaphors for the self-society relation. It allows for the dynamism inherent in recovery as self-transformation and for the way in which recovery involves a conscious re-connection of the self with the social and the natural world. Recognizing the 'sacred' nature of the self also opens the way for a deeper understanding of the undeniable ritual dimensions of anorexia.

The behaviour of people with eating disorders is often called 'ritualistic', using 'ritual' to mean 'obsessive'; but rituals are always more than repetitive, compulsive acts and, if we read them anthropologically, they are full of personal and social meaning. The rituals of anorexia, bulimia and compulsive eating may be seen as ceremonial attempts at self-transformation; efforts to create rites of passage from one stage of personal and social life another in a society which no longer provides such rites (Chernin 1986: 172ff). They can also be interpreted as purity rituals (Garrett 1992b) designed, like all purity rituals (Douglas 1966) to protect against existential chaos, to achieve spiritual salvation and as an unconscious reflection and maintenance of social concerns (especially the widespread distrust and fear of women's bodies as 'impure'). Anthropological theories of asceticism, ritual and religion offer a way of conceptualizing anorexia and recovery as linked stages in a profoundly social transformation of the individual self. They also make it possible to identify and describe the sources of recovery in contemporary society. Some of these anthropological theories have provided a basis for the new explanation of anorexia and recovery in this book.

Experiential voices

In my study, participants were understandably alert to the ways they feel falsely represented in discourses about the condition from which they have recovered or are recovering. In our conversations, they were often critical of clinical terminology and of many of the theories I have discussed. I asked them what it was they thought they were recovering from. Their responses unsettle some assumptions of eating disorders theorists. The headings under which I discuss participants' interpretations indicate the groups into which they placed themselves, rather than those in which I might have placed them. I have respected their own assessment of the extent to which they have recovered, since this is not something that can ever be 'measured'.

'Unrecovered' perspectives

Of the seven participants in the 'unrecovered' group, none had been treated specifically for an eating disorder. Two, Freda and Patricia, were now obese and attributed their compulsive eating to their earlier experience of anorexia. Five would be considered anorexic by medical standards. Of these, Lauren, Philip and Victoria believed they had some degree of recovery, though they were still plagued by eating difficulties; Michael and Jennifer spoke as if they were still anorexic and would probably remain so. When members of this group spoke of anorexia, they did not mention any 'objective' scientific criteria. For them, the defining features of their condition are those they believe they must overcome if they are to recover: self-loathing, developmental stagnation, ongoing problems with food, unresolved questions about death and detachment from other people. At the same time, the thin ones were proud to have achieved an anorexic body and its social acceptability makes it harder to give up. As Freda says: 'You admit to *anorexia*, but not to alcoholism or madness'. She knows, having experienced all three. People in this group are well aware of the dangers of what they call their way of life; a form of identity with its own rewards. Michael has lived like this for thirty years, protecting his ego, without nurturing his 'self':

It's skeletal, the appearance; waif-like . . . But anorexia is a continued vehicle to enable you to investigate this existential style of living. It's a mode of behaviour, a mode of living . . . existentialism, stoicism, redemption through suffering, the higher pain of awareness . . . I want a sustained, heightened awareness and I feel that ideal, the body image, the incarnate of the solitary mountain trekker going alone to look for the higher level of existence, will be stripped away if I suddenly become normal. I'm gratified that this existential pursuit, solitude and suffering . . . and all the things that go with it, has come to me through the vehicle of the torture of my body . . . but having said that, I realize that is an extremely dangerous condition, because you develop a remoteness that just becomes more and more out of touch with reality. It's just an empty void, your existing . . . because you've lost touch with everybody.

None of these people had a fully coherent account of the reasons for their behaviour. They mentioned tragic events (deaths, emotional abuse and neglect), but did not connect them directly with their present suffering, as if a link were missing from their narrative. Several told me they did not know or did not believe that you could recover. The most pervasive element in their conceptualization of the anorexic state was self-loathing: 'I get the feeling I truly don't like me, you know? – most of the time – and you don't look after yourself', said Freda. This attitude to self is expressed through hatred for the body and reluctance to eat. Victoria says 'The initial thing that triggers my depression is the way I look. I'm not happy with my fat stomach today. Food has ruined my life.' Even Sheena, who tells me she is recovering and that she has made real progress in overcoming self-hatred, still says with vehemence: 'Food bores me to death. I hate the hold it has on me; that I have to eat three times a day.'

Sheena speaks of anorexia as a kind of developmental hiatus; a way of indefinitely retarding the confrontations with self and others which are involved in the changes of adulthood. She says: 'I also think that anorexia has an enormous amount to do with some kind of immaturity and inability to grow up. It's something you grow out of.' But as she speaks, her movements and her clothes are childlike and coquettish, her body is frail and she makes her coffee with skim milk, for fear of gaining weight. Ability to list the tasks of psychological development does not translate easily into their fulfilment.

Several participants referred to anorexia as 'a form of slow suicide' and, when we look at the connection between asceticism and death later in this book, it will become clear that much lies behind this cliché. Nicki (recovering) says of her anorexic period: 'You think you're worthless anyway, so what's the point?' But Jennifer, desperately unable to recover, came closer to expressing the fears about death which are such a strong component in anorexia. She told me she did not want to die but to live life to the fullest, yet she believed she could only do this by 'going back to where I was at fourteen' and dealing with her father's death. Living life to the fullest, these people know, would involve changing the form of their relationships with others. All mentioned having cut themselves off from people; even in their marriages and with family members. They know that to grow (literally and metaphorically) requires social reconnection, and they are afraid of the changes this would involve. Michael says he is simply 'too caught up in my own body image and awareness to sustain relationships with other people'. All these explanations for their suffering are fragmented; they contain echoes of the theoretical voices discussed earlier in this chapter, but no sustained narrative about their lives.

'Recovering' perspectives

Where some of the 'unrecovered' group were stuck half way down in their descent into anorexia, 'recovering' participants were often stuck half way up: Ariel, Margaret, Marilyn, Joanne and Sheena had turned a corner, but never completed the rest of their recovery journey. Margaret, for example, though she spoke of 'progress' in other areas of her life, was still obsessed with thoughts of food. These women's interpretations of anorexia were not very different from those of the 'unrecovered' group. The remaining members of this group, however, were at a different stage: Lesley, Jacqueline, Marjorie, Nicki and Susanna had all recently emerged from a long period of suffering and were feeling optimistic about their future, though aware that they were still at the beginning of their recovery. Their ideas, like the stories they were still constructing about their experience of anorexia, were in flux, though more defined than those in the previous group. They stressed the importance of naming and reinterpreting the traumas which preceded the onset of anorexia, before 'full' recovery would become possible for them. They also emphasized 'rediscovering' the more fully connected person each feels she was before the trauma which precipitated her eating problems. Their accounts of anorexia, like its clinical definitions and the discourses upon it, are only half the story. Without its second half, the first cannot be fully understood.

'Recovered' perspectives

The fifteen recovered participants had much more to say about 'anorexia' than did those who were still recovering. None of them thought it had anything to do with 'vanity', although the image they projected to others was important to them. All of them interpreted their past eating problem as a vital part of their ongoing transformation. They were grateful for having had the experience, however terrible, and they saw anorexia and recovery as integral parts of the same existential, and usually spiritual, quest. They described their 'eating disorder' (we agreed to use the clinical terms as a shorthand) as a necessary step in their personal evolution rather than a period of developmental stagnation; they recognize that their behaviour was self-protective, not self-destructive.

Vivienne's story also illustrates another important and largely neglected cause of eating problems; the sufferings of poverty.[25] She says she sees anorexia 'very much in a social context'. Coming from a 'very working class family in Britain, where educational and social opportunities were *extremely* limited, particularly for girls' and where class oppression had produced violence, alcoholism and incest, anorexia was her way of 'stepping outside the family definition; the little coffin [she] had to live in in order to survive'.[26] To escape, she says, she had to break her own identity and break out of its context. Anorexia was also a way of simplifying the chaos around her, attempting to create an oasis of perfection and control, or, as she put it: 'converging, closing down, controlling, stylizing, trying to produce a slightly high camp, Algonquin lunch, Aubrey Beardsley line drawing; a two-dimensional world where everyone was just so. And *no* messiness.'

An eating disorder, like alcoholism, was often a necessary mechanism for coping with otherwise unbearable pain. Vivienne, who used both, thinks that without her anorexia, she would have ended up 'wacked out on Valium and doing mental hospitals for the rest of my life'. Anorexia 'jet-propelled me to find an alternative way to live'. Kate, too, 'got anorexia deliberately; to cope with a difficult situation' – her parents' divorce. She says there were other options, like suicide or psychological withdrawal, but she chose anorexia because it meant she could 'be something'. 'It was a survival choice, in many ways. If I hadn't done that, I would really have gone mad. It was like focusing my madness down to one part. A desperate choice, but still one of survival.'

Several participants also interpret their anorexic stance as a way of communicating their distress – an attempt which misfired. Kate says she thought: 'OK, nobody can help me at this point in time; nobody can understand what's happened to me and what's going on and I don't understand it either. This, at least, will reformat it in a way that most people can understand that there is something wrong.' Then, she thought, people would assist her to overcome the problem. Instead, anorexia itself became the problem – and she was shocked when she could not reverse it.

The quest theme emerged strongly in all these conversations, almost always conceived as spiritual quest. People in this group now talk of anorexia as a 'hunger for meaning'.[27] Ilse says she 'didn't realize the hunger for knowledge or the hunger for experience [she] had then – definitely a spiritual or religious searching'. Kate, too, thinks anorexia is often 'a quest for your own meaning, whatever that may be – for whatever didn't make sense and for whatever reason it didn't make sense – often a quest for spiritual meaning'. Meredith remembers feeling 'lost, alone and empty', 'not knowing what you're doing or why you're here'. During her anorexic period, agnostic, she sought meaning working for a church-run social welfare organization.

In the long term, for this group, anorexia itself did not deliver the meaning they sought. As Zoe put it 'anorexia wasn't working to satisfy my needs – to have a sense of meaning in my life. I didn't have it at all!' It was only with this realization, however, that recovery could become the next stage in their construction of meaning. They still expressed their gratitude for having been through the experience: Ilse thinks it saved her from suicide: 'It was the sensible thing to do, because it stopped those things I couldn't cope with'. Pip sees it as 'a very real, very significant thing in my past, a learning process, not a denial process, something to go through and from'. And Meredith believes that anorexia was a great gift, because she learned so many things from it.

These voices, from the centre of the experience and from the perspectives of recent and long-term recovery, challenge the narrow medical terms which seek to define 'anorexia nervosa'. Even when they use the medical term 'anorexia nervosa', they are in sharp contrast to the 'objectivist' scientific approach of most clinical definitions. Instead, they begin to reveal the existential and spiritual pain which is at the root of self-starvation, as well as some aspects of the social context which produces it. Most importantly, it is those who have been through both descent *and* recovery who are able to give the fullest, most coherent, accounts of both aspects of their experience.

5   Reinterpreting 'recovery'

Introduction

Popular myth has it that anorexia is a fatal disease,[1] in spite of empirical evidence that only about 4 per cent of sufferers die from an eating disorder.[2] When William Gull gave anorexia its contemporary name at the end of last century, he had seen several deaths from anorexia, but even he asserted that however frustrating the situation: 'none of these cases is really hopeless whilst life exists; and for the most part, the prognosis may be considered favorable'. He also thought that 'the medical treatment probably need not be considered as contributing much to the recovery'.[3] Such optimism and modesty are rare in the medical literature today. The popular belief is not surprising because death from anorexia stands out as a particularly tragic and mysterious waste and information to counteract the misconception has been hard to find. For this reason, I offer a very brief summary of the clinical, the scholarly and other, more accessible, literatures about recovery, for comparison with my own findings and conclusions. Research studies by clinicians have been of two kinds; 'empirical' (attempting to measure recovery) and 'phenomenological' (understanding recovery in the terms described by those who experience it). The non-clinical literature on recovery (influenced by feminism, but not exclusively feminist) is phenomenological too.

Recovery studies

Empirical studies

Psychiatric and psychological accounts of the long-term follow-up of patients treated for eating disorders usually become publicly available only through brief journal articles written primarily for fellow clinicians.[4] Nevertheless, as 'expert scientific pronouncements', they carry more weight in the discourse on anorexia and recovery than any of the more 'anecdotal' (and consequently more detailed) phenomenological evidence available in autobiographical, biographical and fictionalized accounts.[5] Empirical studies treat 'anorexia nervosa' as an objective disease entity, without recognizing their own part in creating it as such or the power of their own discourse to define the meaning of 'recovery'. They usually ask the question 'do anorectics get well?' (Schwartz & Thompson 1981) and expect a yes/no, or at least a quantifiable, answer.[6] Clinical studies are most concerned with the success of their treatment programmes, on which further funding frequently depends. Consequently most researchers follow-up their own 'clinical cases' in order to improve or justify the treatments they have administered.[7]

To measure recovery, most of these studies use the broad criterion areas outlined by Dally (1969): weight, menstruation, psychosexual development, degree of independence and mental state; yet clinicians themselves have been critical of the lack of agreed aims, methods and definitions in these studies and their consequent failure to provide much guidance for treatment.[8] Strangest of all is the absence of what they call 'positive outcome indicators'; the factors most likely to *assist* 'recovery'; explanations of *how* people recover. Instead, the focus is on the negative; what might *prevent* recovery. Factors patients themselves regard as important are not considered. Interview questions and questionnaires are predetermined. Potentially complex responses are simplified to fit categories chosen by the researchers; a relatively small group of fairly like-minded people. These articles make no reference to the growing scholarship on eating disorders outside clinical medicine and psychology; longer analytical articles[9] are treated as speculative until their theories have been subjected to 'scientific trials'. The call for uniform 'measures' of recovery masks a call for uniform *theories* and makes it difficult for genuinely new insights to emerge. Theander's comments on the state of 'scientific' knowledge about the outcomes of treatment summarize the problem:

Many questions regarding outcome and prognosis of anorexia nervosa remain to be answered . . . Are our therapeutic measures today . . . really effective? Or are we still trying measures not much better and not much more rational than aromatic bags and bitter medicines? (Theander 1983: 173)

Recovery remains mysterious[10] to these particular clinicians largely because of their failure to trust their patients.[11] Studies of anorexia and recovery which *have* trusted the ideas of their 'objects' and given them a voice have provided far richer understandings of the recovery process. Written in a more narrative form than the 'empirical' studies, they also offer more detailed knowledge and more carefully elaborated ideas.[12]

Phenomenological studies

Several influential clinicians have published phenomenological accounts of recovery as parts of their own or edited books. Perhaps the best known of these are the pioneering works of Hilde Bruch (1973, 1978, 1988). Bruch's therapeutic approach was based on the need for her patients to rediscover (or discover) a lost (or never adequately experienced) self and especially to experience a 'unified, not split concept of self and body'. Her posthumously published *Conversations with Anorexics* contains a full chapter on recovery where she emphasizes that 'the questions of what is involved – by what signs progress can be evaluated and how far the anorexic condition is accessible to treatment – are complex ones that can be answered from a variety of theoretical viewpoints'. 'Treatment results based on amelioration of the psychological factors, some very subtle', she points out, 'stand in contrast to results based on an exclusive emphasis on the state of nutrition and the return of menstruation.' Recovery is a process, not an isolated, measurable event and because anorexia itself results from complex causes, recovery is also necessarily complex. For her, the most fruitful understandings of recovery come from recovering anorectics themselves. As she puts it: 'Observant and sensitive anorexics are aware of the changes in themselves, and by the end of treatment some can describe in detail how events now affect them differently' (1988: 185–8).

Therapies like Bruch's, which concern themselves with the problem of 'being-in-the-world' (how to live; how to structure time and space) address what is fundamental to the problem of anorexia; the issue which is broader than food and deeper than family interaction, although it expresses itself through both. These existentialist accounts quote their patients at length, to illustrate the changes which take place during recovery in people's orientation to their surroundings; to people, to time and to nature. Palazzoli (1963) was especially fascinated by the potential of existential philosophy to explain her patients' experiences, but although these supply raw material for a theory of recovery, her book does not develop one.[13] Feminist therapists also use their patients' knowledge of recovery but they are more interested in seeking for causes in the patriarchal nature of society than creating a theory of recovery which might draw on other aspects of the same society – those which exist beyond or beside patriarchal oppression and are accessible to either sex. Neither existential nor feminist therapists have elaborated a meta-narrative about the recovery process – a theory of how and why recovery occurs. Feminist 'treatment models' (like most of those in Fallon, Katzman & Wooley 1994)[14] usually assume that therapy is necessary for recovery, despite evidence that people often recover without its benefits. Consequently, non-clinical studies offer a far richer picture of the recovery process.

Non-clinical studies

Although there are no books exclusively devoted to recovery, Karen Way's *Anorexia and Recovery* (1993) includes three chapters describing its elements, stages and turning points; Fallon, Katzman and Wooley's *Feminist Perspectives on Eating Disorders* has an important chapter on recovery from bulimia (Peters & Fallon 1994) and Becky Thompson's *A Hunger So Wide and So Deep* (1994) sets her participants' detailed accounts of recovery in her wider, multiracial view of eating disorders. Many of these authors write from personal experience, enriched by their conversations with other former sufferers. As a result, they hear about and describe parts of the healing process which remain unheard and unspoken in most clinical research. They focus on 'what the person feels and who she is rather than on what she does' (Herzog, Hamberg & Brotman 1987: 546).

Thompson, especially, emphasizes that to be free of an eating disorder it is not mandatory to articulate its origins. Only a few women in her study sought therapeutic help. Instead, like the women in mine, they developed their own healing methods to recreate what was destroyed by trauma. Just as their traumas resulted from the combined oppressions of class, race and homophobia, so their recovery required access to time, money and support; that is, political, economic and social solutions were necessary to make psychological recovery possible. Her participants also found healing through narrative, when they heard the recovery stories of others and when they wrote their own in journals. Narrative helped them place their own experience in a wider framework, often a spiritual one. For some, this was the spirituality of Overeaters Anonymous, for others, a return to their own religious tradition. Often they moved through both to discover new forms of spirituality.

Phenomenological studies like these contain rich material for understanding anorexia and recovery, but they have not yet developed a sustained *theory* to account for the self-transformations they describe or their commonalities among women *and* men, in many cultures throughout history. My contribution to such a theory begins here, with my study participants' descriptions of what was most significant in their own tranformation. The rest of this book draws on further evidence from my study to elaborate a meta-narrative that accounts for the transformations themselves.

Elements of recovery

'Criteria' for recovery suggest measurement and the possibility of ultimate perfection and closure. Participants in my study rejected the idea that their lives could be evaluated in this way. Instead, they spoke of what I shall call 'elements' that were essential to their conception of recovery. Even this was often difficult, because many of them resisted the use of the word 'recovery'. No longer wanting to believe in or strive for perfection, they were very conscious of the need to avoid anything resembling over-achievement. Recovery, for them, is not about perfection, control, resolution or closure, but about continuing transformations. 'I don't like the word 'recovery' for anorexia', said Jacqueline; 'It feels like too final a term and that there is an expectation in myself to always be perfect'. People who had been struggling with eating problems for years, sometimes denied that there was such a thing as recovery[15] even as they expressed a longing for it: Jennifer says she would love to live life to the fullest and 'sort of' looks forward to the day she gets well. Freda, although still full of self-loathing, says she is 'very determined to stick around' until she likes herself. A few accepted that it was possible for others, but not for themselves because they were 'too set in their ways'. Some took an agnostic position, uncertain whether anyone really recovers, but interested in trying to define what recovery might be. Several participants were happy to appropriate the word, but had not used it as a framework for understanding the changes in their lives as their eating problems disappeared. Eloise, for instance, thought of the process as 'part of the continuum' of her life; a 'coping mechanism' she no longer needs and has 'outgrown'. Any definition of recovery must therefore allow for these meanings.

All participants agreed that the fundamental elements of recovery were:

(a) abandoning obsession with food and weight
(b) strongly believing that they would never go back to starving, bingeing or purging
(c) developing a critique of social pressures to be thin
(d) having a sense that their lives were meaningful – existentially or spiritually
(e) believing they were worthwhile people and that the different aspects of themselves were part of a whole person
(f) no longer feeling cut off from social interaction.

In its most obvious sense, recovery is about 'normal' eating, but the concept of 'normality' varies with its context. Participants in my study were especially dismissive of the notion of 'normality' which the clinical criteria presuppose. Sue, the only participant who says she has not spent much time thinking about her recovery, thinks she 'feels like anybody else' and simply 'presumes' she is 'normal'. People used the word 'normal' to mean either an abstract ideal ('eating differently from the way I eat now') or a comparison with others ('it's normal for women to worry about their weight'). The first meaning is conducive to recovery while the second, like clinical criteria for recovery, prevents people from transcending current social expectations; from 'stepping outside the stereotype of what's appropriate for women in our culture', as Vivienne put it. For those who had fully recovered, normality meant losing their obsession with food; being able to concentrate on other aspects of life and taking cues about the body and its needs from internal feelings, instead of looking for approval from others. These obvious issues of eating and body size came up at some point in every conversation, but even people who had not recovered knew that they were symbolic of more fundamental aspects of recovery.

To believe that recovery is possible is at least one further step in its direction. To know you will never return to the extremes of an eating problem is another. Jacqueline expressed the complexity of recovery when she said:

> I would say that I simply have the remnants – I have the war wounds – of having lived this way for a long, long time; and probably the fear of being that way. But I know it's not a real fear, because I know I would never, just simply not – I've moved too far beyond that. If I occasionally lapse, or lose my appetite, it's because I have a vulnerability in that area. There were times where I felt my goal was to never be plagued by anxiety about food and I came to discover that it was pretty unrealistic.

Although she is still very thin and afraid to gain more weight than she has, she knows not to push herself beyond the limits of her current recovery. Underneath her scars there is further pain waiting to be acknowledged and resolved, but Jacqueline also knows how far she has come and rejoices in that knowledge. Attempts to 'measure' recovery cannot convey this kind of complexity. In conceiving recovery as a linear progression, they miss the subtleties of its stages and turning points and fail to convey the process involved; the 'how' which clinical studies awkwardly call 'positive outcome indicators'; the sources of recovery.

Stages and turning points

'Stages' and 'turning points' are only established as such in the retelling of the recovery story. They are necessary markers of time and change in the narrative. They are also metaphors for the transformed attitude to time and space which takes place in the recovery phase in contrast with the chaos of the eating disorder.[16] Without them, there would be no story. The story is not only about changes in belief (in personal myth) but also about specific practices (or rituals) which brought about change.

For those who say they have recovered, recovery is never a fixed point but always an ongoing process. 'Progress' is not steady and there are many setbacks. It often feels like 'two steps forward, one step back'.[17] This realization is itself part of recovery, as Eloise pointed out. She said 'I came to an understanding that it's not an instantaneous project. It's actually an ongoing thing. Maybe that's all I needed to do.' Pip spoke of recovery as a kind of education; 'something to go through and from, not to deny'. Jodie also alluded to the continuity between anorexia and recovery when she said: 'You can't separate yourself from your past. It's like asking a widow if she's recovered from the death of her husband.' The fact that self-starvation leaves emotional and often (but not invariably) physical traces, does not negate the choice to continue active self-creation as a 'recovered', non-anorexic person. Scars can be reminders of the difference between the rigidity of 'then' and the continuing growth of 'now'.

Way (1993: 83) identifies an origin of recovery; when anorectics 'realize that they are out of control', that they are being controlled by their obsessions and that they want to change; but participants in my study made it clear that knowing and wanting to recover are only necessary, not sufficient, causes of change. Many of them had reached the realization and desire Way mentions, but felt incapable of turning them into action. Freda, for example, told me 'all the time at the back of your mind there's this nagging; 'I don't want to be like this'; but I'm not going to change that thinking in an interview!'. Kate wishes clinicians would stop putting the responsibility for recovery onto individual sufferers by telling them 'you don't *want* to get better yet', and look at the failure of their treatment programmes instead.

The real turning point usually occurs when people must choose between life and death.[18] This choice is not necessarily conscious. It can take place through ritual or bodily practice which is only later established as a belief. Nicki says: 'I couldn't break the cycle. It was a really awful point; sort of do or die' and for Eloise: 'Something tipped the balance and made me think: 'I can't continue to do that'. In part, my body said: 'you can't do this anymore'; it was too destructive.' None of the other participants remembers making a conscious choice to live, but allowing themselves to eat again *was* that choice. Meredith, now a food writer, says: 'Food is life, isn't it? Food is a symbol of life.'

For some, like Kate, there was a sudden switch in consciousness after which nothing was ever the same again. In her case it came during a therapy session in the last of fourteen hospital admissions, when she found an origin for her anorexic behaviour. For her, the origin was a frightening episode years earlier, when she had almost bled to death. From the moment she connected her anorexia with this memory of loss of control, everything changed very fast: 'For me, it wasn't that slow incremental progress. I just got out of it rapidly. As much as things had gone bad for me earlier, now things went well.' In retrospect, her recovery seems sudden and miraculous, but she says she still had a lot of 'catching up' to do after many years in and out of hospital; learning to eat differently and learning about relationships, for instance. The fact that she did all this quite rapidly does not detract from the general point that recovery is never instantaneous. Vivienne's story, describing transitions and setbacks, is more typical:

I knew there were certain things that wellness would entail, like being better at looking after myself . . . and I thought, in true anorexic style, that I would put all those things in place in my life and hey presto! 'betterness' would appear! And what I had to accept was that there was going to be a long transition where I tried to do the things that would help, and I still carried on binge-vomiting or occasionally attempting to slip back into starvation.

Sue placed the origin of her recovery at the point where others (doctors, her mother, hospital staff) gave up the attempt to help and allowed her some self-determination. The turning point for her was 'when everybody stopped nagging me and started to leave me alone'; but 'it was still a very slow process after that and it took a long time'. Some participants identified a number of beginnings, rather than a single origin. Zoe referred to this as 'rock-hopping'; a kind of goal setting. For Rosalie, there were two turning points: starting work and moving in with the man she eventually married. My own recovery was episodic, constantly renewed and I thought of it as 'learning' and 'changing', rather than 'recovery'. In all these recovery stories time is cyclical, not a linear progression. There is no necessary beginning or end associated with recovery, but there are points when the same issues reappear and are given new meanings.[19]

Return of the repressed trauma

Sometimes, as Kate's story illustrates, the new understandings which made recovery possible could only emerge through a re-encounter with earlier suffering. For several women this happened during a period of post-partum depression or marital problems and divorce. Many now see these 'setbacks' as opportunities they had to 'work through'; to recognize and abandon painful past experiences, often of psychological and sexual abuse in childhood. Once they lost the obsession with eating or not eating, other feelings had to be faced more directly and some of them still recur.[20] Meredith's story is typical:

I feel a lot stronger and much more connected with the world around me and with people, but arising within me each day come up old patterns . . . Recently, on a gastronomic tour overseas, I stayed with people who were extremely generous and wonderful cooks, but it brought up so much for me. It brought up: 'I don't want to be forced or feel I have to eat three meals a day with other people'. I was not in control and I got very ill in my stomach.

Susanna, too, is sometimes anxious about eating out, but she now recognizes the source of the feeling, detaches it from the present, and goes out anyway. Accepting recovery makes episodes like these part of the process, not evidence of 'illness'. The same feelings people had during their eating disorder come back, but because they are understood, they no longer incapacitate. Miranda described this as 'converting bulimia into other, less harmful, forms of control'. Each time she finds a new way to cope with the return of her trauma, the feelings become a little weaker. She hopes that eventually, she can trust her surroundings enough to let go of deliberate control mechanisms as a way of feeling safe in the world 'and just let myself exist'. When the 'traumas' return, as they inevitably do, the new beliefs and practices are brought into play; not to deny the reality of the repressed, but to counteract and transform its meaning.

The return of 'mystical' awareness

Recovery always implies a return. Participants often spoke of 'going back' and 'rediscovering' something they had lost; the 'self' they experienced before their eating disorder; a self connected through relation to the 'Other' including people, nature and an awareness greater than both. Stories about recovery from traumas (accidents, torture, rape, incest, illness) frequently refer to spirit and soul, whether spirit is conceived in psychological, humanist, or theological terms. At the very least they mention some form of 'transcendent experience' which transforms lives.[21] Lesley experienced her recovery as a return to her lively, energetic ten year old self. Jacqueline spoke of a revelation; her rediscovery of a joy and pleasure she thought she had lost. Meredith described her new awareness as 'coming home' and in my own story, friendship, sexual relations, birth, breastfeeding, meditation and yoga were all felt as returns to some original lost wholeness and connectedness; the experience before the traumas which led to the spiritual limbo of anorexia.

There is a Freudian explanation, with several un-Freudian twists, for this sense of return to something always known. It can be found by combining Freud's theories of hysteria (which eating disorders closely resemble)[22] with his attempt to explain 'the oceanic myth' (the derogatory term he used to describe mystical experience). In Freud's meta-narratives, based on his retelling of his patients' stories, recovery from hysteria occurred through 'the talking cure'; bringing to verbal consciousness memories of a trauma which had been repressed by the strength of the trauma itself. The talking cure therefore involved the return of the repressed: a linkage of the present with the past through the creation of a narrative about the repressed trauma. This often led to the 'abreaction' of hysterical symptoms. No longer needed, they vanished; their silent bodily witness replaced by the narrative which explained them. An important part of Freud's theory was that for hysteria to occur there must have been not one, but at least two traumas (or sets of traumas); the first (the original trauma) occuring in the pre-Oedipal period of early childhood and the second around puberty. This second trauma (for Freud, always sexual in nature) acted as a mask for the first. The question Freud did not ask was 'what positive experience (of very early childhood and of pre-puberty) has been repressed by hysteria only to re-emerge when hysteria disappears?'

The answer might lie in his sketch of the origins of religious feeling, also in the pre-Oedipal period. Freud had great difficulty in accounting for the religious impulse on the individual or the social level, in part because of their association with the maternal; 'the sphere of the first attachment to the mother . . . so grey with age and shadowy and almost impossible to revivify – that it was as if it had succumbed to an especially inexorable repression' (Freud 1977: 373). Could it be this very feeling – the experience of union and bliss of the child at the mother's breast, when all its needs are met – which is the template for all mystical experience? It seems to be this bodily sensation of oneness which underlies such religious concepts as Faith and Grace in Christianity, Atman or Self in Hinduism and Nirvana in Buddhism.[23] It transcends the rational consciousness the child acquires through entry into language. It is the 'semiotic chora' to which Julia Kristeva refers as the source of creativity; mysterious and unnameable, containing the terrifying space of the 'abject' (1980) and the source of sacred texts (1984; see Grosz 1989: 44, 49, 84). A comparison with mystical experience in a variety of religions suggests that Freud and Kristeva are referring to aspects of mysticism, including the 'dark night of the soul' (Johnston 1995).

In recovery we experience not only the traumas (including our entry into language) which cut us off from our original sensations of oneness, but also some echo of that feeling of oneness itself. The only way this awareness can begin to be expressed is in poetic, metaphorical form; the form that enables us to hold in our minds simultaneously the experience of our bodies and our perception of external reality. The story of recovery is not about overcoming self-starvation itself, but transcending the traumas which preceded it; creating a new way of being that draws upon a narrative of connectedness 'before the fall'. In this sense, recovery has the 'newness of aftermath' rather than 'the newness of Edenic immediacy' (Said 1975: 371).[24]

Reconnecting with the world

It is not only perceptions of time that change during recovery. Space, or people's relation to their surroundings, is experienced quite differently too. The boundaries between 'self' and 'nature' become more flexible. As Aleisha put it,

As I recovered, I started to believe that my body wasn't separate from nature and I really love nature. Not nature like I have to go and sit among the trees; just nature like what it is. I don't think anybody anywhere is separate from nature, and your food represents your relationship with the universe. My relationship with the universe is one of acceptance and peace now.

Descriptions of this relationship with nature are also inevitably poetic, since it is poetry that puts into linguistic form the interconnections which are part of all mystical awareness. Even Michael, without benefit of recovery, has episodes of connectedness which feel like momentary healing: 'You learn from the mountains, because there's a unique aura about them that makes you unravel the complexity of your self'. Ilse told me that spiritual life for her had always been connected with nature and that her recovery involved accepting that human suffering and growth was just like that of animals and plants. As she put it: 'There's an inherent wisdom in the lifecycle – a life-force'. This metaphor, connecting human knowledge with a life-force in nature, is one element in the creative narrative which has made recovery possible for Ilse. Even those who did not speak directly of nature as 'spiritual', emphasized its importance in their ongoing recovery. Pip, for example, has compulsive urges to go to a beach for periodic mental renewal; Naomi describes her gardening as a form of meditation; something which allows her just to 'be' in the present and in her immediate surroundings.

Even though 'nature' can only be known through the lenses of culture which creates it as an object, there is also a sense in which the 'being' of nature, its spirit, 'breaks through' culture to 'infuse' our own being. Our conceptions of nature and our relations with it are a vital part of the narrative of recovery. The 'reality' of this connection cannot be denied. It may also lead us to postulate the presence of spirit in nature, for in this relationship 'something real takes place to the extent that a person places his or her spiritual body more immediately in contact with the natural universe – and this real something can be limited to neither a bodily nor a mental process' (Kovel 1991: 159).

Travel, too, is about boundaries between self and otherness and for several people in my study it seemed to speed up the process of self-transformation; but only when they felt ready and freely chose it. For some like Jacqueline, whose parents took her on a European tour at the height of her anorexia, it was terrifying. For others like Naomi and Sue, it provided opportunities to experiment with new identities and a different time-frame within which to do so. In removing people from the surroundings where they had begun their self-starvation, travel took away many conventional social expectations and revealed their inconsistencies. It often led to enjoyable interaction with strangers and to the development of greater self-confidence. Often (though not always), participants' eating habits became more relaxed when they travelled. As Victoria says of people in the horseriding country she loves: 'They don't understand how you could say no to a fresh-baked scone' and, of her visits to her husband's homeland: 'People there don't constantly notice what you eat or don't eat'. Significantly, those who say they have not recovered often avoid further travel: Freda says cynically: 'You can be somebody else when you're away for a few weeks – so the idea is not to travel, right?'

Travel can be a helping metaphor for our own self-transformation. Even to read about the journey of recovery is to discover new images of ourselves. It fulfills a psychological need to view ourselves from a different perspective. The images of otherness which we gather during our travels bring about these changes because 'concepts are static; images are alive; they lead us on to ideas of ourselves that we have never entertained' (McMaster 1993).

Reconnecting with people

Increasing social contact and a sense of belonging with other people usually began with one particularly significant and unconditionally accepting relationship; sometimes with a therapist but often outside therapy. Often, too, participants had to break away from a confining relationship (particularly with mothers, but frequently from the unrelenting standards of their fathers) in order to establish wider social connections. These experiences of human connection were potential catalysts in recovery, as this episode in Jennifer's anorexic adolescence makes clear:

I went on a beach holiday with one of my friends. Her mother was a very wise woman and when she found me lying in the sand, at the end of my tether, she popped me on her knee and said 'You're very thin, you're also very loved'; just a gentle way of consoling me and making me feel better. I messed up their holiday, but I slowly started eating. It didn't last long, but that was the closest I came to recovery.

Relationships often became a positive substitute for the importance of food. Social acceptance broke down isolation and restored self-worth. Meeting and participating in groups with others who shared similar political or spiritual values strengthened the sense of meaning the recovering person was beginning to create. Participants described the way they were transformed in their interaction with others. This interfusion of being always opens up transformative possibilities, either for domination or liberation; most powerfully in sexual relationships. One meaning of sexuality *is* this openness to others and to the world, which is why sexual experience was often a vital part of recovering.[25] Friendship came in many guises, one of which was in the professional relations of therapy; with nurses, counsellors and sometimes teachers, as well as with psycho-therapists.

Therapists

Several participants mentioned that therapy can only be effective at 'the right moment'. For many this moment did not come until long after they had resumed relatively normal eating: 'I don't think I was helpable', said Margaret; 'everyone was concerned about me, but I don't think anyone could have done anything.' Patricia, however, suggested that her continuing resistance to therapy may be the very reason why she constructs her past therapeutic experiences as totally negative: 'I don't know that it didn't work', she says. 'I've conveniently blocked off what actually happened, but I don't know if that's me just saying: "Oh yes, but I've done all that".'

Psychotherapy and psychiatric treatment, in general and for anorexia in particular, have now received considerable criticism[26] and during the course of my conversations I heard horrific accounts of force-feeding, of inappropriate gynaecological treatments, of behaviour therapy and of hospital psychiatrists who were more interested in the 'case' than in the person; 'just really ugly experiences', said Eloise of hers. Freda for example, was threatened with certification as a mental patient and permanent incarceration if she did not gain weight. She complied out of sheer terror, was unable to stop, and is now obese. Rosalie remembers that the psychiatrists who treated her in hospital were 'as much at a loss as I was; any insight into what was happening didn't help, because there wasn't any insight into how to recover'.

When participants did have positive memories of psychotherapy, it was the person and the relationship which they remembered as having been important, rather than any particular therapeutic technique. The power of successful therapy lay in having one's being recognized by the other; the essence of satisfied desire (Kovel 1991: 126–7). For Nicki, during her four months in hospital, it was the friendship of other patients and of the nurses which had the most impact on her recovery. She accepted them as 'role models', even as models of how to eat 'normally', because they treated her 'like a normal human being' and talked to her 'on an ordinary level'. They also listened, with cumulative effect. Susanna interpreted her therapist's listening to mean: 'I am here for you and I accept you for who you are', and his calm presence had a very powerful influence. Several participants still think of their ex-therapist as a friend and of their relationship as a model for the friendships that continue to sustain them. Veronica Coopman, once anorexic and bulimic, and now working as a therapist herself, captures this all-important aspect of therapy – the way the relationship itself transcends the individuals engaged in it – in her poem 'The healing force':

> If
> you come to me
> for treatment,
> revere
> the work
> done through yourself
> Do not refer to me
> or my learning
> for if you do
> I can feel only
> me
> and that which
> heals
> eludes us both.   (Coopman 1991: 118)

Children

Another potential 'healing force' is the experience of having children. Pregnancy and motherhood drew very different responses from each participant, depending on the stage when they occurred. Childless women who had not fully recovered feared pregnancy and the loss of control over their bodies which it would entail: To Nicki , 'the whole idea of being pregnant just sounds revolting. Having to put on weight makes you feel really fat and gross.' Jennifer feels the same, but she is also aware that she is depriving herself of something she really wants:

My deepest wish, when I was a little girl, was to have about four kids. The reasons for not having children are not what's really in my heart. It's in my head: Really the reason is I don't want to be pregnant, I don't want to eat, I don't want to not be able to have my laxatives, and I couldn't bear to be fat while being pregnant and I don't want the responsibility of a child – which is, to me (I look from an outside point of view) an awful excuse for not having children.

Some participants who had not fully recovered but did have children described pregnancy and motherhood as traumatic events in their lives. Victoria, who has three children, loathed the weight gains of pregnancy and her increased appetite. In her first pregnancy, she dropped five kilos below her starting weight and was delighted. She was so obsessed with physical beauty, that her mother was afraid if she had a less than perfect baby, she would reject it. Her first son was premature and tiny and she says 'it took me a good six weeks to like him. He was lucky I didn't fling him across the room. He was very lucky I accepted him!'

In contrast, people who had fully recovered when they had children, spoke of pregnancy and living with their children as opportunities for new awareness and further self-transformation, even when some, like Miranda, had a few doubts about it at first. Being pregnant took away all the residual anxieties about her body, 'because there was an absolutely legitimate reason for being bulky', but at the same time, she was terrified that she would 'make bad what was within me' and that she wouldn't be able to contain and nourish a child for the full term when she had been so bad at nourishing herself: 'I had brought up everything I put in there, so how could I hold a baby for nine months?' Margaret has three children and, like several other participants, she referred to the potential intimacy, transcendence of self and physicality of motherhood as healing experiences:

I enjoyed all the physical aspects of the pregnancy and I breastfed them all and I enjoyed that and felt good about it. It's great intimacy with another person and it's giving to another person and having to be open about your physicalness. I feel a great deal more sense of at-easeness with my physical person than I did before.

Parenthood, perhaps more than any other experience, has the potential both for the return of negative repressed traumas and for the re-experience, this time from the parent's perspective, of the deep intimacy of the original spiritual experience. It is not an experience of pure union, as it was for the infant; but an adult's opportunity for renewed awareness of one's body and its capacities, for connection with another being and with rhythms of nature and cycles of birth and death.

Creating recovery

There is a crucial relationship between creativity, spirituality and recovery. The creative endeavour of self-transformation is inseparable from its expression in 'works of art'; each is part of the other. Although I have emphasized the place of narrative – of story-telling and writing – in recovery, the process is also accompanied by other creative acts. Participants had various ways of describing this relationship: Dominic saw recovery itself as a form of creativity, of 'restructuring your time'. For Naomi, quiltmaking and elaborate knitting represented her commitment to living: they were antidotes to depression and suicide. Jacqueline's artistic project; to paint 200 shades of grey, was the beginning of her exploration beyond the black and white world of her anorexic existence. Zoe's recognition of her desire to create was her turning point. Because anorexia 'eked the life' out of her, her conscious decision to be 'fruitful' was totally incompatible with being anorexic. She speaks of her creative desire as a spiritual energy and appetite. When she enrolled in art school, still severely anorexic, she also spent a lot of time in the church nearby:

I must have been the only art student in Sydney who went to Mass! The college was just behind the church, and I used to sneak out to the church! I was still very thin at that stage. I'd go out to Mass and I'd go back to the art school. I wouldn't let anyone see me go . . . And all the time that I was doing that I was reaching out for that spiritual food that was going to feed me.

The creative impulse is the search for salvation and at the same time, the means towards it. It is about creating our own images of God; making aspects of our life into sacred ideals towards which we strive and expressing them in concrete form. In this sense creativity is present in the 'negative cult' of anorexia as much as it is in the 'positive cult' of recovery. But sacred ideals are not always life-enhancing. Many participants identify the beginning of their anorexia with the cutting off of their creativity. Freda for instance, became anorexic when her father, against her teacher's better judgement, told Freda she would never be 'good enough' to be a professional musician. Those who cannot face the prospect of recovery usually avoid creative activities. They are afraid of the unknown which is entailed in re-creating themselves. Patricia has been told and knows that she 'thinks creatively' and 'could be a very creative person', but she does not allow herself to try; to 'cut free and loosen up', as she puts it.

People do not necessarily stop being creative during their anorexic period, however. It is obvious from the life stories of many creative artists that they were in no sense 'recovered' from their addiction or madness and that many died of it. Perhaps, for these artists, since creativity is about abandoning ego, the experience can be too intense to sustain without the crutch of an addiction or madness (or the apparent control of anorexia). The person who creates in this way, creates in spite of the ultimately disabling crutch; but in the end may be destroyed by it.[27] What participants do make clear, however, is that just as the notion of 'distorted spirituality' is fraught with the possibility of inappropriate judgments, so the idea of 'repressed creativity' fails to recognize the personal satisfaction and often the social recognition that is available to people in the midst of their suffering, including during their anorexic period. It was Kate, the poet and novelist, whose discussion of creativity made this point most sharply and provided me with a way out of this theoretical dilemma: Kate never stopped writing during her anorexic years, but she now sees that her writing was mono-dimensional; 'I got stuck and could only see the world in one way and I knew that I must try and shift myself and try and see it in different ways.' Even today, she can still become 'stuck' in a particular way of seeing the world. Her current task, she says, is to extricate herself from the constraints of the poststructuralist theory she adopted during her postgraduate studies.

These examples suggest that creativity plays a vital role in recovery, not because creativity is always lost during self-starvation, but because self-starvation ultimately ends one's creativity through self-destruction. Even Virginia Woolf, who wrestled with the complex relationship between creativity, self-starvation and despair, believed that 'you can only really create when you are well fed and have uninterrupted time and space in which to do it' (Woolf 1974). The fact that she could not fully live up to this ideal does not detract from its importance as a goal. But it is Kate's account (above) of the ongoing conversions of her own creativity which best explains how relative the notion of creativity can be; for it is equally possible for the 'recovered' artist in all of us to become 'stuck' in a single way of seeing reality. It is, once again, her appeal to the non-linear, non-evolutionary nature of both creativity and recovery which makes it possible to understand their relationship more clearly. Creativity, like desire and spirituality, is a potential force for transformation but, at the same time, it always exists in a social context; that is to say, it flourishes in response to the creativity of others and draws upon the discourses and practices (the 'technologies of self')[28] available in any given society.

The means to recovery from eating problems are fundamentally the same as the ways people recover from suffering of any kind; they are the activities through which human beings create and recreate themselves. The only difference is that with eating disorders the transformations and the scars (if any) are food-related. Recovery is no more mysterious than anorexia and no less mysterious than the questions that can be asked about life itself. That these practices and the changes they bring about are named 'spiritual' by the majority of participants is an indication of their enormous power and of their origins in shared social experience *and* spiritual energy.

6   Recovery stories

Introduction

The stories of Jennifer, Lesley and Vivienne illustrate the differences between each of three stages in the journey through anorexia and recovery: the negative phase of the anorexic quest, the turning point into recovery and the ongoing discoveries of the positive phase of re-emergence. These stories demonstrate two aspects of recovery that call for more than selective quotation: the coherence of recovery narratives and their mythological structure. Here, I tell each story in approximately the same sequence as I heard it, using as many of each speaker's words as possible and including their own extended definitions of 'recovery'[1]. Each story concludes with a brief summary linking it to the general observations of the previous two chapters.

The coherence of recovery stories depends upon a structural sequence from 'eating disorder' through a 'recovering' period (however brief) to a conviction that one has recovered; although the transformations of recovery continue even after this conviction has been established. The coherence of the story helps create the coherence of the experience. The sense of flow in both comes from retelling and polishing the story until it is smooth. This does not mean that recovery stories contain no gaps or inconsistencies, much less that recovery allows for none. Instead, recovery includes developing an ability to accept gaps and inconsistencies (in memory and in understanding); to resolve paradox by moving to a higher level of abstraction which narrative makes possible; a transcendence through story. A coherent experience, like a story, is communicable. It is also *connected* in several ways: first, its elements join into a sequence that points to the relations among them (e.g. cause and effect); second, it presupposes an 'author' capable of holding the story together; and third, its similarities with other stories about humans and nature join it to mythology; the sacred narratives underlying experience. These connections are also features of my provisional definition of spirituality as a sense of inner connection and meaning, connection with others and connection with nature and the cosmos. In narratives of recovery, 'spirituality', coherence and mythological structure are therefore inseparable.

Certain myths appear in widely different cultures as organizing principles behind personal and social life. Whenever people tell their stories, they draw upon and help perpetuate these archetypal myths. They are clues to understanding the relationship between the development of the individual psyche, the social context within which it occurs, and the ways in which human beings understand their purpose in the cosmos. Many stories about gods and heroes concern trials and tribulations that provide the necessary initiation into the full stature of adulthood. They are generally concerned with the specificities of a male or female initiation process. Each story in this book echoes myths of initiation, relationship and salvation; myths of self transformation.

Myths of death and rebirth, descent into hell and re-emergence into light abound in human civilization. In western culture, one of particular relevance to women is the myth of Persephone, in which the virgin heroine is dragged down to the underworld by the god Pluto, eventually to be rescued through the maternal love and supplications of her mother, the Earth-goddess Demeter, in a complementary version of the father-son mythology of Christian resurrection. Significantly for stories of recovery, in the Homeric version of the myth, it is Hermes, god of communication, who brings about Persephone's rescue[2]. A much older myth, the Sumerian myth of Ishtar-Inanna, contains even more powerful images of the recovery process which forms part of women's 'initiation' (Perera 1981)[3]. In this myth, the goddess Inanna (archetypal woman) descends to the underworld to join her 'dark sister' Ereshkigal in mourning for her husband. Inanna's entrance to the netherworld is marked by the stripping of all her upperworldly regalia piece by piece as she descends through seven gates. On her arrival in this place of death and nothingness – the primal chaos – she is killed and hung on a peg 'like a side of green, rotting meat' (Perera 1981: 9). When Inanna fails to return, her trusted female executive, Ninshibur, appeals to the great god Enki for assistance. Enki is the god of water, wisdom and creativity; a father figure with wonderfully maternal attributes. He lives in the waters of the abyss; engendering both semen and amniotic fluid: Enki's wisdom flows with, breaks up; it releases the inertia and rigidity of the underworld . . . His waters restore the wasteland, symbolic of the never-ending flow of life's energies. Like the flow of libidinous affect, these waters carry us back into life after a deathlike depression (Perera 1981: 67–8). Enki represents the spiritual wisdom that is an essential element in recovery. From dirt under his fingernail, he creates two tiny mourners/helpers to slip unnoticed into the underworld and set about Inanna's rescue. Perera sees these unobtrusive figures as archetypes of the therapist; 'present, accepting and letting be, expressing the truth of the dark affects, waiting with patience, going deeper and waiting together with Inanna until the time is ripe for her re-emergence' (p.74). In recovery stories, the helpers who have some of these qualities are sometimes therapists and often friends or understanding and accepting acquaintances.

In the stories that follow, I will be pointing out fundamental similarities with this and other myths of self-transformation. The first story (Jennifer's) begins in the tight control and concealed despair of anorexia. She is caught in the first phase of descent and return; deep inside the pit, but not yet touching its base; unable to find a way down or out and with apparently no-one to help her do so. The second (Lesley's) is told from the edge of the pit, looking back after her recent emergence. The last (Vivienne's) is the most coherent and complete, but only temporarily so as Vivienne, fully recovered, goes on to the next tasks in the construction of her life; including that of assisting others to make the part of the journey she has now completed.

Jennifer's Story: 'I control my little hell'

Jennifer did not immediately strike me as thin, unhappy or obsessed. On the phone and face to face, she seemed bright and even relaxed, but in the apartment she shares with her husband in a fashionable suburb, everything matches and nothing is out of place. Ushering me in, she talks about her job in the fashion industry and her active social life; but even before we are seated she says: 'You see; I keep up the perfect front' and begins a kind of confession whose cynicism still shocks me.

Jennifer has been starving and purging with laxatives for thirteen years. She married Anthony on the explicit condition that he would not interfere with, or even comment upon, these twin rituals around which her life revolves; but her implicit hope was that Anthony would recognize the extent of her suffering and help her escape from the prison of self-discipline into which she has locked herself. She bitterly denounces his failure even to try, at the same time telling me that he must work out for himself how to save her, for if she told him, the magic would not work. She pretends, even to him, that they have a perfect marriage.

She illustrates her 'story' with photos – a slightly larger Jennifer ('I hated myself then – managed to lose it all in a couple of months'), with Anthony ('I broke up with him once, because the relationship interfered with my dieting'), her much older siblings ('I want to punish them; look what their ignorance has done!') but none of her parents. Her mother suffered from such severe post-natal depression that she was institutionalized after the birth of each child. Her father spent his last two years in hospital (when she visited, he would say: 'It's Jenny; my little angel from heaven'). He died when she was ten and there was no mourning ('the next morning, Mum told us, and then said: "Now eat up your scrambled eggs"''). Her mother suffered a prolonged emotional breakdown and her siblings escaped by leaving home. Jennifer felt abandoned, unloved and unloveable. Self-denial through starvation was her way of coping with self-hatred and pain. She points to a shelf full of books on eating disorders and says 'they confirm me in how I want to be'. For her, they are 'how-to', not 'self-help' manuals.

When participants told me they did not consider they had recovered, I asked them what they thought recovery might mean for them and mentioned the clinical criteria for recovery. Jennifer rejected them immediately because of the problem of defining 'normality'. She said: 'I have surface normality. That's nothing. You can pretend you have normal eating habits and you don't. My husband sees me eat a big meal every night but if he actually counted how many calories in the lettuce, cucumber, tomato, bit of beetroot, tinned asparagus! . . . Honey, it adds up to seventy calories!' She described her understanding of recovery, but not how it might be reached: 'Basically, it's letting people get to know you. Allowing yourself to be hurt. While you're still hurting, you just don't want any more hurt. The more years that people build up and hold on, the harder it is. It's opening up. It's letting go of all the hurts'. She knows, too, that 'the bottom line is people need to talk – to express their problems, before they can even think of dealing with them'. She showed no interest at all in how other people had recovered and has strenuously avoided seeking help, but she did say wistfully: 'I'd love to be healthy. My biggest wish would be to eat when I want without having a hang-up; but I know I haven't really faced up to the problem or to any of the emotional things that could have accounted for it'. When she adds 'I've never talked it through with anyone', could her reason for contacting me be a step she is deliberately taking towards recovery? She isn't sure: 'I can go on as I am, you know, but I sort of look forward to the day when I can get well. I've been saying this for ten years. I don't want to go on saying it for another ten years. But at least I'm living. People don't know anything's wrong. I control my little hell'.

Jennifer has a fantasy in which she loses so much weight that she has to give up work and 'throw herself' into hospital; to get worse in order to get better. The fantasy involves retribution; she would love to write to her 'friends' and say: 'Greetings from the eating disorders clinic. Look what you've done! Look what your lack of talking to me and understanding and learning about the problem has done!'. 'It's a bit of a punishment to them and my sisters and brothers and Anthony.' Unaware of the resources in herself, she waits for others to break into her prison and rescue her. They must find a way to transform her through their love, yet she is incapable of telling them how. Her anger with their failure is palpable.

Jennifer did not really tell me a story and certainly not a recovery story. She did not follow a chronological or any other narrative sequence. Instead, she constantly came back to her obsessions; weight, diet and laxatives. Although she has a story about how her self-starvation began, she cannot speak of turning points, stages or transformations in her recovery because she is still locked into her account of suffering and its causes. The makings of recovery are present in the way she speaks of its possibility and in her awareness of a few of its elements (the need to go down in order to re-emerge fully, to re-examine repressed aspects of her trauma; to lose her obsession with food and weight, to be open to genuine interaction with others; to be able to talk about her pain and to feel accepted and worthwhile). In using 'you' and 'they', rather than 'I', when speaking about recovering, she distances herself from the possibility of contemplating her own recovery[4]. Rather than identify with other people who share her 'anorexic' experience, she chooses to objectify them and thereby objectifies herself.

Jennifer has reached the state of Snow White in *The Snow White Soliloquies*, the novella Sheila MacLeod wrote during her own recovery from anorexia: 'I don't want to be born again. I don't want to have to go through it all again. Let me be. My life, or half-life if you prefer, is ideal. For me. And if it is ideal for me, why should it be changed? It's my life. I'm not hindering anyone' (1971: 21). She is also like the Fairy Melusina, a much more powerful and complex character than Snow White[5]. While Snow White patiently awaits her prince, Melusina has married hers, but she has also told him never to spy on her in the privacy of her bathroom. When he does, he discovers her dreadful secret; that she has the body of a serpent from the waist down. He is angry with her, she with him, and she turns into a dragon, flying away round the battlements of the castle making a terrible noise and battering the stones. Jennifer's tiny body also hides a dark secret. Should her husband Anthony allude to it, her wrath will know no bounds. He knows her strength, since she shows it daily in her superhuman restraint of appetite and appearance of normality. But at the same time, she longs for him to discover the Beauty within her threatened Beast (a reversal of the gender roles in Beauty and the Beast) and to release her to be who she is truly capable of being. From the point of view of the Inanna myth, Jennifer's anger with Anthony and her family has made them scapegoats for her suffering. The final part of the myth requires Inanna's consort, the charming but as yet spiritually unaware

Dumuzi, to go to the underworld in her place for part of each year, to achieve her permanent release. On the sociological level, this requirement expresses the necessity for men to recognize and take upon themselves some of the psychological burden of the women they love; to undertake their own difficult spiritual journey before they can be full partners with women who have passed through suffering and initiation.

To sum up: Jennifer's apparently 'normal' (socially approved) size conveys the (also socially approved) message of control. Few people in our culture can read the other part of Jennifer's message; that this control confines her to a narrow 'little hell'. Jennifer's story illustrates several common elements of anorexia and recovery which have not received the attention they deserve in the literature on eating disorders. They include the following: Eating problems are not about vanity, but a way of coping with trauma (including, in her case, unresolved grief). To resolve the eating disorder, we must find other, less damaging ways of dealing with past hurts. 'Knowing' about the causes of anorexia is not enough; it can merely confirm an anorexic 'identity'. Anorexia is a negative, protective ritual; its resolution requires different, positive rituals of engagement with the world. Clinical criteria for recovery do not get to the heart of the matter, especially not to the question of what is 'normal' eating behaviour, in a society where the majority of women (and increasing numbers of men) diet. The recovery process, in either sex, is enhanced by the understanding and participation of the other sex. Recovery must include self-recognition and self-acceptance. These come from deep engagement with others and the 'talk' which makes it possible for the sufferer to reconstruct personal narrative from a partial to a fuller account of her life. The next story represents the early stages of this remaking.

Lesley's story: 'It's been a roller-coaster'

Lesley's story is pivotal in my exploration of recovery, because I met her at a major turning point in her life; within the first two years of her marriage and of her medical practice. In the six months between her first phone call and our meeting in person, she had gained seven kilos and as a result she told me: 'Everything has just radically changed and I can't really put my finger on anything now'. After years of study and internship, she was beginning to enjoy a social life. For the first time in fifteen years, she had left psychiatric treatment and stopped taking anti-depressants. She talked of being in a period of adjustment, but used the same expressions ('never again') as participants who identified themselves as 'recovered' and was optimistic about her future.

Lesley strongly believes in the value of telling one's story. She says she has never discussed the issue of her anorexia, despite her years of psychiatric treatment, because the treatment focused purely on depression. She was hospitalized for anorexia when she was eleven years old, but once she moved away from her home town, she did not mention anorexia to any of her later psychiatrists and none of them asked. Like many of the 'recently recovered' people in my study, she is afraid she might express too much emotion and worries that her story might be painful for me as well. She welcomes the opportunity to order her thoughts in a 'concrete framework' and 'get some idea' of the part of her journey she has now reached and what the next steps might be, though it also makes her realize 'you might not have got as far in all this as you thought you had'. She mentions her need to sort out the 'rush of unsorted emotions' of her current stage; but hers is the chaos of transformation, not the rigid despair of Jennifer's anorexia. Hesitations and repetitions as she speaks express the confusion she is experiencing and her active search for structure and meaning within it. Lesley pays close attention to the eating side of her recovery, but mainly to make the contrasts between her past and present attitudes and practices. Her work, her marriage and her friends have now become more important than obsessive food control but she qualifies her growing confidence with a reminder of what is still to be overcome and doubts about her ability to do so (another common feature in the stories of people at this stage of recovery).

The flow and change in what she says are absent from Jennifer's conversation. Because my interview with Jennifer the day before is so vivid in my memory, I also immediately notice the difference between the marriages of the two women: Jennifer's is based on secrecy, Lesley's on greater openness. Although she does not think her husband Mark really understands what she has gone through, they seem to be negotiating the food issues (and no doubt many others) in a way which forces her to change some of her established patterns. Mark knows, but is not very concerned, about her 'anorexic past'; 'he thinks it's something that happened ten years ago and it's over'. Lesley does not like Mark treating her like a child in relation to food, reminding her when and what she must eat, because it brings to mind her parents, but she is glad he cares. Unlike Jennifer, she has not made her husband's co-operation essential to her recovery. She accepts full responsibility for her eating behaviour and the recent changes in her attitude to food: she has put on weight for her own sake and not to please him. She says: 'I allowed myself to put on weight [and] I find now that I'll just eat because I have to eat to keep going, but before I was always hungry and I'd always say: 'No, no you're not allowed to be hungry. You can't have anything to eat'. So I respond more to the feelings of hunger than I ever did before.'

The pattern Lesley describes recurs in each of the stories of recovered participants: the gradual acceptance of bodily needs and the importance of relationships ('for so long I repressed every social feeling I had'). She also alludes to the return of a previously repressed and now remembered pre-anorexic happiness: 'Before the anorexia I was a very bubbly, lively ten year old and I feel I'm slowly starting to come right round again. I hope so.' When she goes out socially, people tell her they are glad to see her and she uses this social contact to enhance her self-esteem, to confirm her subjective feelings of growing confidence and worth, whereas Jennifer and each of the other 'non-recovered' participants discounted compliments because they did not fit with their own negative self-perceptions. Lesley used to feel 'I may as well not be here – I'm of no value to anybody', but 'that's certainly changed now'.

Lesley was brought up in a Lutheran family and community. Her ideas about spirituality have developed along lines of her own today; but her anorexia, like mine, may have been influenced by a Protestant form of anxiety and a consequent perfectionism.[6] When I ask Lesley what religion means to her now, she mentions the sense of being fundamentally acceptable; of her life having some purpose – the feeling she lost during her long anorexic period. She says she would like to explore her Christianity further one day, but that it plays no direct part in her current stage of recovery. This does not mean there is no connection between her religious belief and her emergence from depression and starvation. On the contrary; just as she draws on the social acceptance which part of her has always known would be available when she was ready for it, so she is beginning to reclaim her spiritual awareness; feeling that her existence matters and making up her mind about where she fits in the overall scheme of things.

The sense of journeying, of quest, of change, even if it is slow, now imbues her narrative, in contrast to the static accounts of people who have not yet reached a turning point. Even in referring to her recent ideas about recovery as 'wishy-washy,' she is using a fluid image. Lesley's concluding remarks anticipate, however tentatively, those of fully recovered participants: 'I'm sure there are some people who don't want to let go of the strings of the past; it's comfortable to keep on going with what you know, rather than trying to move on. But I certainly don't want to keep on the way I was.' Whereas Jennifer's story concerned her descent into the underworld and her realization that she had not gone far enough into its 'negative cult' to justify her return to the upper world; Lesley's is told at the point where she has just emerged from the underworld. She is conscious, in her remarks about an unseen power that knows what's best for her, of the intervention of a force beyond and within her: Enki's

wisdom. Eating and drinking again, she is, like Inanna at the corresponding stage of the myth: 'revived; sprinkled with the food and water of life'.
'There is an anointing or libation of the oral, good stuff, a granting of value
and validation in sprinkled doses'; the approval Lesley mentioned from
her friends and colleagues. Nevertheless, at the moment of return, she
feels 'simply befuddled and dizzy like an infant, new before life' (Perera
1981: 78).

In my retelling of her story, Lesley's husband Mark is an ambiguous
figure; part helper, part liberator; part challenger, part sexual complement. In terms of the myth, he is a Dumuzi figure. Dumuzi, the consort of
Inanna, is blithely ignorant of her journey to the underworld, necessary for
her sexual and emotional fulfilment, and a scapegoat for her anger as she
discovers the extent of her power. In other words, their relationship is not
an easy one. The way Lesley speaks of Mark indicates something of their
struggle towards the more equal, mature relationship she hopes for. She
told me that she saw herself in ten years, 'still married, and with children'.
Recovery involves developing a commitment to intimacy and the Innana
myth is helpful in outlining some of the spiritual tasks this commitment
requires. They are spiritual, because they are about the self's ongoing
development of soul at the expense of ego. Lesley's story clearly shows
that she is aware of the challenge and links it with the process of recovery.

Summing up: from the vantage point of recent recovery, Lesley is
beginning to make new sense of her story and even create some of its
missing parts. She realizes that depression and anorexia stemmed from
the same problems and required similar resolutions. She can see that it
was other sufferers who taught her new ways to 'be anorexic' during her
childhood period in hospital and that there is a need for models of
recovery instead. Her own recovery has included rediscovering and
incorporating 'that bubbly ten year old' she once was. She emphasizes that
there comes a time when you must 'take responsibility for your own
recovery' and that do so involves 'giving yourself permission' and having
faith in something beyond yourself as well; 'someone there, even if they're
very much in the background, that doesn't judge you; that accepts you for
what you are'. Although she apologizes for 'not getting very far with the
story', it is no longer the disorientation of despair, but that of change and
growth which makes her story sound chaotic, especially in contrast with
the next story; Vivienne's.

Vivienne's story: 'Thinness is not a prerequisite for engaging in life'

When I first met Vivienne, she was training to become a Jungian
psychotherapist. As I write, she has been working in that capacity for

eighteen months. Without her anorexic experience, she would probably not have chosen this path – an extreme version of the recasting of a life story. Not all 'recovered' narratives were as smoothly controlled as Vivienne's, but each flowed because its narrator, having told it many times before, had confidence in its basic structure. Few other recovered participants had such a detailed rationale for their recovery, because few had been through Vivienne's intense self-analysis. Vivienne's recovery is also comparatively recent; others, looking back over several decades, were more detached from their anorexic past. I have included this story, however, because it illustrates so vividly the elements, the coherence and the mythological structure which were always, though usually to a lesser degree, features of other recovered narratives. Most people in this group took the initiative in recounting their stories of recovery, with very little questioning from me (unrecovered and recovering participants asked many more questions of their own, too). Typically, they told me in their letters or phonecalls before our meetings that they had a story of recovery to tell and wanted others to hear it and Vivienne was more than prepared when I arrived for our meeting.

In Vivienne's home, every compact disc and every book has its place and the kitchen counters are unencumbered. I am almost afraid to disrupt this order by leaving my jacket on her sofa. She immediately understands my hesitation and its sources and says: 'when my internal chaos is high, I like to have order in my external surroundings. Right now, I'm going through a lot in my therapy training'. She settles into a storytelling position, legs crossed beneath her in an armchair, and almost immediately begins. She speaks with dramatic intensity; using pauses, changes of rhythm and breathing and accompanying facial and eye movements that enhance the sense that I am witnessing an artistic presentation. Her narrative emerges in strict chronological order, broken only by her reflections on the meaning each episode has for her in the present.

Vivienne's story begins with a working-class childhood in Britain during the sixties, with very limited educational and social opportunities and a family background of alcoholism and incest; 'a classic anorexic, extended, fuzzy-boundaried family', with an emotionally and often physically absent father and a controlling and intrusive mother of whom Vivienne says: 'She came from a family where there was no real affection and was therefore not able to pass it on. Her relationship with me was basically a war about whose needs were going to be met and she always won. I was given food instead of affection.' By the age of eleven Vivienne was overweight, very clever at school and determined to break the family pattern through academic achievement and control of her size. Over the next few years she began 'sliding very slowly into anorexia and loving it'. She felt 'in control of the universe'; but at seventeen her body rebelled and, unable to keep up her rigid starvation, she began routine bingeing and vomiting. By the time she arrived at university, she was also severely addicted to alcohol:

When I got to the end, when I got to the point that most alchies do, of 'I cannot continue to drink and I can't not drink, so I just can't exist anymore and I can't die', my body wasn't giving up quickly enough on me and though I actually wanted to die, I've always had a sort of prohibition on suicide, from the Buddhist point of view of 'I'll just have to come back and do it all again' and that would be infinitely worse than anything else; I ended up in AA and got sober and I've been sober for in excess of eleven years.

At the same time as she joined Alcoholics Anonymous, referred by the university counselling service, she entered a long period of psychotherapy. Her first therapist, Jill, plays a part in Vivienne's present story, as well as in her past; she represents the kind of therapist Vivienne herself wants to be. Her relationship with Jill is the necessarily idealized model towards which she strives in her own life: 'Jill is not a controller. She has her own religious beliefs which are immensely supportive for her, but she doesn't ram them down anybody's throat.' When they first met, Jill provided an example of someone who 'accepts life on its own terms and believes that she has enough resources to meet the day'. Vivienne had not met such a person before. Slowly, over a period of time, she noticed 'something like progress'; she began to realize some of the roles she had been living and the extent of her vomiting declined a little, but whenever she visited her parents, she would still 'lose consciousness of self and just fall back into the black hole immediately'. What Jill finally helped her realize was that there would not be a sudden end to her problems; no final binge, no return to starvation; 'it would just peter out and I would get left wherever I got left'. As she came out of binge-vomiting, her weight continued to rise stone by stone. She was becoming everything she feared and hated – out of control – and she was terrified.

Vivienne is a large woman for her height and, to recover, she had to accept this. She continues to do battle with the negative consequences of her size, but in a quite different way from before. She no longer expends 'massive amounts of energy in compensation' to make people believe that she is not 'a fat, lazy, ugly, derelict, selfish slob' – the social connotations of her larger size. Instead, she has disengaged from these connotations altogether. As she went through the maelstrom of her emergence from anorexia, bulimia and alcoholism, Jill was her reference point and her support; she continued to say: 'It's all right. It's possible to continue living outside of the framework which you have designed as possible life.' To emerge from the 'little coffin' she had to live in to survive in her family,

Vivienne had to break her own identity and break out of its context. She says: 'It sounds really easy until you actually have the emotional experience of the roof caving in and like being in a three dimensional oceanic chaos and not knowing where you're going to be beached or if you're going to be beached *if* you are going to ever surface again'. One of the things Jill taught her was that in every recovery, it is only possible, at a given moment, to do certain things: 'It's pointless saying to someone with anorexia: 'You could do this, or this, or try that', because if the self-caring mechanism isn't there, there's no way in the world you can do it.'

Recovery, for Vivienne, was a kind of miracle; 'something that shifts at a fundamental level' so that the changes can 'build up very very slowly'; 'It's one of those bizarre things where it's chicken and egg. Over time it was almost like somebody dripping water onto a stone, building up a stalagmite'. These two juxtaposed metaphors show up the impossibility of 'defining' recovery through measurement. Instead of criteria for recovery, Vivienne offers a kind of baseline, which is 'freedom from obsession'. To achieve it, she first had to give up her need to control her size. Once she gave up this need, the obsession disappeared and was replaced with many other interests. Having reached this baseline, she felt free to effect other transformations in her personality. Instead of concern about how others perceive her, she is now more interested in how she feels about the world and within herself. She says: 'The size I choose to maintain is a kind of passive choice. I cannot control my size now, so I just eat three meals a day and get on with my life. Food is not a priority.' Recovery also means

embracing life; entering into the fray and into the messiness, without this attempt to simplify, control and structure experience. Instead, you do different work; you do what's necessary and you leave the outcome to the power greater than yourself that is whatever you happen to envisage. It doesn't have to be a personal God. The outcomes are not your personal responsibility and you can't run the whole show.

The order Vivienne creates in her story is very openly retrospective. It contains insights she could not have had at the time, including the story's periodization. It is this order, too, which enables her to make frequent comparisons between 'then' and 'now'; comparisons which are essential to recovery. The Buddhist perspective she has adopted gives Vivienne a means of explaining her reluctance to commit suicide, but it also provides a non-linear way of thinking about time. She inserts breaks for reflection in the story now and again, where its 'perfection' is interrupted, with deliberate effect, to remind herself of the imperfection of its outcome. She says 'I still have problems' and goes on to explain why; but she also explains that she now understands them as socially induced rather than internal; that they are the constraints within which her ongoing recovery must be continually re-established. She has developed a detailed and articulate critique of the contemporary western worship of slenderness against which she mounts her own daily struggle; reading, writing and talking about the issue in preparation for a doctoral thesis.

Vivienne insists that the discovery of meaning never stops and is never simply cognitive. She concludes that it is only through story that we can escape what she calls 'scientific reductionism' and express the 'connection and dynamism' she sees as essential to meaning. For her, 'dry analysis of fact' destroys true understanding, and anorexia and other attempts to control the body are metaphors for this destruction; 'like taking a human body apart and then discovering you can't put the bloody thing back together again because you've lost life'. Yet she also warns against too much storytelling; against 'creating a myth of recovery which itself generates attitudes capable of producing anorexia'. I think she is referring to the 'recovery' movement and its compulsion for confessional narratives which can be as distorting in their own way as the original experience. Mythology is essential to recovery, she says, because of its potential 'to embody a wider diversity of women's ways of being in the world than does our culture'.

When Vivienne read my first transcript of our conversation she was alarmed, amused and sobered. She wrote me a letter which said, in part:

> It was very odd to read my transcript: I was mortified by my seeming arrogance and dogmatic statements about 'how things are'. It was quite confronting! Still, that's probably no bad thing. The other thing which struck me is that you see the coherence in my account whereas I see the contradictions and superficialities in my world view.

Then, with irony, 'nothing anorexic about my mentality, is there?'

To summarize: Vivienne has emphasized the role of her extended family, her absent father and controlling mother in her descent into anorexia. Her story also demonstrates that anorexia, bulimia nervosa and compulsive eating are not separate, but simply possible shades of response to existential questions. In her case and for others from similar backgrounds, alcohol, like her eating problems, was another 'way out of no way' (Thompson 1995). For her, reaching that place where there are no choices and confronting her own death was the beginning of a 'miracle'; of abandoning control to something beyond herself only to find eventual safety and meaning there. Although she now has her own critique of the methods of AA and OA, she firmly believes in their emphasis on personal narrative and spirituality – and that spirit is inseparable from the material reality of the body; which is one reason why she has just taken up belly-dancing.

Part III

Spirituality

Spiritual pain is not so much a problem to be solved as a question to be lived. (Adapted from R. M. Rilke)

Society and spirit

_____

> Religious beliefs, however strange their appearance may be at times,
> contain a truth which must be discovered.   (Durkheim 1976: 438)

Introduction[1]

What do people mean when they speak of their recovery as a spiritual
process, or a process with spiritual components? The elements, stages and
turning points my study participants described contained a spiritual
subtext I asked them to draw out. This co-presence of the spiritual and
recovery in their stories most often occurred before I mentioned spirituality at all; nor was there any allusion to spirituality in the newspaper article
which attracted their attention. Participants were therefore not simply
telling me what they thought I wanted to hear. This chapter begins with a
discussion of their responses and goes on to consider the implications of
these responses for an understanding of the relationship between individual spirituality and spirituality in society as a whole, using classical and
contemporary sociological and psychological theory to do so.

Participants' accounts of spirituality

All participants acknowledged some form of spiritual belief and referred
to practices they associate with spirituality, although their interpretations
of 'spirituality' varied considerably and only some of them had this
consciousness when their recovery began. With the exception of Sue
(whose response I discuss below), those with the longest period of
recovery had the most developed accounts of their own spirituality. Most
distanced their interpretation of spirituality from formal religion, though
some had found it expressed there. They spoke of anorexia and recovery
as parts of a spiritual quest.

Anorexia and recovery as spiritual quest

Those who were still anorexic referred to their quest as a repetitive and misguided searching. Michael, for example, used a dramatic image often associated with anorexia; the pilgrim on a lonely quest for meaning, in his case framed in the masculine mode of an 'upward' quest for salvation. His main ritual practice, apart from his 'spartan' diet and 'monastic' lifestyle, is mountain trekking on less than 800 calories a day. He does this annually, as a form of atonement and purification. 'I have to punish my body and suffer', he says, 'looking for some sort of enlightenment and salvation'. His desire to 'know' has the intensity of religious zeal; for him, the mountains are 'a didactic presence' and his expeditions 'an education process'; 'There's an aura, a uniqueness about them, that makes you unravel the tortured complexity of your self'. Having said this, Michael immediately adds: 'but I don't want to digress off anorexia'. Several other participants also spontaneously revealed aspects of their spiritual lives but did not directly connect them with the story of their anorexia to form a single narrative of spiritual search and discovery.

Most of those who had not recovered, or were still recovering, related similar on-going, repetitive quests and used religious terms to describe their self-starvation as a wrong direction they did not know how to reverse. Patricia spoke of a 'constant battle' with herself, 'a self-discipline: the struggle between the physical body and the spiritual self; a control of the temporal: not enjoyable, but virtuous'. Lauren says she has done 'a lot of meditation and affirmations and visualization', but they have not helped much because she has not 'given them enough time'. She believes 'there's something out there which can touch you, and it's also in there (pointing to herself)', but 'it's a matter of drawing it out,' and she's been 'squashing it'. Margaret chose food restriction 'to become a better person'; motivated by the example of Lenten fasting and the idea that eating was sinful and sacrifice pure, even though such ideas and practices were not emphasized in her own religious community. Although she thinks they are irrational, these attitudes continue to influence her emotionally. Ariel still has episodes of bulimia and compulsive exercise, but she too is engaged on an explicitly spiritual quest. When her religious needs were not met by the Anglican tradition she'd grown up with, she started exploring Judaism; first through reading, then by attending different synagogues, until she found her spiritual home among members of a Jewish Reformed community. By the time we met, she had decided to convert to Judaism and spoke glowingly of the Jewish attitude to the body, to food and to the family; but she could not yet see the connections between this search and her years of starving and purging; her need for recognition and acceptance. Lesley did not make explicit links between her recovery and her religious beliefs either, but she does acknowledge a divine presence 'even if it's very much in the background', 'that doesn't judge you; that accepts you for what you are . . . some unseen power that knows ultimately what's going to be best for you'.

All those who have fully recovered (except Sue) now have some form of spiritual belief, but not all of them see its development as flowing from their anorexic experience. Rosalie, for instance, became a 'born again' Christian when her mother died, long after she had recovered from anorexia. She is open to persuasion that there was a spiritual element to her eating problems, but she has not thought of them in that way before. Her grief at her mother's death precipitated an existential crisis that might also be interpreted as a return of the repressed; Rosalie's early asceticism can be seen as one attempt to resolve questions of life and death, and her conversion to Christianity years later as another, more satisfying alternative. Sally, now a member of a Zen Buddhist community, describes her anorexic adolescence as a time of spiritual searching, but she does not make a direct connection between her recovery and her spirituality either. She does say, however, that if she had had 'some kind of faith or some sort of spiritual refuge' in adolescence, she 'might not have been through such a confusing time'. Jodie and Sue were the only participants who denied any interest in spirituality, but Jodie identified herself as a humanist and located her recovery in the same threefold connection as the others and Sue has had limited access to discourses which could assist her to answer the many questions about recovery that prompted her to participate in my study. The absence of spiritual language does not signal an absence of spirituality.[2]

Most participants emphasized the on-going, non-linear aspects of their recovery and its dependence on the 'spiritual' discourses available to them at various points in their lives, including Buddhism (Zen, Tibetan and Mahayana), Judaism, charismatic Christianity, more traditional Catholicism and Protestantism, and New Age spirituality. Simone, for example, anorexic during the late 1960s and 1970s, drew upon ideas available to her in the Human Potential Movement to explain what she was doing: 'When I was a hippie, there was stuff in the counter-culture about fasting: I thought my full potential would be reached if I ate perfectly and ate exactly the right things and fasted. It was my version of spirituality. It was the best I could do under the circumstances.'

Those who have fully recovered also emphasized that the beginning of real spiritual awareness only became possible as, and to the extent that, they abandoned their obsession with food. Meredith said: 'As I go along, the more deeply convinced I become that the spiritual aspects really have been at the heart of it'. Vivienne made very direct links between spirituality and recovery, explaining that one of the problems for women is that men are held to be spirit, while women must embody soul. As a result, she thinks, there is not much room for women to develop spirit; except perhaps, vicariously through a man (symbolized by Christ). She uses this theory to explain her desperate spiritual need in adolescence, why it was so difficult to satisfy in western culture, and why the difficulties of women's spiritual quest are therefore most likely to be 'embodied' in the form of anorexia nervosa.

Recovery as connected spirituality

If anorexia was the beginning, and a vital part, of a quest for meaning, recovery involved the discovery of spiritual meaning, even if only in retrospect. The spirituality participants described having found holds the three-fold sense of connection they all mentioned in some form: connection within oneself, connection with others and connection with the natural world or the cosmos. It also includes experience of a transforming power beyond themselves.

Connection with oneself meant a sense of inner linking among different manifestations of the self including the body, mind and spirit; in contrast with the experience of a 'split' self during the anorexic period.[3] Participants who felt they were 'on the way to recovery' had most to say about this inner connection. Marjorie thinks 'anorexia and recovery have certainly been a search for the whole person'. Marilyn has begun to 'feel the split', 'as if', she says, 'there are three parts to me; the logical part, the emotional part and the ego, and it's as if I've repressed my self for so long and suddenly I've given myself permission to nurture myself'. Most significantly, Ariel is beginning to accept her body and says: 'The body is sacred. It's not meant to be [felt as] dirty or unhealthy.' Those who had fully recovered were especially emphatic about the reconnection of body and mind and spoke of it in spiritual terms: 'Connection with my body is being part of God', said Aleisha. 'I discovered, as I recovered, that glorifying God was loving the body and not separating it but treating it like it was some sort of prayer.' Meredith, who now follows Tibetan Buddhist teachings, told me: 'Look – the body and spirituality go hand in hand. After all – and more and more I begin to see this – Jesus and Buddha and all the great teachers are incarnations. They are bodily manifestations!'

The second aspect of spirituality to which participants referred was their awareness of *connection with others*. This included personal (and sexual) relationships and also a sense of community, often with specifically spiritual associations. Ariel's Jewish Synagogue gives her the spiritual community she craves. She says: 'It's a complete way of re-learning a whole lifestyle. I don't have many friends except the people I know at the Temple, whom I can be communal with, to learn more about it. And it's so family oriented. I love it!' Eloise, who has little interest in religion, finds the same connection with people who share her 'left-wing, feminist social analysis'. This has become a means of creating her own framework of belief and practice: She told me: 'If I want to maintain a sense of recovery and not revert to anorexia, it's had to have been (through) a sense of control over my life outside of just my own body but actually in my relationships to work or with my friends. And I guess I like seeking out alternative images, as opposed to just staying within the mainstream.' For Miranda, recovery involved social connection through participating in choral and orchestral groups. She says she found her community and her spiritual context in music; 'and that was instrumental in my recovery; that I had that community of musicians and of music'. For Kate, too, 'there was something spiritual about recovery'. Although she is uneasy with the word, she says her spirituality is in the love she has for other people; something she was incapable of experiencing while anorexic and which, for her, is 'tied up with Christian values'. She speaks of her developing commitment and relationship with her partner as the most spiritual part of her life.

The third element in these accounts of spirituality was the *connection with nature*. Reconnecting with the body included reconnecting with the outside material world and this was often experienced as a rediscovery of and participation in nature. Ilse told me that her spiritual life had always been associated with nature but that her recovery involved something more; accepting that human suffering and growth was just like that of animals and plants; beyond human control. She says: 'There's an inherent wisdom in the life-cycle – a life force; like we had a lot of rain this summer and the trees on our land have grown something like thirty centimetres. So in nature if you've got a chance, you go for it! I think those gumtrees have actually taught me a lot.' The fact that this three-fold connection was experienced as a '*re-connection*' is important too. The return to childhood memories and their retrospective sanctification is not simply an imposition of the present on the past. It draws upon powerful bodily experiences – the original 'oceanic feeling' I have already characterized as the physical foundation of spiritual assurance.

The fourth and most controversial aspect of recovery is threaded through the other three; an *awareness of a greater power* than the self, the social or nature, though it is present in each of these. Lesley feels it as 'an unseen power that accepts you for what you are, knows what's going to happen and ultimately what's going to be best for you'. Miranda describes it as 'a spiritual holding'. Kate recognizes it as Love. Aleisha, though she has no religious affiliations, unself-consciously calls it 'God'. The second part of this chapter examines some of the ways modern social theory has

attempted to explain this power, suggesting that although the Enlightenment rationalism of classical social theory has restricted our understanding of it, postmodernism can open new possibilities for reintegrating it
within academic and popular consciousness.

The meanings of spirituality

Recovery clearly involves more than an intellectual search for philosophical certainty, since it is a physical transformation and since emotions akin
to those of religious conversion are involved. Participants' accounts
demonstrate that the conviction of a re-connection (inner, social and with
nature) is as much 'felt' as 'known'. The concept of spirituality is essential
to my analysis of recovery because participants used it themselves; most
often spontaneously, sometimes only after I had questioned them about it,
and often in order to examine it critically. They used it because it has
become a popular word to describe the metaphysical side of personal
existence; to speak about the soul and to cover those experiences and
feelings for which there is no other commonsense language outside
religious terminology. Had they spoken to me in the 1960s, they might
have used the term 'existentialism' instead. The theories which seem most
suited to explaining this aspect of anorexia and recovery are those of
existential and transpersonal therapy,[4] but even transpersonal psychology
does not explain *how* 'spirit' acts in society to bring about the personal
transformation which is recovery. Part of the theoretical problem arises
because existential and transpersonal theories have not adequately explained the relation between ritual, society and 'spirit'; the relationship
this and the following chapter examine. The remaining difficulties come
from making too rigid a distinction between the terms 'existential' and
'spiritual'. Philosophical existentialism, theistic or atheistic, derives not
only from Kierkegaard's struggle to understand human freedom in
relation to a deity but also from Hegel's attempt to define the meaning of
Spirit in human history. Consequently, existential questions are always, in
the sense in which I have defined spirituality, necessarily spiritual
questions. A de-spiritualized existential approach to therapy leads to
paradox and contradiction:[5] the anorectic's apparent choice of death is in
fact a bid for life, but this 'existential freedom' not to eat, carried to its
extreme, ultimately denies free will and makes a mockery of existential
responsibility. Without some notion of a power beyond the self, 'recovery'
demands that sufferers pull themselves up by their own bootstraps.

Until recently, it was difficult to write about 'spirituality' in academic
texts because academic thought was shaped by the Enlightenment idea
that real knowledge is rational and scientific; set apart from expressive

ways of describing reality through the emotional and physical media of the arts. One of the benefits of poststructuralism is its critique of this false distinction. Rejecting the Enlightenment thinking which has characterized the modern era has allowed a return to an interest in more 'mystical' ways of knowing; to the idea that language arises from and expresses bodily experience and emotion and that it is always shaped by narrative; by the kinds of stories within which knowledge is articulated. Once again, it is becoming possible to speak of Divinity, not as a 'thing', an object of study, but as a question we ask of existence and for which we find answers in experience.[6] This interest in spirituality is found not only in the New Age movement and its healing rituals (Heelas 1996: 80ff) which I discuss in chapters 8 and 12, but also in the 'new mysticism'[7] of established religion (e.g. in the Catholic Church) and the 'mystical' interests of such poststructuralist writers as Luce Irigaray (1986), who do not hesitate to use the word 'Divine', broadening it beyond the conventionally religious and returning it to its original status as a 'mystery'.

Going back to the classical texts of early modern social and psychological theory and reading them from a late twentieth century perspective is another way of understanding 'spirituality', its relation to 'reality' and to each society in which it occurs. Each of the writers whose theory of religion I am about to outline – Durkheim, Weber and James – has made a significant contribution to the creation of modern narratives concerning spirituality or, as they called it, religion. These narratives draw on deep and usually unarticulated myths about human existence; myths which always have cultural resonances. For example, in societies where Christianity has offered the dominant myth, stories about recovery rely on the underlying narrative of the resurrection of Christ, itself subtended by older myths of death and rebirth that give meaning to the changes of the seasons and the generations. In modern academic work, spiritual experiences have been treated as objects of study instead of sources of understanding, but not without discomfort. William James acknowledged this problem when he wrote that 'in the metaphysical and religious sphere . . . our articulately verbalized philosophy is but the showy translation into formulas . . . of our inarticulate feelings of reality' (1958: 73).

There are three major theoretical problems in claiming that recovery is simultaneously a spiritual and a social process. Durkheim, Weber and James each contribute to the solution, but each has his own forms of blindness to the answers I ultimately propose. The first problem is whether the 'spirit' and the 'spiritual' (to which participants in my study refer) is a purely social construction, or whether it has any existence outside the social. The second problem is on one hand, whether the asceticism which I take 'anorexia nervosa' to be is a form of 'distorted' spirituality and recovery a kind of 'balance' which 'corrects' the distortion; or on the other hand, whether this is a culturally and historically biased judgment which should be abandoned. The third, related problem, is the problem of how to write about spiritual experience and spiritual forms of knowledge in the same book as social theory; whether it is even possible to do so without diminishing the meaning of spiritual experience or without sounding anti-intellectual. The answers offered in this book owe a large debt to Joel Kovel (1991), whose reflections on spirit and society help bridge the gap between the 'founding fathers' of sociology and psychology and contemporary thought in these areas.

Durkheim's sociology of religion

In *The Elementary Forms of the Religious Life* (first published in 1915), Durkheim wanted to demonstrate that what we call 'the religious', the powerful impetus towards moral self-improvement, 'the raising of an individual above himself'(1976: 424) with all its associated ideas and practices, was wholly produced by social forces. Far from rejecting religion as a mere epiphenomenon of a material reality, however, Durkheim insisted that religious phenomena – myth and ritual – were the idealized forms of the processes essential to the continued reforging of social bonds and that these social bonds were the essence of the social. In other words, religion was essential to the continued existence of society itself. For Durkheim, spiritual forces, whatever their emotive, intellectual and practical power, remain firmly within the social. He saw no need to posit a God, gods or Spirit Being greater than or outside society because, for him, sociology itself was capable of explaining the spiritual. This positivism (his desire to set sociology on an equal epistemological footing with the natural sciences) hampered his attempts to explain something that is, by its very nature, 'occult' but whose foundation lies in the sacred stories that infuse our personal narratives; something constantly revealed through the body and the emotions as well as the intellect.

Durkheim was especially interested in the rituals which maintain religion; nurturing the bonds among members of a society and creating their personal and social identities. He referred to 'ascetic' rituals, those which involve suffering, as 'negative rites'. Anorexia and recovery can be read as ritualistic attempts to construct the self. The descent into anorexia can be understood as a negative rite and the return (recovery) as a positive rite. This approach resolves a great deal of the 'mystery' surrounding eating disorders and recovery. It opens up a whole new way of construing the narratives of participants in my study. It helps us to interpret the 'stages' in their transformations as stages in a sacred rite of passage: As ritual, anorexia nervosa itself is the separation phase in the initiation of the individual into full selfhood; a chaotic, liminal period; the apprehension of nothingness out of which the future must be created. As part of this ritual, the taboos on certain foods are purifying; they are attempts to pay homage to social proscriptions on 'fattening foods' and to transform oneself, by self-control, into a more worthy person in the eyes of the community.

Recovery, with its accompanying rituals, is the reconnecting part of the rite, when the individual returns to the community, strengthened through suffering (1976: 299–323). The negative cult (the eating disorder) is therefore 'a means in view of an end'; a condition of access to the positive cult. For Durkheim, 'fasts and vigils or retreats and silence' are 'nothing more than certain (social) interdictions put into practice'. These 'ritual abstinences' are also means of individual and social transformation. The experience of a temporary asceticism confers greater power on the individual once that individual is reincorporated into society. It is 'a sort of preliminary initiation which introduces (the individual) progressively into the social world' (p. 309). Durkheim's account of the social construction of spirituality explains how spiritual concepts and practices, both liberating and not, come to have the power they do within culture; but his analysis cannot fully explain the apparently private nature of anorexic rituals nor the ways in which 'recovering' anorectics define their transformed selves against (i.e. as different from) much of collective mythology and ritual. For this, both psychoanalytic and dialectical approaches are essential.

Kovel's liberating spirit

Kovel's project in *History and Spirit* (1991) is to question the power of science (including social science) and to show the roots of social conflict (domination) and the dialectical means by which it may be overcome as it recurs throughout history (liberation). His discussion of the meaning of spirit helps resolve my first problem; the relation between spirit and society, with his hypothesis that spirit is both shaped by and breaks through society to transform it. He also assists with the second; the relation between spirit and individuals (is anorexia a distorted form of spirituality?), by suggesting that the more 'spiritual' people's lives become, the more they lose their narcissism. At the same time, he consciously recognizes the place of the body in this transformation.

Kovel's extended meditation on the meaning of 'spirit' – his own 'quest' (1991: 21) – is not hampered by Durkheim's commitment to making sociology capable of explaining everything. Like Durkheim, he explores religious phenomena from outside, but without Durkheim's social reductionism. Spirit, for Kovel, exists as a vital force; in desire, power, being and liberation; in the individual soul and as that which shapes history even as it is shaped within history. He describes individual and historical processes as transformations which arise out of a dialectic between splitting (domination) and the overcoming of splitting (liberation). Spirit is 'basically critical of power and domination' (p. 5). It is present within *and* beyond history, as the direction of a generalized human self-consciousness towards Being (p. 171). This is the 'spiritual quest' to which people in my study referred.

Spirit works in individual lives through the overcoming of Ego and the development of Soul; a greater openness to the Other, including humanity and the natural world. Spirit also works through the material body, rebelling against its domination; an idea of great relevance in explaining recovery from anorexia. Whereas for Durkheim the soul was 'distinct and independent of the body (though united to it by the closest bonds)' (1976: 242), the soul sacred and the body profane (p.262); for Kovel, the body itself *is* spiritual; flesh is the spiritually imbued body.[8]

Weber's mystical rationality

My third problem – how to write about spirituality within the academic discipline of sociology without diminishing it as a form of knowledge or claiming that it is a superior way of knowing – is also the problem of what can be taken to constitute rationality. Durkheim, Weber and James attempt to deal with this problem 'objectively', claiming to leave their own questions and emotions out of their texts, while Kovel makes his personal position and its antecedents explicit and weaves them into the story of his own quest. Nevertheless, Max Weber's work includes ideas about rationality, asceticism and mystical knowledge which together make up a story about knowledge and salvation.[9]

Rationality, in Weber's sociology, is the wellspring of human, social, action. It can take several forms: it may be instrumentally rational (concerned with measurement and the means towards achieving a particular end), substantively rational (concerned with the ultimate ends of the action, as in the pursuit of an ethical goal), affectual (motivated by positive or negative emotion) or traditional (determined by ingrained habit) (1978, 1: 24–5). Although different societies and historical periods seem to emphasize one over the others, all these forms of rationality are always present. Salvation, in this life or a future other-worldly existence, therefore has a highly rational motivation. In *Protestantism and the Rise of Capitalism* (1906/1971) Weber focused specifically on the desire for 'salvation' in the after-life as a basic motivation behind the rise of capitalism in western society. It is increasingly evident that modernism (the height of capitalism) has been dominated by instrumental rationality; the worship of the means, and the suppression of the other three forms of rationality, or ways of knowing.

Salvation, according to Weber, can be achieved by a variety of means, including through the believer's own efforts and through divine intervention over which the believer has little or no control. 'Salvation' is always towards 'becoming', towards self-transformation and perfectability – in the eyes of others or of an unseen transcendent power (which in Durkheim's story amount to the same thing). It is the personal efforts of the believer in this direction which are associated with asceticism and mysticism. One means to salvation, for Weber as for Durkheim, is through ritual. Each time ritual is used, it creates the necessary mood for the alleviation of guilt, the transformation of the self, and the creation of new meanings about the world and one's place within it. Ritual makes a sacred time and space which is able, through sheer 'manipulation', to redeem the individual from guilt (pp. 530–1). It is associated with salvation through self-perfection, in which the individual strives to make him or herself as close to godlike as possible; a form of self-deification. Rituals, based on this search for perfection, in turn create a meaningful relation to the world (p. 535). To achieve this state, according to Weber, has usually required the individual to be separate from the 'ungodlike' body and the everyday world, often through 'hysteroid states' which induce visionary spiritual phenomena. Significantly, Weber associated this approach to personal salvation with the increasing rationalization of religion in the modern world; with instrumental rationality, centred on means, calculation and control (p. 536). He already foresaw both the 'New Age' belief in self-deification and its frequent embrace of capitalist values (Heelas 1996).

The foundation of *asceticism* (of which anorexia and bulimia are examples) is, for Weber, a rejection of worldly values and affairs. He contrasted it with *mysticism*, in which the aim is flight from the world and the search for non-rational forms of knowledge known as *gnosis*; the perception of an overall meaning in the world, accompanied by the assurance of a religious state of grace (pp. 544–6). The possession of this knowledge, or the desire for it, 'sets the believer against the intellectual strata' who either deny the importance of religious phenomena altogether, or seek to explain them through rational means. In my study, *recovery* from anorexia strongly resembled the movement from an ascetic to a mystical path (but without a rejection of the intellect).

James and the experience of conversion

The 'spiritual' perspective described by participants in my study includes personal experience of a power beyond both the individual and society. The parallels are striking between participants' accounts of recovery and the conversion experiences described in William James' classic *The Varieties of Religious Experience*. *The Varieties* provides fascinating evidence of the part played by spiritual conversions in recovery from mental and physical suffering; stories that lend weight to the vitality of the spiritual myths underlying them.

First, James shows that religious experience is *frequently associated with some form of pathology*. He also notes the recurring use of food imagery to describe the hunger and thirst for spiritual experience and to convey its satisfaction.[10] By 'pathology', James not only means that certain 'extremes of religious behaviour' (asceticism, for instance) are a kind of illness but also that disconnection from the spiritual is itself the pathology from which he traces the movement of recovery; from the 'sick soul' to 'saintliness'. What he describes is the difference between the personal existential burden of the self and the belief in a transpersonal force; the attitude that 'turns our moral death into our spiritual birthday'. Secondly, James represents *recovery as conversion*. The conversion experiences he analyses may be instantaneous (crisis) or more gradual (lysis) in the same way that participants described both their recovery from anorexia and the growth of some form of spiritual belief. Thirdly, James describes the spiritual experience as *a sensation of union*; of a direct connection with the cosmos, with humanity, with nature and with Divine Energy. This element of union, or reconnection, is an essential feature of the spiritual experience participants describe in my study. James insists, however, that religious conversion is not the only means of reaching this unity and that 'remedying inner incompleteness and reducing inner discord is a general psychological process . . . which need not necessarily assume the religious form' (James 1958: 146–7). Nevertheless, in my study, even when the 'turning point' between anorexia and recovery was brought about by 'an opposite affection over-poweringly breaking over us' (as when participants fell in love) or 'getting so exhausted with the struggle that we have to stop. So we break down' (p. 173) (the experience of attempted suicide or the decision to seek treatment), each of these turning points involved placing our welfare in hands other than our own; trust in a process beyond individual will.

The spiritual energy that makes recovery possible is, of course, located in the social and made possible through it but, with Kovel, I do not think it can be explained solely in terms of the power of the social; its source is in the energy that gives the social itself its strength. This is, in fact, the final point which James makes about spiritual healing: that it includes *'a belief in the reality of an unseen order and in the human need to be attuned to it'* (p. 58). All participants claimed that recovery requires an experience of something (a material reality and/or an energy) beyond the self. They named it 'spirituality' or referred to it as 'love', as God, or as Nature. James calls it a product of 'the human ontological imagination', thereby asserting the irreducible reality of that which is understood through poetic (metaphoric) descriptions.

James' account, like Durkheim's and Weber's written at the turn of the century, makes the same distinction they did between rational thought and mystical experience and, as they did, emphasizing that the latter is mainly apprehended through emotions and the body. Like Durkheim, James was attempting to translate experiences he believed to lie beyond rationality into the narrower realm of social 'science'. Today, social theory's renewed interest in the body and its emotions[11] is beginning to expand our ideas of 'rationality' to include another possibility; that since bodies and emotions are necessary for full human understanding, knowledge is not fully rational without them. The task of contemporary social theory is to recognize not only the meaning in the language of mystical states, but the additional form of knowledge they contain.

Conclusions

To return to the problems with which I began this discussion of spirituality and to whose answers Durkheim, Weber, James and Kovel contribute: firstly, the question of whether spirit exists outside its construction in culture and history. Durkheim's explanation of the power of ritual and belief (as that which establishes and maintains social bonds) is entirely adequate to explain both anorexia and recovery, especially given the emphasis participants in my study place on social reconnection. But to exclude the possibility of an existence of spirit outside the social is to deny the connections between all forms of knowledge, 'scientific' and 'mystical' (more 'poetic'), and to go against Durkheim's own injunction to take seriously what people say about the 'supernatural' dimension of their experience. Since it is more obvious to us today than it could be to Durkheim that the barriers between disciplines and forms of knowledge (including between 'social' and 'natural' science) are themselves historically determined, I prefer the more exciting possibility that spirit, as the fundamental energy in both society and nature, may act within historical processes, on the individual and on the collective level.

The second problem is less tractable: to posit the superiority of 'recovery' over 'anorexia', in the context of the spiritual, seems like spiritual pride. It also makes 'anorexia' into a kind of false consciousness and 'recovery' just another ideology. It raises difficult questions about good and evil, liberation and domination, to which Kovel's meditations do not necessarily offer a solution. Well aware of spiritual pride as a form of Ego, Kovel is loath to make judgments about other people's spiritualities, especially since all humans are, in his view, essentially spiritual beings. To speak of asceticism as a type of 'historical domination' does not leave much room for free will where spiritual pathways are concerned. I am tempted to agree with him that self-mortification (of which anorexia nervosa is one form) is a denial of the self, an attempt to possess the body (a part of the natural world) and hence a frustration of the desire for being. Having spoken of asceticism as a form of spiritual distortion, however, Kovel concludes that 'if a spiritually inclined person . . . is so configured by historical and personal accident as to require an ascetic denial of flesh to fulfill his or her particular pathway, so be it' (1991:161). While this formula at least leaves room for understandings we have not yet reached, it does not take us far enough towards them.

There is another, more speculative possibility. I have already argued, using Durkheim's concept of ritual, that anorexia and recovery are both moments in the same spiritual process. If we abandon the western concept of linear time and think, instead, of spiritual Being as having its own form of time, then anorexia does not necessarily have to be viewed only as a precursor to recovery, but as a spiritual journey in its own right, with its own end in this life, which may or may not be in recovery. The concept of linear time prevents us from seeing, as Tibetan Buddhism, for example, sees very clearly (Rinpoche 1992), that death itself may be another way of being and thus another spiritual pathway. While this may not be a satisfactory answer for people whose commitment is to healing, or whose human need is for the survival of a loved other, it does accord with the acceptance of death by many who have not recovered from anorexia and by those around them (e.g. Dunbar 1986; Pétrement 1976).

This explanation still seems too passive a solution to an essentially political problem. Like many clinical, sociological, and feminist theories, it makes anorexia, rather than recovery, a protest against domination. While there may be an important place for such forms of political protest as self-immolation and hunger fasts, stories which seem to offer these as successful solutions to political problems do not serve contemporary anorectics well, since they do not have the same meanings they may have held in other historical periods or in other cultures. Perhaps we need to retain the possibility that, for some rare individuals, self-starvation and death can be another way of being. At the same time, this possibility should not deflect us from the creation of theories of recovery which choose the more life-affirming alternative.

In relation to the third problem, of how to write rationally about spiritual forms of knowledge, Weber's discussion of alternative forms of rationality is invaluable. I make use of Weber's distinctions between forms of rationalities wherever the problem of rationality arises, and particularly (although he did not use it in this way) in relation to the changes in bodily states and awareness (the knowing body) discussed in part IV. At the same time, I emphasize that these rationalities are connected and that to adopt one of these at the expense of the others distorts knowledge. While poststructuralist theory has loosened up our epistemological possibilities with respect to spirituality, it also benefits from close re-readings of the classics of modernist thought on the topic. Each of the writers considered here presents us with a challenge this book takes up in constructing a new narrative about the spiritual dimension of recovery:[12]

Religion expresses nothing which does not exist in nature. The only question is to learn from what part of nature these realities come and what has been able to make men represent them under this singular form which is peculiar to religious thought. (Durkheim 1976: 70)

Spirit does pertain to nature, and we should not hesitate to engage in radical speculation to try and understand how this may be so; but radical spirit enters human existence only through history and we must also try to understand why this may be. (Kovel 1991: 2)

Mystical knowledge is not new knowledge of any facts or doctrines, but rather the perception of an overall meaning in the world . . . [From] such gnosis . . . there may be derived a new practical orientation to the world, and under certain circumstances even new and communicable items of knowledge. (Weber 1978, 1: 545)

[Mystical states] tell of the supremacy of the ideal, of vastness, of union, of safety, and of rest. They offer us hypotheses we may voluntarily ignore, but which as thinkers we cannot possibly upset [and which may be] . . . the truest insights into the meaning of this life. (James 1958: 328)

8   Rituals of self-transformation

One dimension of mental illness may arise because an increasing
number of individuals are forced to accomplish their transitions
alone and with private symbols.   (Kimball 1960: xvii)

Introduction

Prolonged fasting was once seen as an expression of spiritual or political
courage and sometimes still is.[1] Even sociology and feminism have tended
to glorify the self-starvation of anorexia and neglected the importance of
the recovery period. Yet participants in my study, recovered or not,
invariably regarded their anorexia as a distorted form of spirituality and a
misguided way of life. What does this apparent contradiction mean and
how can it be resolved? My answer is in four parts that progressively reveal
new facets of anorexic asceticism from the point of view of recovery. The
first (The negative rite) poses two questions which relate to this problem:
is 'not recovering' a form of spiritual asceticism today? and in what ways, if
at all, is it connected with the spiritual asceticism of medieval women's
religious fasting? My answers draw upon evidence from historical and
contemporary sources, including the experiences and views of participants in my study. In the second part (Contemporary meanings of
asceticism), I introduce four different solutions offered in recent literature
on anorexia nervosa. The third part of the chapter (From negative to
positive cult) is the core of the book, using the anthropological theories of
Durkheim and van Gennep to provide a new explanation for the
asceticism of anorexia; an explanation which makes sense of recovery as
well as anorexia itself. The fourth part (Some theoretical resolutions)
returns to the contemporary literature to demonstrate how this new
explanation resolves many of the difficulties encountered by previous
scholars. The final part of this chapter (The positive rite) discusses
parallels between recovery from an eating disorder and other contemporary forms of self-healing, since the rest of the book is devoted to expanding
the notion of recovery as the positive phase of a ritual of self-initiation.

110

The negative rite: asceticism, suffering and death

Not all anorectics recover. If anorexia and recovery are really parts of the same quest, how are we to understand the apparently *unfinished* quest, when people descend into anorexia, but do not return? How should we interpret this asceticism, permanent or temporary, and its relation to suffering and death?

Not recovering: spiritual asceticism?

The life and death of the French philosopher and mystic Simone Weil is a story of non-recovery which, perhaps more than any other this century, contributes answers to this problem. Weil identified with the Gnostic tradition, persecuted as a heresy by Church Fathers across the centuries, which held that the material reality of the body and the world was evil and could only be escaped by death (Murray 1981: 57–61). Plagued by physical pain for most of her life, she identified with suffering in all its forms, but especially with hunger (Pétrement 1976: 233, 245). For her, fasting was a way of testing the limits of human mortality and hence the limits of earthly reality. One of her meditations on this subject reads:

Food is the irreducible element . . . the point where the very mind which conceives finds itself degraded to being one out of the number of appearances . . . Fasting constitutes an experimental knowledge of the irreducible character of food, and hence of the reality of the sensible universe. (Murray 1981: 61)

Anyone who deliberately fasts to extreme is testing the limits between life and death, but not all share Weil's carefully articulated rationale. Her doctrine of extreme dualism was inspired by her admiration for the twelfth-century Cathars and her identification with their sufferings from persecution. As her contribution to the world, she felt compelled to maintain the split between her body, her spiritual longing and her critical intelligence; continually attempting to transcend her bodily limitations, separating critical thought from mysticism and refusing to abandon the former in favour of the latter (Pétrement 1976: 471). She died of tuberculosis in 1943, because she refused to eat more than her com-patriots in occupied France at the time. The coroner's verdict was 'suicide . . . by refusing to eat' (Pétrement 1976: 537). Perhaps, for her, this was the ultimate form of mystical sacrifice (Murray 1981: 60). To call Simone Weil's asceticism misguided, a waste of a life, or a distorted form of spirituality would be an intolerable form of spiritual pride. Instead, I am forced to consider the argument that anorexia need not necessarily be viewed as a precursor to recovery, but as a spiritual journey in its own right.

Not all deaths from anorexia in the twentieth century are as self-consciously spiritualized or intellectualized as Weil's, but however the meaning of anorexia is expressed, it is always (like hers) a struggle between life and death. Catherine Dunbar, who died from anorexia at the age of twenty-three and whose story has been told by her mother (Dunbar 1986) certainly recorded in her diary a kind of spiritual agony which resembles that of her medieval namesake and the physical and emotional 'afflictions' of Simone Weil. 'I am so scared and mentally torn inside', she wrote. 'Dear Jesus, please help me' (p. 58). Her longing for death was finally accepted by her family and friends, who felt that their only recourse was to assist her to prepare for the end. Like Weil, she had a strong consciousness of the presence of evil and her struggle with anorexia was an attempt to confront the meaning of death. The Christian interpretation her family placed upon her peaceful acceptance of her own death had as powerful a meaning for them within that framework as did the deaths of ascetic saints within *their* social context.

In contrast, the death of Karen Carpenter seems to have had no articulated spiritual rationale. Her anorexia partly stemmed from her lack of self-confidence and her perfectionism; the desire to be a better person in the eyes of her public.[2] Her death was the abandonment of that moral struggle. Yet she too, has attained a kind of secular sainthood through her suffering. Inpatients of eating disorders units listen obsessively to her music[3] and in popular culture there is a kind of mystique associated with her tragedy which glorifies her pain in retrospect. It is a complex blend of envy for her thinness, horror at its result and awe at her apparent determination to suicide. Where Weil's anorexia is the object of reverence for some intellectuals, Carpenter's provokes a similar reaction in a wider audience. Each sacrifice is taken to exemplify a particular contemporary cultural problem; in Weil's case, the sufferings of factory workers and people in war-torn nations with whom she identified; in Carpenter's, the suffering imposed on women by western expectations of slenderness. Both women have become cultural symbols, used differently in different social groups, to represent facets of a collective suppressed fascination with death.

Historical studies of asceticism: continuity or discontinuity?

Asceticism has been approved in most religions (though not without qualifications) as one of several permissible spiritual paths, but what is its meaning today? Especially among people who are not members of a religious community and do not expect or find a religious sanction for their views and actions? The self-starvation of Weil, Dunbar and Carpenter can be further understood in the light of a growing literature which compares the practices of medieval and later ascetics with contemporary anorexia. The question which has most commonly been asked in this literature is, to put it simply, whether or not medieval fasting women saints were 'anorexic'. The more important question, which has not been addressed, is whether and in what sense contemporary anorectics are 'saints'. In other words, instead of asking whether the fasting of 'anorectics' is 'the same phenomenon' as that of religious fasting in the middle ages, we need to ask what contemporary anorectics share with medieval fasting women;[4] not 'were they the same as us?', but 'are we the same as them?'

Most historians point out that since both sets of behaviours are culturally produced, they must be entirely distinct; that 'anorexia nervosa' is a modern medical diagnosis which did not exist in earlier times and that, in any case, there is not enough historical evidence from the past to apply contemporary medical and psychiatric diagnoses accurately. They have therefore focused on what women's starvation meant in medieval European culture. Their arguments are quite compatible with my theory that self-starving is a ritual that constructs meaning for the individual and her society, creating boundaries between the pure and the impure, however purity and impurity are defined in that society (Garrett 1991). They say nothing, however, about the meaning of recovery. It is relatively easy to understand why people might adopt rituals of self-starvation (and there will be different reasons in different cultures), but harder to explain why such people would then abandon them. If asceticism is spiritually meaningful, what is the spiritual meaning of recovery?

Historians, anthropologists and clinicians who have addressed the question of continuity or discontinuity between medieval ascetic fasting and contemporary anorexia fall into two camps. Bell (1985) and Banks (1992) argue for some 'continuity', while historians Bynum (1987) and Brumberg (1988) and clinicians Vandereycken & van Deth (1995: 220ff) insist that there is none. Here, I briefly examine their arguments. The earliest of these studies, Rudolph Bell's *Holy Anorexia*, takes a largely psychoanalytic approach to explain both behaviour patterns as 'a desperate effort to establish a sense of self' in societies which deny full selfhood to women (1985: 58):

The medieval Italian girl, striving for autonomy, not unlike the modern American, British, or Japanese girl faced with the same dilemma, sometimes shifted the contest from an outer world in which she faced seemingly sure defeat to an inner struggle to achieve mastery over herself, over her bodily urges. *In this sense the anorexic response is timeless.* (1985: 56, my italics)

This explanation does suggest the dialectic of domination and liberation that plays a part in anorexia, but it has little to say about how recovery is also possible in these societies. Although Bell's focus is not on recovery, *Holy Anorexia* contains important evidence of its occurence in the medieval lives he examines. Bell describes how a young woman who used her anorexic behaviour to escape the psychological domination of her father would frequently enter a convent where, in her late twenties or thirties, she would recover and become active in the affairs of the convent, often being elected its head. 'She would learn to fast rigorously, but in a fully self-controlled way and the 'devils' which plagued her earlier would make way for more reassuring presentiments' (p. 56). Saints who fit this 'recovery' pattern include St Veronica and St Clare. In the process of recovery, Veronica suffered some early relapses, and 'she always adhered to the spartan but not unhealthy regimen set out for everyone in her (religious) order', but her later life was considered 'wise, moderate, outwardly calm and passive', concentrating solely on her religious devotion, and she warned the sisters of her order against the more extreme manifestations of spirituality (p. 80). Likewise St Clare, having recovered from the illness brought on by her not eating, became a prioress and, according to Bell: 'explicitly backed away from her earlier excesses, displaying much the same experiential wisdom shown by present-day recovered anorexics' (p. 125).[5] St Catherine of Siena, on the other hand, was unrelenting in her asceticism, of which she eventually died. Bell writes that she 'courted death' and that despite her strong social and political activism within the Church (like Simone Weil's political activism in the French Resistance), she was eventually 'exhausted by her austerities and broken emotionally by her failure to reform the Church' and (like Weil) 'her will to live gave way to an active readiness for death' (p. 53).

Caroline Banks (1992) establishes even stronger similarities between medieval asceticism and anorexia. Using interviews with contemporary 'recovering religious anorectics' and material from their diaries, she looks for the Christian 'cultural norms' which influence contemporary fasting, rather than focusing on the usual assumption of researchers that dieting and secular ideals of slimness are primarily involved. She concludes that 'it is an open question . . . whether the related processes of medicalization and secularization are complete on a subjective level for all anorectics even in the late twentieth century'. Banks' argument and her evidence concern fasting which has an explicitly *religious* rationale (each of the women in her study uses the language of Christianity) instead of the wider notion of *spirituality* employed in my own approach. It is not only the stated religious beliefs of anorectics, however, which make their asceticism 'spiritual' but, as I argue more fully below, the relation which both their beliefs and actions bear to cultural ways of dealing with death. They need not emanate from a specifically religious form of discourse. Medicalization and secularization do not eliminate spirituality; they simply contribute to its relocation outside institutional religion or perhaps rediscovery in movements other than religious ones; liberation movements like the environment movement, feminism, anti-colonialism and the continuing development of the human spirit in art, music and literature. The 'culture-bound' nature of the anorexic rationale (p. 867) can be better understood as a 'western' failure to provide rituals of social re-incorporation after a period of liminal asceticism; rituals explored in the second part of this chapter.

'Discontinuity theorists' are right, however, not to ignore the important cultural and historical differences which mediate the expression of spirituality. Carolyn Bynum, especially, warns us not to assume that apparently similar behaviours have the same meanings in different historical periods and, specifically, not to apply to the past causal connections derived from contemporary medical and psychological theories.[6] Bynum is usually cast as a 'discontinuity' theorist because she has insisted on the *differences* between medieval and contemporary fasting (Counihan 1989). Her *Holy Feast and Holy Fast* (1987) stresses that medieval women's abstinence symbolized collective rather than individualistic values, and was associated with a religious imagery of feasting and food which were intrinsic parts of medieval society. She also insists that medieval 'miraculous fasting' in its own cultural context was always seen as suffering, and that 'suffering was considered an effective activity, which redeemed both individual and cosmos' (p. 207). She sees this as a significant difference between the medieval fasting saints and today's anorectics; but nothing in her careful consideration of similarities and differences between medieval female fasting and today's anorexia nervosa contradicts my argument about the spiritual basis of both. When Bynum writes that 'eating and not eating became more than metaphors for grace and desire; they became actual modes of experiencing' (p. 114), she is describing the same processes which occur in all societies, whereby metaphors (in this case food metaphors) are used in concrete as well as in more abstract artistic and linguistic forms, to effect ritual transformations at the individual and at the social level. Her evidence could therefore be adduced to demonstrate that the continuity between asceticism and anorexia lies in the use of food and fasting as a symbolic attempt to confront the universal problem of one's own mortality.[7]

Vandereycken and van Deth, a psychiatrist and a psychologist respectively, having read Bell and Bynum but not Banks, conclude that the question of 'whether medieval saints were anorexic is irrelevant' (1994: 225) for two main reasons: first, because problems of historical methodology make it impossible to discuss the (religious) past in contemporary (secular) terms, and secondly, because of the different definitions of 'perfection' in each society (they find none of the contemporary anorectic's relentless pursuit of thinness and fear of fatness among medieval fasting saints). Their arguments are based on an oversimplified dichotomy between (in their words) theological 'giving of meaning' and medical-scientific 'explanation' which dismisses the former as inevitably 'superstitious' and elevates the latter to the status of truth, as if it were not itself ascribing meaning by its own discourse on the world. The real situation, I am arguing, is far more complex.

One historical study of women's asceticism that also explains the social significance of suffering (without aligning itself with either continuity or discontinuity theories about anorexia) is Sarah Maitland's re-examination of the life of Rose of Lima, the seventeenth-century patron saint of South America. Maitland (1990) argues that Rose's self-imposed penances (horrific to the modern mind) were not, as she had previously claimed (Maitland 1987) evidence of 'the extreme body hatred and guilt that a patriarchal religion lays upon women'. Instead, she says, if we look for the meaning Rose and her culture ascribed to her behaviour, we find that Rose's suffering was highly meaningful in its social context, the recently colonized New World, where she witnessed 'some of the most squalid examples of materialism and petty colonialism and also one of the most defeated and culturally mutilated people that history offers us' (p. 65). Rose's penitential practices gave her an unusual degree of autonomy, were deeply appreciated by her own community and offered her the consolation of believing that she was performing a socially useful task in taking upon herself the sufferings of her fellows; earning their salvation through her self-torture. This interpretation of the meaning of fasting certainly has resonance with the life and expressed motivation of Simone Weil. It also invites us to consider the possibility that the fasting of contemporary anorectics expresses their distress at their own social situation; not only at their lack of control over their personal circumstances, but also a more general introversion of a cultural malaise about death and the mortal body.

Another example of a holy woman whose fasting took on an important social meaning is found in Brenda Meehan's (1993) account of the life of Russian hermit and ascetic Anastasiia Logacheva (1809–1875). Influenced by the model of the Desert Fathers, Anastasiia withdrew from the world in order to devote herself to the spiritual life. Her asceticism was not so much self-denial as an attempt to live in the 'eternal paradise' which was also to be found on this earth:

As she emptied herself of bodily longings, she developed the translucent radiance of the true ascetic . . . A radical transformation of personality, the goal of monastic and contemplative life, took place within Anastasiia, clearing her of attachments and petty strivings and making her a willing vessel for the divine, a mediator between the temporal and the infinite. She shone with a radiance that attracted followers to her even in the depths of the forest and led many to sense in her the power of a deeper reality. She was sought out as mediator, model, counselor and staritsa (holy woman). (1993: 58)

Meehan's beautiful description of Anastasiia's 'jarring translucence' is explicitly written 'to offer spiritual guidance for today'. Her reading of the stories concerning Anastasiia is as much about contemporary spiritual sensibilities as it is about the spiritual longings of Anastasiia's place and time. Reading Meehan's work in this light uncovers a modern version of longing for transcendence. Meehan makes no claims about anorexia in the present, but she believes that women of the past may have used asceticism as a deliberate means of achieving both spiritual power and temporal influence. She implicitly suggests that asceticism should be taken seriously as a possible spiritual pathway in the late twentieth century.

I would argue further; that women seeking spiritual pathways today need ways to transform the negative cult of fasting practices into the positive cult of bodily, environmental and social connection, in order to reach the kind of spiritual fulfilment that a life of asceticism currently denies them; since spiritual fulfilment of this kind usually requires community recognition and approval. Whereas medieval religious ascetics were often explicitly presented as role models for young women, contemporary anorectics, even when they draw upon religious discourses to rationalize their actions (as do those in Banks' study), are not given religious validation. Instead, the respect and even envy they sometimes command is in tune with twentieth century individualistic competition and achievement. In fact, excessive fasting today constitutes a parody of contemporary values in relation to the body, thereby revealing the splits such values create between body, self and spirit. Perhaps the most neglected aspect of the continuity/discontinuity debate, though, is the fact that most of those who have fasted to excess in earlier times and still do today, recover. They are less likely to be remembered for their normal eating than for their apparently prodigious restraint, but theirs has been the more complete pattern of descent and return of which asceticism in all human cultures is but one part. Participants in my study were aware that their eating problems were only one episode in a fuller story, and anthropologists' narratives about the structure of ascetic rituals provide the blueprint for that story, as we shall see later in this chapter.

Participants' views: asceticism as distorted spirituality?

The problem remains that participants in my study, recovered or not, spoke of their anorexia (as opposed to their quest) as a distortion of the fuller lives to which they aspire. If we accept that the terminal asceticism of someone like Simone Weil is a valid spiritual pathway, what should we make of participants' assertions to the contrary? Those who are still practising an ascetic way of life, with or without a theological rationale, acknowledge its problems and long for an alternative. Others in this group have been unable to sustain their asceticism and have abandoned it for an equally self-hating pattern of compulsive eating. Their anorexia, in common with Weil's, is part of a quest; but unlike her, they have no conviction that it is divinely ordained or that it forms part of a pattern of wider human suffering. The examples of Michael and Philip will serve to show the attitude of this group to their own asceticism.

Michael consciously identifies with Weil (having seen the BBC TV documentary on her life), at the same time admiring and questioning the logic of her sacrifice and his, saying:

You feel you don't merit any more. If the children in occupied France can survive with this diminished food intake, why can't you? Purposely and deliberately you reduce your amount. It's any *absurd* sort of parallel, but it's true. The key word is sacrifice. You feel you've got to make this sacrifice in going without, because maybe you haven't merited any more. It's a discipline. You feel you're living under wartime conditions.

Like Weil, Michael believes he is testing the limits of life and death. Both his self-starvation and the mountain climbing which accompanies it express an ascetic impulse; a way of living out his questions about the value of his own existence:

I like this exciting risk area, but not to the point of danger. It's like traversing a glacier where there's a crevasse, but not naively plunging down one. I like crossing this voyage of the unknown, too, because it heightens your sense of your own awareness and you learn from it. But you've got to be in very rigorous body mode; fired up for it and not carrying any excess weight.

Weil made her historical contribution to twentieth century intellectual life in spite of her lifestyle, but Michael recognizes that his way of life actually prevents him from contributing much to the world. He says 'I'm dreadfully immature', 'I don't know why I'm doing it', 'there's no capacity for change'. A part of him also wants to recover. He asks me 'how did you recover?' then says 'I envy you'. But he concludes 'I don't feel sorry for myself. I've learned to bear it. It's my burden in life. It's the cross I have to carry.' Is this meaningful sacrifice, or a sadly distorted spirituality?

Michael seems to think it is the latter; an 'absurdity', as he implies above. He also refers to the triviality of most social relationships and concerns as the worldly domain he wishes to transcend rather than as the sociality which might give a new meaning to his spirituality.

Philip, too, is in no doubt that his position is 'distorted'; that his practice does not accord with his belief. His professed Christianity leads him to conclude that his own behaviour is wrong, but he simply does not know how to escape the contradiction. He admires people like Cherry Boone-O'Neill (1982) who speak of their Christian faith as the key to recovery, but he has not found a way to apply his beliefs to his own situation:

I think [her book] is great, because that's what the Christian faith is all about. God in his wisdom doesn't want us to be sick and really when you are doing that, starving yourself, you're committing a sin against the Holy Spirit, so therefore you should be treating your body like the temple of God. That makes sense to me, that I should be treating my body correctly.

Participants who have just begun to recover also condemn their own earlier fasting behaviour. Lauren thinks that her anorexia has been a denial of spirituality through an excessive respect for rationality. For her, recovery involves a movement away from her own form of logic towards greater acceptance of what she calls 'the emotional level'. She describes the struggle between these two levels in these terms:

Much to my horror – I really don't like the thought of having done that – I really have worked largely at the intellectual level, and the logical level, rational level. But logically and rationally I know what I've done is wrong; what I'm doing is wrong. So I've been trying to open up my imagination a lot more to let my emotions out, by doing a lot of relaxation-type techniques. I do talk openly about the spiritual and the emotional level and all that sort of thing and the universal power and the energy. And there have been times when I have actually used it and it has worked.

Participants who have fully recovered look back on their anorexic period as a necessary, but temporary, 'distortion' (unsurprisingly given the choice of spiritual path they have now made). Eloise, for example, speaks of her behaviour then as 'self-destructive', 'misdirected energy' and 'confused'. She captures the spiritual longing to develop soul (as the opposite of ego), when she says:

I think that on one level, I was quite energetic, but not at all to my potential. My desire to be involved in so many things was enormous. My desire to actually *be*. And my desire to achieve was extreme. But it was going hand in hand with something that was quite destructive.

Jodie also speaks of her incredible energy and occasional heightened awareness during those years as a frenetic and somehow desperate way to be, in contrast with the peace she now experiences as her more usual mode of being:

I had something then, it was just going in the wrong direction. When you're really hungry, your awareness of things is heightened, so it was appreciation, but it wasn't joy like what I have now; it wasn't comfortable or peaceful; it was agitated, hyperactive.

'Going in the wrong direction, frenetic, destructive, incomplete, absurd, sinful, wrong' are not descriptions of an ultimately satisfying, empowering experience. However, we must also consider that the very availability of alternative stories – stories of recovery – forces these participants, recovered or not, to reconstruct their story in this negative mode. But is this all that is involved? Just as the key to Weil's 'sacrifice' was in her intellectuality (she chose logical thought over the body and the emotions and stoicism over epicureanism), perhaps the key to participants' negative interpretations of their asceticism is in their awareness of an alternative, broader form of rationality that takes account of the body and the emotions and which they meet in part through widespread 'New Age' ideas.[8]

There are at least three possible reasons why participants in my study experience or remember their asceticism as spiritual distortion. They do so firstly because all discourses on their behaviour today construct it as a form of pathology, even when (as in feminist discourse) the intention is to criticize the medical formulation. Secondly, they do so because there are no theological rationales for such extreme forms of behaviour which would make it acceptable (though still unusual) in contemporary society and thirdly, because their awareness of the emerging discourse on recovery (if only through their contact with me) has suggested alternative ways of creating meaning in their lives. For them, the development of spirituality seems to require acceptance and nurture of the body rather than its transcendence; more direct communion with others than solitary meditation, and a full acceptance of the natural, material world and their connection with it.

Contemporary meanings of asceticism: evaluating the theories

To return to my original questions about the meaning of spirituality in the lives of self-starving people: is contemporary anorexia the expression of a meaningful asceticism or a distorted form of spirituality? and are today's anorectics the analogues of medieval fasting saints? I shall consider the merits of five available explanations that I have called (a) 'the ascetic ego ideal', which adopts a psychoanalytic interpretation, (b) 'symbolic social suffering', in which anorectics take on the sufferings of the world, (c) 'hidden death themes', in which they play out the unwillingness of western society to face death, and (d) 'exceptions to the rule', in which asceticism is an inevitable by-product of particular social conditions for certain individuals. Explanation (e) 'from negative to positive cult', offers my own solution (inspired by the anthropology of Durkheim and van Gennep) in which anorexia is part of a ritual movement designed to resolve all of the previous possibilities.

The ascetic 'ego ideal'

In this explanation, anorexia is interpreted psychoanalytically as one manifestation of adolescent developmental crisis (at whatever age it takes place, for developmental stages need not be firmly associated with chronological age). Some clinical 'eating disorders specialists' have favoured this model in their attempts to find similarities and differences between their clients' behaviour and religious asceticism. The feminist psychotherapist Marilyn Lawrence (1984: 32–5), for example, points to the moral kudos associated with ability to limit food intake, at least in the western tradition. This is one of its attractions for adolescents in search of social acceptability and self-regard. Mogul (1980: 155) also suggests that anorexia nervosa may be a more pronounced version of 'normal' adolescent asceticism – a youthful response to the existential dilemmas faced in adolescence. Rampling (1985: 89) explores the ascetic dimensions of anorexia within a psychiatric model. He postulates the same 'ego-ideal' for both asceticism and anorexia, but does not take into account the possibility of 'soul' with which this ego (and its ideal) might be in conflict. Each of these analyses, however, fails to explain why some adolescents carry their ascetic experimentation to such extreme conclusions while others appear to abandon it. The definition of asceticism is, clearly, one of the issues at stake.

Symbolic social suffering

The Varieties of Religious Experience gives us a more precise definition of asceticism but with an accompanying value judgment. James, trying in his own way to be as scientifically objective as the clinical paradigm, wants to avoid pathologizing asceticism and to rehabilitate its religious meaning. He admits that 'the scrupulosity of purity may be carried to fantastic extremes', but even in these he sees a kind of social usefulness, for the ascetic mortification of the flesh is 'one response to the problem of evil in the world':

It symbolizes, lamely enough no doubt, but sincerely, the belief that there is an element of real wrongness in this world, which is neither to be ignored nor evaded, but which must be squarely met and overcome by an appeal to the soul's heroic resources, and neutralized and cleansed away by suffering. (1958: 281)

The ascetic, according to James, finds 'a profounder way of handling the gifts of existence' and symbolically takes on the sufferings of the world. His explanation accords with the meaning I have ascribed to the lives of saints like Rose of Lima and Anastasiia Logacheva, and even Simone Weil; but it does not go very far in explaining how this symbolic purpose comes to be understood as such in the minds of their contemporaries, nor how this might differ in different epochs and societies. If contemporary anorexia nervosa fits this description of asceticism, it does so unconsciously for the anorectic, for whom fasting is most likely to be about *individual* redemption from guilt and salvation through self-perfection (as described in the work of Max Weber 1978: 530–1).

Hidden death themes

Another model helps to account for the unacknowledged processes involved in the symbolism of anorexia. Within a psychological paradigm, Craig Jackson (1986, 1989, 1992) has elaborated a carefully documented argument that anorexia results from the contemporary western denial of death and its symbolic equivalents – separation, loss, unresolved grief and severe trauma. Jackson (1989: 1) argues that the anorectic's apparent courting of death is in reality 'a meticulous denial of death' which 'buys freedom from anxiety about death' (1986:1). He suggests that eating is inevitably about death, since we eat dead material and since if we do not eat, we die. In her refusal to eat, the anorectic therefore acts out the twin meanings of a social taboo. He believes that his analysis of anorexia has been ignored by researchers because of their own resistance to dealing with death-related issues.

There certainly is a symbolic relation between anorexia nervosa and death, but it requires a fuller development than Jackson's arguments provide: In the light of recovery, the anorexic courting of death acquires an expanded meaning. There are clues to this meaning in one of the empirical studies which Jackson cites in support of his theory: Kenneth McAll (1980: 368), a doctor of medicine, believes that inadequately mourned grief leads to anorexia. He has reported his successful treatment of anorexic patients using a Christian mourning ritual, claiming an 83 per cent recovery rate in a four-year follow-up. Identification with the dead, especially the mother, has often been found to be related to the genesis of anorexia (Ceaser 1977; Raimbault 1971; Falstein 1981). The desire to understand death (which may appear as a longing for death) is simply the other side of existential questions about life. Hence to recognize death in a formal way is also to value life. This is probably what McAll's ritual achieved. 'Cognitive restructuring' without the physical immediacy of ritual would not have had the same effect. The purpose of the grieving ritual, especially since it involved the material reality of shared bread and wine, was to provide the bodily and emotional dimensions of mourning; the symbolic creation, by material means, of links between life and death.

In Jackson's argument, the individual with an eating disorder is also conceptualised as a survivor by proxy of a relative (usually the mother) who is the original survivor of traumatic events. Carolyn Quadrio (1989) has written of the links between survival and anorexia in her discussion of anorexic daughters and grand-daughters of holocaust survivors. She emphasizes the way in which 'family ghosts' of continuing fear and survivor guilt can haunt the following generations. In my study, Susanna, the daughter of a Jewish death camp survivor, became anorexic in her late twenties with the break-up of an important relationship. Her interpreta-tionof this experience confirmed both the generational transmission of guilt and the power of the death theme in her own life, suggesting that they are intimately bound up with her sense of self and existential meaning. She did not see it as a 'cause' of her anorexia, but as one of the meanings she now attributes to her starvation:

One of the concepts the children of survivors talk about is that you get a double dose of guilt; you get the normal Jewish guilt and you get the holocaust guilt, so you're constantly guilty about everything you do and are [laughing]. One of the post-holocaust traumas that people suffer from is guilt at surviving: why did they survive and others who were so much more worthy don't? . . . My father passed all that on to me. I had no right to exist, to be alive. There was no concept that I as a human being had every right to be alive; that I could be a valuable person just for being who I am.

Jackson's work, therefore, focuses on a neglected aspect of the anorexic experience; the general repression of death in the culture that produces anorexia: He writes: 'Most non-traumatized individuals with healthy psychological defences remain blithely unaware of the close interdependence of life with death and death with life – they are able to transcend this harsh reality' (1992: 1). Transcendence, I would add, means integration rather than escape, and it is this integration of death into life which is the outcome of recovery from anorexia. Direct confrontation with death, as in near-death experiences (Ring 1980; Ring 1984; Sutherland 1992) and anorexia can convince those who have them that their lives are meaningful, and in this way enable them to live fully and confidently in the present. All societies need rituals which enable them to acknowledge death and make it serve socially positive and transcendent purposes (Kessler 1985). Our own society, in which 'death is the great unmentionable, the imperative taboo' has been less than successful in elaborating such rituals (Kessler 1985: 15). Instead, anorexia, and more particularly recovery, are made to serve this purpose (among others) in western societies today.

Exceptions to the rule

The problem of 'spiritual distortion' remains: Can asceticism ever be considered a valid form of spirituality and under what conditions might this be its meaning? The difficulty arises from the definition of spirituality which I have adopted in which the movement towards greater spirituality and less of its opposite, ego, requires an integration of self, body, nature and society. This is not the meaning of spirituality for most committed ascetics, for whom the body is inherently sinful – to be controlled and transcended (though some, like Anastasiia Logacheva, might simply abandon the body to God's care in nature). As well as awe and reverence, Christian asceticism has always attracted the charge of heresy, because of its attempts to reject the body whose importance is affirmed in Christian theology. Simone Weil's confessor and friend, Father Clément, did not conceal from her his opinion that she was a heretic (Pétrement (1976: 458). Asceticism implies a lack of balance; an aberration from a 'normal' pattern. In spite of this, asceticism as heresy can be of social value, for heresies challenge established doctrines and force us to confront and re-evaluate orthodoxy: what is considered 'acceptable' behaviour. Anorexia parodies the orthodoxy that 'thin is good'. Participants in my study, in speaking about their anorexic stage, were actually confessing to a heresy (excessive thinness) in the same way that the body reduction and diet industry forces its many acolytes to confess excessive indulgence (Spitzack 1990).

To affirm the importance of recovery, we must therefore reject the desire for 'purity', since it splits the body from the self and denies the centrality of bodily experience in spiritual life. When the demand for 'purity' through over-control of the body itself becomes orthodoxy, as it has in western society today, then its opposite, recovery, is the real challenge. The symbolic value of anorexia as a parody of western attitudes to the body is not to be denied, but if the symbolism is to acquire its full 'spiritual' value, it requires the completion of recovery; the re-acceptance of the body with all its messiness and unpredictability, including the inevitability of death.

Joel Kovel's statement that 'the practice of a violent asceticism often brings about what it tries to suppress' describes exactly the well-known transition (experienced by many study participants too) from strict anorexia to bulimia. As he concludes; 'the results [are] full of misery'. Kovel wants to include acceptance of the body as an irreducible element of spirituality, but recognizing that 'transcendence' may also be achieved through confrontation with the terror of non-being, he allows that for some human beings, under certain circumstances, the latter pathway may be the only one open to them (1991: 160–1). This, as we have seen, was also Weil's conclusion. It is the best available conclusion for the consciousness of the 1990s, for it fits Weil's life, recognizing its flaws but accepting the symbolic *social* importance of her sacrifice, without suggesting that anorexia is a superior *personal* solution to questions about life and death.

From negative to positive cult: symbolic death and rebirth

The most convincing explanation for the asceticism of anorexia comes from classical anthropology. Durkheim's conception of ritual can accommodate recovery because he sees asceticism as having two different phases and multiple meanings: The negative cult is the necessary prelude to the 'positive' rite of initiation into the deeper mysteries of life and death. 'Fasting is an expiation and a penance; but it is also a preparation for communion; it even confers positive virtues'. From this perspective, the lifelong asceticism of the medieval fasting saints is as a permanent form of liminality; of remaining stuck in the ritual's negative phase.

Another 'classical' description of ritual, upon which most subsequent anthropological accounts have been based (most famously that of Victor Turner 1977) is found in van Gennep's *Rites of passage* (1960/1909), published six years before Durkheim's *Elementary Forms*. Here, I point out the parallels between these rites of passage and the rite of anorexia/recovery (italics indicate van Gennep's and Turner's ideas):

a) Like initiation rites, they are not just about physical puberty, but about *social maturity*. (van Gennep 1960: 65)
b) The initiand withdraws from society during the pre-liminal phase (van Gennep 1960: 10) for the purpose of '*self-scrutinization of the central values and axioms of the culture*' in which the withdrawal occurs (V. Turner 1977: 167). This scrutiny is what feminist and sociological arguments about anorexia call social 'rebellion'. If recovery is the next

phase in the rebellion, the scrutiny leads to a different way of living from that prescribed in 'normal' social relations; the recovered anorectic rejects the social imperative to constant vigilance over her shape and size.

c) During the withdrawal period, initiands *frequently adopt masks (of animals, nature spirits or witches), or go naked, to demonstrate that as liminal beings they have no status, property, insignia*, etc. Similarly, it is the anorexic mask that is most obvious to observers: It conceals and protects the developing person within. Instead of stripping the body of its clothing, anorexia strips its flesh to reveal an essential vulnerability. In recovery, the anorexic mask is discarded and a wider range of personae become possible.

d) Also during this period, *the paradoxes created in social relations are exhibited and symbolically challenged* (V. Turner 1977: 176). For women, anorexia ritually challenges current demands that they be slim yet fertile; submissive yet autonomous; devoted mothers but high achievers in the workforce. It may also challenge power relations between generations.

e) *Dietary taboos* are frequently involved (van Gennep 1960: 81). For people with anorexia, the taboos being followed are those of their particular society. As well as reducing the amount of food eaten, they avoid particular foods as 'unhealthy' and the interpretation of 'unhealthy' varies from decade to decade following the dictates of the discourse on diet (B. Turner 1982).

f) *Sexual prohibitions* are involved in order to create a condition of 'purity' which will enable access to the sacred, in cultures where sexuality implies impurity (van Gennep 1960: 169). In my study two participants (those who did not associate sexuality with the impure) remained sexually active, and two (who were married) 'tolerated' sexual activity, while none of the others engaged in sexual relationships. This strongly suggests that social, rather than uniquely hormonal, factors are involved and that there is a reciprocal connection between them.

g) Initiation rites often involve status reversals in which the initiands, especially when they are young, 'mobilize affect-loaded symbols of great power' (V. Turner 1977: 175–6) *to test their strength in relation to superiors, particularly parents.* The anorexic refusal to eat is such an 'affect-loaded symbol' which also acts as a dramatic means of questioning adult authority over that particular individual. When this authority has not been sufficiently tested in adolescence, anorexic behaviour may be the means of challenging the 'authority' of dead parents or of other authority figures in that person's life.

h) *'Life-crisis liminality'*, in the Christian tradition, has often been preached as the *pathway to salvation* (V. Turner 1977: 198). This perspective views life itself as a liminal period before the 'reincorporation' of the risen body into eternal life. It is therefore not surprising that in western culture, which is so heavily based on Christian values, asceticism should be chosen for this purpose and (in earlier times) understood as a permanent way of life. Anorexia draws upon this understanding, whereas recovery appears to understand 'salvation' to be obtainable during an earthly lifetime.

The usual sequence of events in the recovery process bears out these parallels between rites of passage and anorexia/recovery. The acute anorexic period is like the 'preliminary initiation which introduces the initiand into the sacred world' through fast, retreat and silence, which are 'no more than certain interdictions put into practice' (Durkheim 1976: 310); in this case, social interdictions against particular foods regarded as fattening and consequently unhealthy and impure. The initiation therefore starts with the *separation phase* when the fasting rituals begin.[9] Unless the 'anorectic' is unable or chooses not to move out of this phase, the final stage in the ritual is the phase of *reincorporation* into the community, accompanied by a gradual resumption of normal eating patterns for that community, full membership of the society and greater participation in its activities. Between these phases, however, there is a remaining period of *marginality* or *liminality* (very roughly corresponding to the stage reached by the 'recovering' people in my study), when the newly initiated person is still fragile and disoriented following her ordeal: 'When the individual is no longer what he or she once, and quite recently, was but is not yet what he or she, emerging from this intermediary and literally transient state, will soon become' (Kessler 1985, 139).

Durkheim says that religious (hence spiritual) impulses are highly contagious. This may help explain the common phenomenon of 'copy-cat anorexia' (Brumberg 1988; Wolf 1991). The fear of contagion is also partly responsible for the frequent remark that people in an anorexic phase resemble ghosts, appearing to be not quite embodied or present in the physical or social world. Kessler describes these 'ghost-like' liminal beings in all initiations in this way:

Hovering on the outskirts of everyday society from which they have separated themselves, the initiands are a shadowy or ghostly presence. Not really present in society or part of its continuing life, they are somehow not fully alive, and are thus regarded in some ways as dead. Moreover, in close contact with powerful spiritual forces that ordinary mortals must treat with great care, they are both vulnerable and also, as potential bearers of those forces, endangering; in their spiritually exposed condition, unprotected by mundane social identities or routines, they are both susceptible to and also contagious bearers of potentially death-dealing forces. (Kessler 1985: 141)

Durkheim's analysis also helps to explain why anorexia today is so widely misinterpreted: the same rite can take on different functions in different historical and cultural circumstances. It produces effects which are 'interpreted differently according to the circumstances in which they are applied' (Durkheim 1976: 386). This explains the different historical meanings attributed to ascetic fasting in different historical periods (the problem in the continuity and discontinuity debate canvassed above). In societies which regard religious asceticism as a positive good, Durkheim argues, there is a strong distinction between the religious and the profane world. From this sacred/profane distinction, he says,

. . . comes the mystic asceticism whose object is to root out from man all the attachment for the profane world that remains in him. From that come all the forms of religious suicide, the logical working-out of this asceticism; for the only manner of fully escaping the profane life, is, after all, to forsake all life. (Durkheim 1976: 40)

In contemporary western society, however, there is considerable confusion about what is 'sacred' and what is 'profane'. One undeniable feature of the anorexic mentality involves the splitting of the world and the self into pure and impure components, in an effort to escape the 'impure' and an impossible attempt to transcend mortality (the very dualism which is rejected during recovery when death's inevitability is no longer denied). In the absence of stories about the sacred, however, the negative phase of an ascetic ritual is easily misunderstood as pathology.

Some theoretical resolutions

I have been considering a number of possible interpretations of the 'ascetic' aspect of anorexia. Each of these contributes one dimension to the final explanation I have created using the ideas of classical anthropologists. The 'ascetic ego ideal' posits a developmental theory; that anorexia is the individual's psychological attempt to reach an 'ego ideal'. To this, a Durkheimian perspective adds the notion that developmental stages are achieved by ritual and that ritual symbolically enables us to confront and resolve the issue of our own mortality. It also shows that the 'positive phase' of the ritual (recovery) is the most developmentally important phase. The theory of 'symbolic social suffering' suggests that the asceticism of anorexia fills a social purpose. This theory also draws on the idea of anorexia as a metaphor for society. Some historians, like Maitland and

Meehan, have shown how ascetic fasting, in certain historical circumstances, can confer moral and social powers and privileges on the faster. Durkheim, like James, argues that such people fill a useful social function because they incite us to effort (Durkheim 1976: 311, 316), presumably reminding us of the need for self-transformation. I would add that today it is recovery, the completion of the ritual, which is a more powerful example than anorexia itself.

Writers who have revealed the '*hidden death themes*' in anorexia have tapped into one of the most important aspects of the problem. Durkheim's analysis of ascetic rites as part of mourning rituals confirms and potentially expands their findings. It recognizes that anorexia is an attempt to deal with griefs of many kinds. As the negative phase of the ritual, anorexia is therefore both an initiation and a metamorphosis of the personality which forces a confrontation with death in order to make the choice of life more conscious. This initiation into the mystery of symbolic death and rebirth is only complete in retrospect, during the 'positive phase'. Analysing anorexia and recovery as parts of a ritual initiation process is a valuable way of understanding some of the means we use, individually and socially, to 'manage' death.

Durkheim's analysis also helps resolve the question of whether anorexia is 'distorted' spirituality or whether instead there can be '*exceptions to this rule*'. It allows the possibility that asceticism has different meanings for different people at different times and that, in some circumstances, the exaggeration of the negative cult which results in a lifelong asceticism or early death, might be of great social value. To this I have added that since asceticism today does not have a publicly intelligible religious meaning, the exceptions to the rule are now located in the past. Today, it is stories of the completed rite; from its negative phase through to its completion in the positive phase, which are likely to be of greatest social benefit. Understanding recovery in this way also helps resolve the problem of whether anorectics are like the medieval fasting saints. All ascetic practices share a common rationale; the necessary confrontation with death. There is, therefore, continuity among these practices, but also with all the other human practices that transform our being in the encounter with our own mortality.

The positive rite: ritual self-healing

Initiation is a process of self-transformation, and self-transformation always involves suffering *and* re-emergence into health (or into a more difficult to define 'good death'). Where the negative stage takes the initiand through suffering, its positive stage involves healing. Recovering anorectics, in fact, perform their own healing rituals, so it is not surprising that the stories of recovery told in this book share many of the elements of ritual healing found in studies of contemporary Pentecostalist and New Age groups (Csordas 1983; Glik 1986, 1988, 1990a, 1990b; McGuire 1987).

Why does ritual healing work? Ritual healing succeeds in these groups, McGuire believes, because of certain *characteristics* to which my study also draws attention. First, it is concerned with healing the whole self: it does not make neat distinctions among physical, emotional, social or spiritual 'troubles', but addresses the broader issue of human suffering. Secondly, it implies alternative self-society connections from those of biomedical healing; it usually locates the ill person's suffering in a larger, transcendent order and may also represent a statement against the rationalization of the body and the emotions in contemporary society (1987: 240). Thirdly, it re-establishes order or meaning in the person's disordered situation by a process of symbolic transformation, through ritual words and actions. Finally, the person has a sense of being enlarged, not reduced, by the illness experience (pp. 242–3). Clearly, what is happening in these group-sanctioned rituals is a process of self-transformation through the creation of new meanings about the person's life, heightened by the bodily actions and group emotions of the ritual.

How does ritual healing work? The ritual actions my study's participants used in recovery strongly resemble processes of group ritual healing, drawing on the same 'rhetorical structure' to give them meaning. This structure includes a 'resacralization of the individual's past', 'changing its meaning in the present' and 'healing oppression' in whatever form it has occurred. 'Endogenous processes' like sleep and rest, search for insight, dreaming and dissociation are also essential components of ritual healing (Csordas 1983). The stories in my next chapter show how people in my study used all of these and other processes including meditation, art work, music, etc. Ritual healing, even when performed alone or with only one or two others, always assumes the presence of a wider community to provide the system of thought within which the healing ritual can be understood (Csordas 1983: 333). In ritual healing, endogenous processes are activated by exogenous ones such as persuasion or suggestion. Some form of psychotherapy may be an important catalyst because the relationship with a therapist, or another important relationship, serves as the 'community', validating the meanings participants themselves create through these endogenous processes.[10] Psychotherapy itself is often seen as a form of initiation (Shorter 1987: 40). Like initiation ceremonies and like Csordas' ceremonies of 'ritual healing', psychotherapy provides natural metaphors for the process of psychic transformation; but it can only ever be an exogenous stimulus to the rituals which clients evolve in private, driven by 'a deep psychological necessity'. For Jungian therapist Bani Shorter,

This could equally well be called a religious necessity, for ritual is a confrontation between an 'I am' and a frightening 'I am not' . . . Ritual is a ceremony enacted with a sacred purpose or intent. Here one is always subject to an overwhelming numinous power capable of destroying or re-creating the individual. (1987: 45)[11]

Integrating an initiation like this can become a lifelong task. The stories in my study stress that self-healing is never complete. Recovery is not a linear process, neither is it circular, because 'it *achieves* a centre; the constantly changing, but integrated, self' (Shorter 1987: 40–52, 79–86). Another Jungian therapist, Marion Woodman (1980, 1982, 1985) also sees a woman's recovery as an initiation into mature, spiritual womanhood; the state of being 'forever virgin'; capable of making independent choices about her life and of staying perpetually open to new transformative experiences. Addictions (of which she believes eating disorders to be one) are ways towards self-knowledge for those who choose them: 'In the addiction', she believes, 'is the hidden treasure – the knowledge of themselves – and they can take no other path toward it. It is their particular sacred journey' (p. 99). She describes her own recovery from an eating disorder through a journey to India and the self-sought initiation ritual which took place there, concluding with comments on the ongoing nature of recovery which is also a feature of the stories in this book:

I wish I could say I went through enclosure, metamorphosis and emergence in India, and having gone through my initiation returned in triumph to Canada, a transformed woman, free to *be*. It was not that way at all. Bringing the treasure back from the underworld into life is always the most hazardous task in the fairytale. (Woodman 1985: 182)

9 Spiritual stories

Introduction

The stories of Michael, Dominic, Miranda and Naomi are four of the many that compelled me to look for spiritual explanations of anorexia and recovery. They tell in greater detail than I have so far, and in the context of each person's life experience, what spirituality means to them and its place in their ongoing recovery. They illustrate the relation between asceticism, suffering, death and recovery; and the rituals of self-healing these people have created from a variety of sources. They demonstrate how recovery stories both draw upon and help make up greater narratives about society and spirit.

Michael's story: Looking for salvation

Dear Catherine,
It was with deep empathy that I read the article on your life with anorexia.
I am a 44 year old male who has had periodic battles with this debilitating disease. I too, became depressed after my mother's death at 15 and endured periods of loneliness and contemplated suicide at the age of 22. Like you, I denied myself pleasure and became somewhat existentialist in my lifestyle. I very much want to help with your research. Surveys show that 5% of sufferers are males so I do hope you reach out to this one.
Michael

We met at an outdoor cafe on a Sunday morning. I was touched by the gentleness of Michael's face long before I noticed his slight build. The face matched the voice I'd heard on the phone; the thinness was peripheral. We talked, and still do, like old friends. We share the experience of anorexia and agree about its meaning, but our lives have been different in almost every other way. With no religious background, and without benefit of recovery, Michael has reached similar conclusions to other participants about the spiritual nature of this search: he partly understands the goal of his asceticism, but has not yet found the way to reach it.

Although Michael says his health is 'stable', eating is a chore, not a pleasure. For over thirty years he has denied himself sweet or rich foods, cannot eat in the presence of others, has trouble swallowing and digesting and often vomits after his small evening meal, yet he does not want to overcome these problems because he feels that any extra food would 'spoil' his control and change his body. His frugality started in childhood, before his mother's suicide. He was already introverted, well behaved, shy, sensitive and lacking in confidence. His mother had problems with alcohol and his father was a workaholic. Neither of them was emotionally available to him. His difficulty in eating and the pattern of vomiting started when he was very young. He remembers it as a response to his father's force-feeding him. At school, he already felt like an outsider. When he was twelve, the physical education instructor would make him strip off his shirt, singling out his frail body for ridicule and humiliation in the cold of the English winter. He says still cannot bring himself to expose his body at a beach or in any public place.

After his mother's suicide, when Michael was fifteen, he withdrew into depression; living alone because he did not enjoy people's company, becoming 'serious-minded, conscientious and mildly intellectual', shunning and repressing emotions, discarding 'friends' and avoiding sexual intimacy; fearing and wanting to deny any physical or emotional needs. He says: 'the observation of parents and the attendant misery made me pursue this path of deprivation and constant denial in order to stay alert'. He determined never to marry, have a family of his own or expect a 'normal, balanced life'. 'The family bond fell apart', he says, 'and led to me becoming emotionally starved, which has built up to an extreme level now, of not being able or wanting to focus on developing and sustaining relationships with people – especially women.'

From time to time he has made efforts to change: experimenting with small alterations to his diet, trying to build his muscles with weight training, even taking steroids; with no effect. No doctor, even at the Institute of Sports Medicine, has asked about the sources of his problem or identified it as an eating disorder. They have told him only women suffer from anorexia nervosa. Although he has few sexual feelings, he has occasionally visited prostitutes but, ashamed to be using another person as an object, has discontinued the practice and lost interest even in masturbation. 'Emotional deprivation has stunted my body', he says. 'Regular sex life with a nurturing partner would mean less muscle tension and more contentment and well-being, but I've just completely lost the urge.'

When Michael returned to university to complete his degree in his thirties, he went through a terrible crisis: 'My world became torture. I didn't eat anything, I was vomiting constantly, I was just in a black hole and it was a nightmare and I was totally out of control. I couldn't concentrate, I had sleep disturbances and I became suicidal again. I went through a whole year of university without talking to anyone because I didn't want them to see the plight I was in.' His depression was the return of his repressed traumas: 'During that hellish period', he says, ' I was constantly looking backwards, and I just became almost incapacitated and debilitated.' Too terrified to confront the past, he erected even stronger barriers against it, finding solace in the structured time of the workplace in a job that makes minimal use of his real mental capacities; isolating himself in reading, and refusing to develop any human attachments. When his cat died, he cried for four days; 'I was crucified', he says.

His existence generally feels futile and meaningless, except during the mountaineering expeditions he lives for. Sometimes he describes these as a quasi-religious quest, saying: 'I'm not into meditation or yoga, but you are looking for some sort of salvation.' Sometimes they are a purity ritual and a trial by ordeal: 'I feel I have to do this ritual repeatedly, to cleanse myself and get reaffirmation that I'm still a basically intrinsically good person that's not done any wrong, so I have to punish my body and suffer.' Mostly, he sees them as an existential pursuit that parallels his anorexic lifestyle: 'I want to be on a higher metaphysical plane. Anorexia corresponds with a zealous, not morbid, interest in mountains and existential religions and escaping the meaninglessness of trivial relationships in society. I've found a true quest for meaning.'

Michael's mountaineering has several functions. It gives him 'a purpose, a motivation and a drive' and although he knows that 'the incarnate of the solitary mountain trekker going to look for the higher levels of existence', like anorexia, cuts him off from social connection, he does find comfort in discovering his place in the cosmos. He says: 'being in the grandeur of the mountains makes you more aware of your own uniqueness. It's not egotistical. It brings out humility, because you are insignificant in the panorama of the mountains; just a speck in the universe.' He comes back much less anxious, with a kind of serenity that his acquaintances remark upon. His 'existential high' is distorted only because it is incomplete; it is as if his body had no memory of being held to give him trust in the goodness of the world; to connect positive experiences in the present with their counterparts in the past.

His relation to the world of nature is from the outsider's position; he feels dwarfed and powerless. His feelings about society are similar; he often refers to himself as alien to society, 'not normal', set apart by his small size and his distaste for superficial interaction. At the same time he feels 'imprisoned' in the cage or gaol of his anorexia.[1] He also sees the cage as a protective wall and shield behind which he draws back from others.

Because he is out of touch with people, he says, he is also out of touch with reality. He cannot be interested in other people, because he is obsessed 'not with the ego, but with the body'; isolated by physical and mental pain.

This is not narcissism, but spiritual disconnection; of body from self, self from nature and self from people. Michael knows that recovery would involve reconnecting the split parts of himself: 'because your whole personality feels detached'. He knows his body must change: 'maybe it's purposeful body mutilation, but if I can't look in the mirror and find myself OK to look at, how can anyone else?' It must include social relationship: 'some kind of confidante who would nurture me back, not only to a belief in myself, but to a trust in others'. But the prospect of change is terrifying: even renovating his house, something he would like to try, feels too self-indulgent and makes him scared he would dismantle his own 'painfully constructed identity'. Michael says: 'I'm painfully aware that anorexia is a false mode of living. It's a synthetic constructed existence, sustained and perpetuated by your own denials and refusals and there's a limited capacity to grow in it'.

From Michael's perspective, his story is a rationalized response to unresolved grief and trauma, expressed and lived out in existentialist terms. From the perspective of psychotherapy, he suffers from unresolved grief and 'survivor guilt'. From a sociological perspective, his is a blend of existentialism and 'self-spirituality' influenced by New Age ideas (Heelas 1996). From my perspective, which includes the others, his asceticism is an arrested attempt to come to terms with death and therefore with life. The return of repressed trauma has not been followed by a corresponding return of mystical awareness. He struggles, suffering, towards some kind of release, but although his transformation will require his own efforts, it cannot come from him alone. If he is to live more fully, he must ultimately take the risk of opening himself to the many forms of healing that come from others, as the remaining stories in this chapter make plain.

Dominic's story: 'I was reborn'[2]

Dominic is the same age as Michael and, like him, vomited and starved in his teens and had troubled family relationships. But in his story there are experiences of caring which have been the foundations of recovery and of his current work with dying people. When he was thirteen, working on his family's farm in New Zealand, he was very self-conscious about his excess weight, especially as his older brother was shorter, more slender and more athletic, like their father. One day, as they were harvesting, a pitchfork went into his knee, which rapidly became infected. This event precipitated a crisis. He began vomiting, then restricting his food intake and he was eventually hospitalized, several times, over a period of two years, including a stay in a psychiatric institution from which he convinced his parents to discharge him before he was given shock treatment ('electro-convulsive therapy'). While he was home, his father died, and not long afterwards, Dominic's family readmitted him to the same local hospital ward where this had happened. There, he had the experience that changed his life.

Within a short time of being in hospital, he met an elderly man called Mr Turner and became very attached to him. When Dominic was well enough, he used to shave Mr Turner every morning. One morning, Mr Turner told him to sit down on the bed and said he wanted to have a talk with him. Dominic thought this was 'rather wonderful'. Mr Turner clasped his hand, threw back the sheet and showed him his colostomy bag. He said his life was fulfilled, he was ready to die, he didn't really see the need for any intervention from the medical profession; he didn't like the colostomy bag and he didn't like his powerlessness. He knew he was dying. He had seen Dominic's father die and he described how it happened. Pointing through the window towards the sea, he said: 'That's where you should aim. You'll find meaning out in the world. You won't find meaning here.' Dominic knew he was right.

Five minutes later, Mr Turner died. Dominic suddenly felt very tired. He went into such a deep sleep that the hospital staff thought he too would die; but the next morning, he woke in a side room, looked out the window and felt more alive than ever before. The colours of the garden; its trees and flowers, struck him for the first time and he thought: 'God! this is just amazing! What am I doing here?' That moment was the beginning of his recovery. He returned home, moved into his mother's kitchen and took on 'women's work', since he was still too weak for heavy 'male' farm work. His participation in the domestic sphere gave him an admiration for women and their emotional openness that he never lost. During the next ten months, he gained weight and became an apprentice in a hotel. 'That was when I was reborn', he says. 'My life was beginning. And I knew I was very very lucky, because I was going to be able to shape who I was, because just a couple of days after I turned sixteen, I moved right away from the family.'

For the next two decades Dominic travelled, worked and owned businesses ('restaurants, of course, I'm very good at food!'). His eating patterns stabilized until a period in his thirties when he was living alone in the country, in a house with no mirrors, growing his own food and obsessed with a one-sided relationship. His self-esteem and his weight plummeted before he'd noticed. It was not until a friend came to stay and did not recognize him that he realized what had happened. This time, however, he set out to refeed himself. Instead of giving away the food he grew, he began cooking it and inviting others to come and share his meals. He also determined to find out more about anorexia, reading books and eventually, on a trip to London, attending self-help groups where he was able to draw upon his own experience to help people – especially young men – with the same problem. He is still active in such groups in Australia. In ABNA (the Anorexia Bulimia Nervosa Association) he found people who understood him, he 'didn't feel a freak', he was able to tell his story and hear the stories of others and begin to understand his experience and theirs. Through stories, he says, he realized that 'your life is not stagnant'. He concludes: 'Recovery gives you the world, really. Infinite. It's so precious, the time we have here, that to me (anorexia) seems a silly silly waste. Tragic.'

Dominic's story emphasizes the importance of coming to terms with death as part of recovery. His encounter with Mr Turner was a forceful turning point; the catalyst for a simultaneous resolution of his feelings about his father and an acceptance of death which released him into a fuller life. It also shows that new life crises are sometimes met with an anorexic-like response. In Dominic's case, awareness of the problem, and his knowledge that it could be resolved, accelerated his second recovery.

Miranda's story: 'A potent reconnection'

Miranda's story illustrates the significance of death, ascetic ritual, community and spirituality. Like Dominic's, it shows the way ascetic food rituals can be a means of managing and eventually resolving issues about life and death. I have known Miranda for nearly twenty years and even before we met I heard people speak of her with admiration and affection. She radiates calm, strength, energy, commonsense and perceptiveness. Widowed in her late thirties, she chose not to continue in her work as a teacher and librarian and instead made her children her first priority, working in a variety of part-time jobs. This way of living also gave her opportunities to follow her interests in art, music, languages, special education for people with learning disabilities, psychotherapy, somatic therapies, philosophy and theology. She has never told her children that she was bulimic and few others know, but her years of bulimia were the link between the childhood story she had repressed and the person she has now become. Her ritual vomiting began in her teens and only ended when she married in her mid-twenties. Since then, she says, her interpretation of this experience has changed almost year by year as she has integrated increasing levels of meaning into her story.

For ten years, Miranda vomited compulsively and secretly after every meal. Although on one level she found her behaviour frightening and disgusting and thought she was the only person in the world who did this, on another level, she 'chose' to vomit rather than starve because the symptom better expressed her particular pain: For reasons she only later understood, she had internalized the 'bad' mother; consequently, she felt that anything she took into herself would become bad and had to be expelled. The act of vomiting was her way of preserving the 'special person' she knew was still there behind her apparently flawless public persona; school captain, public speaker, popular with teachers and students. As a child, when people asked her what she wanted to be when she grew up, Miranda would say: 'I'm going to be Miranda'. It was this strong sense of self which her bulimic ritual unconsciously protected: 'When I vomited, a veil would come over my perceptions', she says, 'and stop me from facing something which would have destroyed me.'

Her recovery began through her relationship with Nicholas, whom she eventually married. As this relationship grew, she gradually came to accept her body, her anxiety about eating slowly receded, and she experienced her more comfortable eating habits as a return to the social participation of mealtime rituals which she had denied herself during her bulimic years. Re-connection, through a variety of rituals, old and new, was an essential part of recovery for Miranda. Substituting socially meaningful rituals for the lonely rite she had devised for herself slowly removed the guilt and shame she had associated with eating. Superficially, she had recovered when she stopped vomiting, but vomiting had been a means of protecting her emergent self (the part of her which was 'becoming') and the threats to that self had not yet been fully resolved. She had still not gained access to the source of the pain she was afraid to face. In spite of the improvements in her life, her relationship with Nicholas and the birth of her children, she had a strong feeling that 'the special person' inside her would die. The feeling led her to begin five years of psychotherapy. During this period, her mid-thirties, Miranda made the connection between her bulimia and her feelings about death. She was now strong enough to face the reasons why she had become bulimic; to remember a missing part of her story.

Miranda lived her early childhood in Asia and Africa before she was sent to an English boarding school. Her parents came to Australia together when Miranda was twelve, ostensibly to begin a new life, and she was flown out from England to join them. In reality, her father had no intention of remaining with the family and left them soon after their arrival. One evening, when her mother was out, he came to their house to take away some of his belongings. Full of bitterness against his wife, he tried to explain himself to his daughter. He told Miranda that shortly after her birth, her mother had become pregnant again. She was depressed and distraught at the idea of another child when she felt so inadequate to care for the first. Together, they agreed that Miranda's father (a doctor) should abort the pregnancy. On the night he told Miranda the story, he blamed her mother entirely. Miranda never mentioned his visit. From that day on, she turned against her mother and soon after began vomiting. If her parents could kill another child because she was so much trouble, how could they love her and what was her life worth? The precious self she knew was within her must be protected at all costs.

In her creative attempts to cope with this knowledge, Miranda described a series of 'conversions' from one kind of control to another during recovery and a gradual relinquishing of these controls to a belief that 'the world supports me just as I am'. First, there was Nicholas' love: the relationship was so intense that it lifted her out of herself and her desire to control was 'sort of swept along too' because suddenly someone else had complete control over her life, but in a positive way that reaffirmed her. Nicholas put her on a pedestal. In the long term, this could not work, but at the time, it made it possible for her to see herself as better than she thought she was; 'to crawl out from around the base of the pedestal and start to look at a way of gaining some control'. As her body changed in recovery, Nicholas' obvious delight made the changes easier to accept, especially as they were associated with the pleasure and the emotional release of their sexual relationship. Meals became important not only for their ritual regularity, but also as an expression of intimacy. The ritual element of the meal was very important to Miranda, because all through her teens, when she was bulimic, mealtimes had been of no importance at all in her household, while Nicholas regarded them as ceremonies. This brought her back, in a positive way, to the ritual of mealtime at boarding school, which was the place where she had become 'highly ritualized in every area of my existence', substituting regularity and ritual for real intimacy:

Some of the rituals at boarding school had tremendous significance for me; such as our morning assemblies where we sang – some of those things were wonderful, and even the mealtimes, in their own way. There was always a sung grace and there were very very strict rules about table manners, which lent a certain decorum to the mealtime. So I suppose living with Nicholas actually reconnected me with that regularity which I had substituted for intimacy, but along with that came intimacy. So it was a very potent reconnection.

Miranda had always had 'a tremendous spiritual response to music', especially the church music whose daily ritual sustained her at school. In recovery, her participation in musical groups gave her the same sustenance and the comfort of friendship with people who shared her love of music. It provided the community she craved. Each of these rituals contributed to the strength she needed to enter therapy. For the first decade after her bulimia stopped, she says, she would not have been able to touch the pain, but she knew that unless she did something about it, she would lose her precious hidden self and even physically die. Therapy made it possible for her to tell her story, understand its significance and finally accept the 'specialness' she had known she possessed as a child.

Her direct confrontation with death came not long after this, when Nicholas died of a rapid form of cancer. This trauma helped her to face her fear of death and to come to a new realization of the meaning of her own life. At last, she reached the 'absolute awareness' of herself which she remembered having in childhood. She says 'I was now able to accept the spiritual part of my life as something terribly important, where before, my emotions were so out of my own control and so frightening to me that even imagining that I had a spiritual life was quite beyond me'. Miranda stresses that her healing has made her a better parent; that through therapy and reflection, she has been able to give her children what she knows they need; to heal their own grief at their father's death and to give them what she did not have herself as a child, because she is now fully conscious of what it is.

Miranda has not found a religious movement to which she feels she can belong, but she no longer minds. Spirituality, for her, lies in her sense of belonging to a wider community and of being supported within the 'unseen order' she has increasingly come to trust. 'I think it's absolutely essential to leave the bulimia and then to know that you can regain some control of yourself, before you go on to some other form of letting go; to a spiritual holding.' She emphasizes that the ritual of bulimia was an essential part of her journey to this point; her initiation into a form of maturity which allowed her to face a more than usually overwhelming fear of death. The liminal phase of recovery has now given way to her more fully embodied and connected presence in the world: 'The meaningful life, the authentic spirit that knows how to live, is a life that has accepted Otherness and made itself ready to die. Of course this does not mean that such a being wants to die. Quite to the contrary, a full soul finds life all the sweeter and more intense' (Kovel 1991: 107).

Naomi's story: 'Made up as it goes along'

Naomi's colleagues, in the government department where she works, know her as a warm and sociable, effervescent person, comfortable with her body and, unlike many of them, unconcerned with dieting or exercise. During the week, she is absorbed in the challenges and the rewards of her

senior position. Only her counsellor and a few trusted friends are aware
that her weekends are intensively devoted to a private form of ritual
healing. Without benefit of communal setting or a communally accepted
rhetoric of language and actions, Naomi has evolved her own ways to gain
access to a repressed childhood, confronting its terrible memories with the
new self she has painfully shaped since then. Self-help books have
influenced her to some extent, but her actions are experienced as coming
from somewhere deep within but also beyond her, through nightmares,
trance-like flashbacks, meditative states and strong creative urges. Each of
these processes has been an 'endogenous' one occurring in solitude as a
fundamental part of ritual healing, even though it is sometimes sparked by
'exogenous' means; through regular sessions with her counsellor and
conversations with a very few trusted friends. She is amazed at the wisdom
of her unconscious self which usually saves her from flashbacks during her
working week, reserving them for Friday and Saturday nights, when she
has time to work with and through them.[3]

Naomi has told me her story several times, each time shifting its
meaning with a newly recalled detail, as her memory briefs her only with
what she is able to 'contain' in the present. Her story is complicated by the
fact that she was epileptic from the age of seven.[4] The anorexic period
began when she was seventeen, preceded and accompanied by regular
depressions, and lasted until she was twenty-five. During one of these
depressions, when she was twenty-one years old, a male colleague noticed
her distress and offered to take her for a drive. He raped her. The
depressions intensified until, four years later, she began to have 'horrible'
nightmares. She saw a psychiatrist and decided to leave work and go
back-packing around the world. Travel liberated her from (as she first put
it) 'over-protective parents and the pressure to marry'. She met other
independent women who became her models and she realized that her
anorexia had nothing to do with 'trying to look beautiful', though she only
began to understand its causes much later.

By the time Naomi returned to Australia, she was no longer anorexic
and her depressions lifted for a while; but within two years she experienced the 'blackest and longest' of them all. She thinks it could have been
precipitated by a number of events: a car accident during an epileptic fit,
after which she gave up driving and felt she'd lost her independence;
gastric problems for which she was hospitalized; or the experience of a
gastroenterologist 'inserting items up my rectum'. She held off suicide by
knitting jumpers and making quilts for friends, promising herself that she
would not die until each was finished, then leaving a tiny piece incomplete.[5] In her late thirties, she had surgery that eliminated the epileptic
seizures. I met her about a year later and heard most of this part of her

story. At this stage, her knitting and quilting had become elaborate and beautiful, she was taking piano lessons and avidly listening to classical music. Decorating her house and working in its garden were her metaphors for self-transformation and growth, as well as her means of meditation. At the same time, she was beginning to have flashbacks to her childhood that left her feeling terrified and vulnerable. She knew they were associated with the rape, but that the rape could not have caused her anorexia, since she was already anorexic when it happened.

During the next few months the flashbacks were more frequent and more appalling, sometimes accompanied by vomiting. Naomi started drawing the scenes she remembered and the feelings they evoked; filling several sketchbooks. She felt an urgent need to share these with me because, as she said, she wanted her story to be complete. Then she remembered being anally raped by her father, on many occasions, between the ages of four and seven (when her epilepsy began). In her drawings of these events, she often pictures herself curled in foetal position somewhere close to the ceiling: epilepsy and anorexia had been the ways she'd found to survive 'outside' her abused body. As these memories returned, Naomi devoted every spare moment to her artwork, producing posters, books, models and quilts that told her story in more and more vivid detail. Some depicted its most dreadful aspects and others drew upon the happier and safer events and places of her childhood; creating metaphorical havens in the present. They have been shown in art galleries and some have formed part of an exhibition of work by incest survivors. Her current flashbacks tell her there is still more to be remembered, involving both her parents, but for now she is grateful for the medication which holds them at bay.

Her artistic output goes hand in hand with other rituals that reconnect her with the pleasurable experiences of her childhood. She often makes a meal of her earliest foods; Vegemite, rice puddings and french toast; soft, warm, milky foods that meet her emotional needs of the moment and replicate the symbolism of mother's milk which is a part of the reincorporation phase of many initiation rituals (van Gennep 1960). She has made a model of a fairy house in which there is a 'safe room' to which she retreats in imagination after a flashback, and she is painting one of the rooms in her (real) house the same colour. She confronts death and suffering, no longer through ascetic practice, but through richly creative personal rituals that link her with the wider community of artists past and present.

Naomi's recovery, like most recoveries, is from sufferings of which anorexia was only the mirror and the mask. It demonstrates that rituals can have many meanings and serve many purposes. Like communal religious healing, Naomi's rituals bring painful memories to conscious-ness, give them a new meaning and find ways to contain and live with their terrors. For her, the language of healing is not religious, but it is spiritual because it is the language of the 'whole' self and of reconnection between this self, nature and other people. Although she belongs to no formal community, her recovery is assisted by her network of friends; they provide her with the emotional support which a religious group supplies around more formal ritual healing ceremonies. Her rituals empower her; not only to continue to work calmly and effectively in her job, but also to define and redefine who she is and wants to become. Finally, like the participants in ritual healing groups, she believes her suffering has strengthened, rather than diminished her, and that it has been a way to self knowledge. She says:

> I like this idea that problems are thrown up against you for a reason; when it's right for you to deal with them. If I hadn't gone through this, I wouldn't have had the breadth and depth, particularly the depth, in my experience that I've been through since. Maybe I just wouldn't appreciate just being, or just being me. I would be so bland about that stuff. I wouldn't know what the other bits were. I would have to have all these expectations of where I stood and what I was. I'm glad I know in this lifetime. I'm glad I did work it out in this lifetime [and she laughs].

Early in this book, I recorded Naomi's comment, when she read my first draft of her story, that 'it sounds too elegant as a description of me!! I tend to see what I'm doing as me stumbling along'. My discussion of ritual in the last chapter has opened the way for a fuller understanding of this remark and of our different interpretations of aspects of her story. Her perception confirms a final attribute of ritual, that ritual is 'an arena of contradictory and contestable perspectives – participants having their own reasons, viewpoints and motives'; that ritual, like the narrative to which it is linked, is in fact 'made up as it goes along' (Goody 1977, cited in Parkin 1992: 13).

Part IV

The body

We look at ourselves in the mirror in order to please someone.
Rarely to interrogate the state of our body or 'soul', rarely for us,
and with an eye to our *becoming*.   (Irigaray 1986: 7)

10   Recreating the body

> I came to be able to turn my attention to what I used not to . . . I
> now recognize that my body is alive, is living, as conscious as my
> mind, which I had not *known*, or admitted when I was anorexic. And
> I also realized that there is a constant flow in my body, in my self . . .
> there is no hierarchical distinction between the *inner and the outer*.
>
> (Mukai 1989: 635–6, my italics)

Introduction

Takayo Mukai's moving account of her own recovery appeared in
Women's Studies International Forum in 1989. It includes the passage I have
just quoted, about a new way of knowing the body in recovery from
anorexia. Participants in my study also spoke of the new meanings they
have given to their bodies during their self-transformation; a transition
from alienation to discovery. Their insights about the body's relation to
the self, to the world (of society and of nature), to spirit and to language,
suggest new ways that social theory might understand each of these
relationships.

As Mukai makes clear, recovery involves the creation of a new
subjective reality, with a quite different perception of one's physical self.
The new perception goes hand in hand with changes in bodily shape, size,
strength and abilities. There is no denying the importance of a shift in
emphasis, in participants' accounts as they recover, from an awareness of
the 'outer body' and how others see it, to the 'inner body' and how it is
subjectively experienced. Talking in this way, however, suggests a 'real'
inner body and an 'artificial' outer body, as if we could have access to a
culturally unmediated natural order – a possibility sociology denies, since
it argues that all our perceptions are culturally shaped. If anorexia nervosa
involves a radical splitting of body and self, how can participants
(including myself) be considered to have 'recovered' if we still speak in
such dualistic terms?

Dualistic discourses

The dualistic 'split' between body/ emotions/ sexuality on one hand and mind/ self/ spirit on the other pervades participants' conversation – even when they have recovered. Margaret (recovering) spoke of her body as 'a separate thing from my brain'. 'When I'm having a shower', she said, 'I have this sense of it being just down there under me. And when I'm on a diet, I'm doing things to the body part of me. My mind is in charge of my body. They are very much separate.' Sheena (also recovering) still feels 'fragmented' into sexual and emotional sides that 'got cut off and never expressed' during anorexia. She continues to perpetuate the split in the idea that there actually are 'pieces' to be identified and glued together, rather than interweaving processes to be lived. But even recovered participants talk in this 'split' way of body and self, often referring to themselves as 'I' and their bodies as 'it', like Meredith, who says: 'I'm much more attuned to my body now, to know when it's hungry and when it isn't and what it wants. It will actually tell me it needs a banana.'

Dualisms imply domination and submission. When people had fully recovered, they spoke of their anorexic attempts to control the body with the mind – to 'master it', as Rosalie puts it – and of the way they had gradually lost that need. Marjorie was aware of the roots of her own body/mind dualism in European culture and she expressed the very problem which concerns me here; how to speak and write of the body without splitting and objectifying aspects of human 'being':

To recover, you've got to start seeing your body as part of you. We've split it off for so long. And punished it. This is what I think recovery is: that the whole, all of me, is worth looking after. That's the big change, actually. I blame the European philosophers for this, you know, the body/mind thing; they definitely divided the two. They think the body's something else, that they don't have to look after.

Marjorie is right about the influence of dualistic discourses on our experiences of our own bodies. Western traditions of thought, epitomized by Descartes' *Cogito*; 'I think, therefore I am', make it difficult to speak of 'my' body without raising a host of questions about the way in which other people perceive this body and the influence of their perceptions upon my own. This is one of the problems addressed by twentieth century European philosophy and in particular by the existentialists. Since anorexia nervosa, as I have indicated elsewhere, is partly an existential problem, then existentialist philosophy might be thought to offer clues to recovery. Jean-Paul Sartre, its most famous proponent, tried to eradicate mind/body dualism from his own philosophy, yet his work is full of the transcendent nature of the intellect and its attempts to escape the 'nauseating' body. In *Being and Nothingness* (1966), the body is defined as 'that which is known by the other' (p. 297), 'a thing . . . much more my property than my being' (pp. 401–2), 'lived but not known' (p. 427), 'the psychic object par excellence' (p. 455) and 'nauseous' (p. 468): 'A dull and inescapable nausea perpetually reveals my body to my consciousness. It is on the foundation of this nausea that all concrete and empirical nauseas are produced and make us vomit' (Sartre 1966: 445). This attitude to the body colours his arguments about the body as it does most of that other influential existentialist text *The Second Sex* (1953) for, as de Beauvoir says of herself and Sartre: 'We were encouraged by Cartesian rationalism . . . We believed ourselves to consist of nothing but pure reason and pure will' (cited in Grene 1973: 17). The overwhelmingly negative imagery which Sartre connects with corporeality – the subtextual fear and loathing of the body in his writing – are stronger than the logical arguments he claims to advance against a mind/body dualism. Yet when Sartre writes about 'my body' and 'I' he claims to be representing us all. He is justified to the extent that we all participate in western discourses about the body. I discuss Sartre in this chapter because his philosophy addresses 'the problem of the body in its relations with consciousness' (1966: 1) and the philosophy of Being, which touches on one meaning of spirituality I have adopted in this book; namely, spirit as the process of being and becoming.

In *Being and Nothingness*, there are three ways of thinking of the body; 'the body-in-itself', 'the body-for-others', and 'the body for myself as known by the other' (Sartre 1966: part 3, chapter 2). These are useful, though not exhaustive, ways of thinking about social influences on bodies. Sartre argues that I can only be aware of myself through the awareness of others about myself, and that it is this inescapable situation which produces in me a sense of alienation (p. 462) and a longing 'not to have a body any more, to be invisible' (p. 463). I would suggest instead, that the body is created; shaped and transformed, by *it*self which is *my*self, in an interaction between experience, will and available social meanings. It is the inseparability of *it*self and *my*self which gives participants the feeling of inner dialogue they describe as 'the body speaking to me'. Participants' willing acknowledgment of the discursive influences on their feeling and thinking shows their awareness of the social dimensions of bodily change.

The resemblance is striking between, on one hand, Sartre's description of alienation, longing for invisibility, and nausea to the point of vomiting, and, on the other, the expressed feelings of people during an anorexic phase. It is this description of the 'typical' modern condition which might be adduced as a contributing factor in anorexia (Giddens 1991: 105–7). But Sartre's suggestion that this alienation is the inescapable condition of being human is not borne out in accounts of *recovery* from the 'alienation and nausea' of anorexia. In fact, these accounts suggest that the intellectual alienation from the body which is part of the anorexic condition (the hyper awareness of the body-for-others and the body for others as known by the self) can be resolved through a greater awareness of the body-in-itself; that is, of the body's internal states and of the body as a centre of action; the lived body (to which Sartre fleetingly alludes on p. 427). Despite their own difficulties with dualism, participants seemed to make use of the concept of 'inner' body as a means of escaping the constraints of a merely 'outer' body. That both inner and outer bodies are *imaginary* bodies does not seem to detract from the value of the concepts in resolving some of the problems of the anorexic condition.

Like existentialism, poststructuralist theory also attempts to escape dualism. It does this by positing not two but many selves; not only body and mind, but a fragmented body and a fragmented mind. Lacan's account of the mirror stage in childhood development is the text most often cited to demonstrate the inevitability of these disjunctions (Lacan 1977). He argues that the self is always split into observer and observed; that the self can never live up to the ego ideal; that there will always be a split between the body as felt and the body as idealized. Participants' accounts of recovery, however, show that it is possible to abandon an emphasis on the ideal body; the body for others, in favour of the felt body; the body one trusts *as if* it had a language of its own which one is willing to learn and which will present the world to us in new ways. Recovery, in this sense, is a form of resistance to the self-objectification demanded in our culture. In recovering, mirrors (like weighing) cease to be the dominant measure of one's worth, or indeed of one's reality. The stories participants construct to make sense of their lives include the 'myth' of the inner 'natural' and 'authentic' body, as an alternative to the body they used to believe they 'should' exhibit to meet the cultural expectations of people around them. If participants do not speak of this 'inner' body as equally subject to another, more liberating, form of cultural construction, it is because recovery does not require this degree of intellectual analysis. What it does require, together with transformative bodily practices, is a story that allows people to experience themselves in new and non-alienating ways. Since our language is replete with body/self dualism, it is not surprising that participants' language includes this split; but through their bodily practices and their story of an 'authentic/natural' bodily self, they overcome the effects of this dualism to experience the embodied self as a connected whole.

Irigaray provides two metaphors of great relevance to this problem of 'inner–natural/authentic', 'outer–social/false' in the stories of participants. Her own project has assumed increasingly obvious 'spiritual' dimensions, especially in *Divine Women* (1986). In her attempt to find new ways of writing about women's experience, she uses and transforms Lacan's metaphor of the mirror. In 'And one does not move without the other' (1982), she describes women's relationships with their mothers through the powerful image of swallowing the mirror. 'J'ai avalé la glace' is as much about the internalizing of the mirror in order to see into oneself as it is about taking in, with mother's milk, the image of a woman's body. Irigaray's other powerful image, the speculum (1985), is an even more apt metaphor for women's attempts to know the inner body. It illustrates how, in our process of becoming, we take the mirror within, to come to know our own sexuality. The availability of such images, not necessarily directly from Irigaray, but in the culture from which she distilled them, is an example of ways the metaphor of 'inner and outer bodies', despite its apparent dualism, may serve important transformative purposes.[1]

From 'outer' to 'inner' body: participants' words

When participants made the distinction between an outer and an inner body, they implied that the inner body *contained* the 'real' self to which they gained access in recovery. For Vivienne: 'what you look like, the form, is much less important than who you are, which is the content'. For Simone: 'the more that I felt better about myself, the more I felt pride and the pride translates into body image. The body straightens up and fills out'.

These statements also convey the idea that the outer body *expresses* the inner self; as if others could read off the meaning of one's person from one's bodily appearance. This is a cultural assumption with considerable force, but one about which it is very difficult to be precise, since appearance has such different meanings; not only across cultures, but within a single culture as well.[2] It is, of course, the very problem which may contribute to anorexia; the frequent equation of fat with sloth, lack of control and general moral degeneracy while slenderness is read as control and moral purity. During the course of my research, I certainly found myself using appearance to make judgements about participants' degree of recovery and I was also aware that visual signs could be deceptive in a number of ways. This is one reason why I have used groupings into which participants placed themselves, rather than those into which I might have placed them. I notice, for instance, that Patricia moves her large body with the agility usually associated with smaller women. In contrast, Susanna, the shortest and almost the frailest of study participants, first appeared to me as an imposing presence. Similarly, participants' responses to my body were influenced by their expectation that I had 'recovered', but also by their own needs for me to be 'not too fat' or 'not too thin', depending upon their own desires for themselves. All of which indicates that the notion of the outer body as an expression of the inner self, although accepted by most participants and the culture in which they live, is not as unproblematic as it first appears.

The body-for-others

Participants were most likely to allude to the importance of others' opinions when they were still anorexic or recovering. They longed for the 'inner', 'authentic' self which would liberate them from their fear of other people's critical gaze ; not recognizing that this inner self is also a social creation because, in recovering, we introject the approval of others instead of their disapproval. Lauren told me, for example: 'I used to imagine people were looking at me as I was walking down the street and that sort of thing. So I wasn't being true to myself. I was still being influenced by what other people were saying. I still don't know what the true me is. I'd admit that.' At the same time, when participants were anorexic, they also feared the approval of others, and especially the male gaze. As Marilyn put it: 'I hated the thought of anybody thinking I had a good body. How could he find me attractive – this person who actually likes me – because my body's awful!'

Jodie's story captured both facets of the cultural construction of the body; the introjection of social disapproval in anorexia and the internalizing of social approval in recovery. Jodie is a dedicated cyclist. She explained how the negative comments of a coach who urged her to diet in the early stages of her recovery propelled her into an orgy of self-hatred, insecurity, bingeing and vomiting; but she also says that today, she chooses to listen to her dietician instead and to eat the amount and kind of food she needs to engage in her sport. The 'inner/outer' distinction remains in her thinking, but she transforms it into a positive validation of herself. In case this sounds too voluntaristic; as if recovery were entirely a matter of choice, I re-emphasize that although agency is always involved in self-transformation, so is the availability of discourses and practices which make it possible. Jodie does select a positive from a negative alternative, but she can only do so because the positive alternative is available to her.

The body-for-itself

For Sartre, being-for-itself (hence the body-for-itself) is 'the revealed revelation of another type of being' (1966: 25), and is therefore a different form of consciousness of oneself and one's body. Recovery includes this more conscious awareness of the body. Significantly, only the 'recovered' people in my study spoke at length about an 'inner body'; about the way their body *feels* and what these feelings mean to them, rather than about their bodies as perceived by others. When they spoke of an 'inner' body, it was in the context of the physical practices they now enjoy; the rituals through which they continue to transform the meaning their bodies have for them. The 'inner body' to which they refer, far from being a pre-existing body to be 'discovered', is continuously shaped through practices and language.

This 'inner body' is an *imaginary body*; a body which is also socially constructed. It is the imaginary body which is the object of ritual transformation and this in turn has effects on the biological body. For example, the muscular development which takes place in yoga is not the primary object of the exercise; rather it is the creation of an imaginary body through language, visualization and sensory experience which leads to a new respect for the body as a means to a deeper spiritual awareness.[3] Zoe contrasted her reliance on the judgment of others with her current attitude when she said :

My body feels well. I have strength. I'm strong. I'm a normal weight now, no-one would question that; but I'm strong, I'm springy and I've got muscles! I didn't mean to get those muscles, to develop these muscles but I swim (and I guess that goes in the family). I've learned to respect my body and to give it what it needs. Now I know how to feed it. The more I do this, the more I have faith in my body now. It's looking after itself. I feed it properly and I go to the gym.

So although Zoe still speaks dualistically ('I' feed 'it'), and gives the body a life of its own ('it's looking after itself'), she also reveals the social sources of her 'new' body in her family's habit of swimming, in the 'gym and aerobics culture' of the upper-class suburb in which she lives and even in the importance she attaches to 'normality'; having one of the kinds of body which is admired in her particular cultural milieu. The meaning which 'aerobics' has for her, however, is liberating rather than splitting and controlling. She thinks of aerobics as a way of transforming her awareness instead of as a means of constructing a visually acceptable body-for-others.

Although I have been arguing that the 'inner body' is a cultural creation used to advantage by the recovering anorectic, there is, nevertheless, a sense in which the inner, biological body is directly 'known' and accepted once more in recovery; in the recognition of hunger. Hunger, as Simone Weil so acutely expressed it, is the final demarcation between life and death, being and not being in the world. In anorexia, the bodily sensation of hunger is denied and in recovery it is accepted. To this extent, at least, the body can be said to send messages to which the self listens: 'Before, I would deny that I was hungry but now I will recognize the signals. I'm beginning to respond to hunger and to what your body needs' says Marilyn. Even hunger, however, is culturally shaped: where, when, what and how we 'feel' we want to eat depends almost entirely on cultural factors (Lupton 1996). Recovery from anorexia involves, even more than the recognition of hunger, a re-learning of socially acceptable ways to satisfy it. These facts illustrate the inseparability of the biological body, the imaginary body and the social body; all of which help make up the self.

Ritual transformations of the body[4]

Anorexia and recovery, like all rituals, involve and transform the body. In addition to the mythological elements of narrative, recovery involves practices of a ritualistic nature with (usually unconscious) ritual intent. I now turn to a discussion of some of these rituals as I found them in the stories of participants, to show more precisely *how* the body is involved in the transformations of recovery. Naomi's story told of rituals of gardening, music, model-making and painting, together with the still more physical rituals of eating; her choice of foods which have particular memories and meanings for her. In the stories of other participants, the bodily aspects of self-transforming rituals are still more apparent. They include abandoning ritual weighing, and a new use of activities such as swimming, belly-dancing, bike-racing, surfing, meditation and dancing. Although people who are anorexic may employ some of these activities as a means of weight-loss and as a way of controlling space and especially time, the same activities (and new ones) have quite different purposes in recovery. From being means of punishing and reducing the body, they become ways to experience body and self more fully; ways to experiment with expanding body boundaries. With the greater freedom to relax these boundaries comes the sense of 'connection' that is part of spiritual awareness.

Weighing

Weighing is one of the rituals through which, in the acute phase of anorexia, most 'anorectics' remind themselves to be forever vigilant in the control of their bodies. Some learnt it from their parents in childhood and others from peers and 'health' messages in the media. For participants who are still 'anorexic', the ritual may involve stepping on the scales many times a day; or it may become a weekly, monthly or less frequent event, charged with enormous significance – very definitely a ritual of the negative cult. They describe their weighing ritual as 'paranoid', as part of a 'rationalizing' of the body, and as 'a great trauma'. The 'rationality' which governs this ritual is Weber's 'instrumental rationality'; the calculation and measurement as ends in themselves which, when divorced from the other forms of rationality, become fetishized as if they were the only credible 'reality'. Jennifer's and Victoria's use of weighing illustrate this rationalizing, controlling aspect of weighing and measuring and some of its destructive results, when happiness itself depends on the downward trend of numbers on the scales or of figures on the size tags of their clothes:

Sometimes I feel almost good about myself. I might be at a stage where I've cut back and lost another lump of weight or something, but that particular week I may have had a couple of really sensible controlled meals, so I think that sort of rationalizes you a bit. The only thing my husband notices, probably, is I'm terribly paranoid about weight. [Jennifer]

I had a period when I just never weighed myself. I was happy or unhappy according to what fitted. You know; if a size ten fitted, I was happy. If I had to wear a size twelve, I was unhappy till I fitted back into the size ten. I'm not sure how much conscious effort went into it. I feel happier when I'm not eating, so when I was pregnant and they had to weigh me, that was a source of great trauma. Especially as when you're pregnant your weight is so much higher than you're anticipating seeing on the scale. [Victoria]

Participants in the other two groups either do not weigh themselves or do so only in periods of stress (for reassurance or as a relapse into self-punishment). For many, the scars of this form of instrumental rationality remain. In the three examples which follow, Joanne (recovering) still measures her achievement and her happiness by her weight, even though she has never been other than slim. Marjorie (also recovering) acknowledges a gradually 'changing slant' on her lifetime of daily weighing; and Kate (recovered), even though she welcomes weight gain and looks forward to pregnancy, still finds herself using the language and practice of the scales:

I'm lucky, I seem to be able to eat a fair bit and I don't get fat, but I'm still obsessed to a certain extent. I always keep my weight under eight stone and if ever I do put on any weight I do tend to go into a bit of a panic and think I'm getting fat. Other people never notice. In fact, people say 'have you lost weight?' I sometimes think the only thing I've got going for me is that I have never had a weight problem. [Joanne]

I don't think I could stop weighing myself. Not yet. I've weighed myself the whole of my life. You know? Every morning it's been the ritual. But I suppose the slant has changed, because now this is what I keep telling the young ones that I see:

'You've got to start seeing your body as part of you; we've split it off for so long.' [Marjorie]

In some ways I should just completely and utterly not weigh myself for ten years and just say 'I will be whatever I would have been if I hadn't been anorexic' . . . I don't know what I would have been. Essentially before all that I'd been sixty three [kilos]. I think fifty eight looks pretty fantastic: I think that's good and I should go back up there, but to actually get from fifty six to fifty eight I really have to eat a lot. It's quite a big jump for me. To me I suppose that's my real number of the real woman. So you're denying yourself by not going back up to fifty eight. [Kate]

Weighing oneself, even daily, is (probably increasingly) seen as 'normal' 'health-promoting' behaviour, especially for women. The scales have become more important than the mirror in giving women 'knowledge' about their bodies. They trust them more than they trust their sight, their feelings or their ears. A depersonalized and ultimately unreliable way of gaining information, this kind of weighing is a metaphor for much statistical research and some 'scientific' methodology in clinical research on anorexia which often overlook the limitations of their instruments in providing knowledge about the complexities of human experience. For recovered participants, weighing may be abandoned altogether, or understood as only one form of knowledge – instrumental knowledge – about the body. If it is used, it is as a complement to the many other ways of knowing and thinking; the substantive, ethical and aesthetic rationalities Weber struggled to express in his theoretical work, but which are available to us all unless we have deified one form of rationality (like 'science') and made it sacred in opposition to other, 'profane', knowledges.

Swimming, dancing and other bodily practices

Swimming was one of the most frequently mentioned bodily means of self-transformation in recovery. Many participants spoke of swimming as an activity removed from their ordinary everyday life; in effect a sacred time and space in which they experienced the movement of their own bodies in relation to nature; an opportunity literally to 're-create' themselves physically and spiritually. The fluidity; the sense of being part of a whole, the bodily memories of floating in the womb, all play a part in recreating the 'oceanic feeling' of the repressed spirituality they rediscover in recovery. For these participants, swimming has become a positive, rather than a negative cult. Kate enjoys the 'sensual experience' of riding the waves on her boogie-board. Rosalie says:

We've got a sizeable pool in the back yard that I like to swim up and down every day; but it's because I love that sense of well-being. I find [with] fiddling around the house doing all the sorts of things you have to do as a mother and housewife, it's nice to get in there and just swim up and down and leave all the rest of it. It's not just the physical activity in swimming; as well, it's the fitness. Doing that actually gives me more energy.

It is not, however, swimming *per se*, which alone effects the transformation. Ariel, still suffering from obsessive thoughts about her body and from occasional bingeing and vomiting, continues to use swimming as a form of negative self-discipline, even as she is allowing herself to enjoy its other pleasures. It is the transformation of Rosalie's attitude to swimming (the meaning it has for her), as much as the activity itself, which is involved in her recovery.

For Vivienne, belly-dancing has become a means of altering her awareness of her body and her sexuality. When we first met, she told me (again, in the almost unavoidably dualistic language of 'my relationship with my body'):

I still have big problems with the fact that my relationship with my body is sufficiently screwed that things like dance, lack of physical inhibition are non-existent; though recently I have got to a point where I've got a vague desire to do belly dancing. What specifically I'm after in belly dancing is the sexual – it's hips. It's the fact that I have got large hips and I want to find out what they're about. I rang up (a belly-dancing centre) to ask about it and one of my immediate questions was 'they're not anorexic leotard people are they?' and when she said: 'Oh no, love'; I thought: 'Right. You're on!'

Having been reassured about the non-obsessive orientation of the group, Vivienne has now become a regular and enthusiastic belly-dancer. She thinks of belly-dancing as the antithesis of her anorexic body rituals and as a means of exploring her sexuality.

Jodie began bike-racing with her husband, discovered that she was good at it, and decided that going fast was more important to her than what she looked like. Although it could be argued that she has replaced one form of obsession with another, she sees a huge difference between 'exercising' and 'training'. The former was designed to control the body she mistrusted; the latter is enjoyable in itself (especially since she shares it with her husband and her cycle-racing peers) as well as rewarding her with a sense of physical achievement. Jacqueline, although still struggling with many 'anorexic' aspects of her past, is also beginning to engage in activities that give her a greater sense of her bodily potential for pleasure and power and an altered perception of her bodily boundaries. From the 'iron will' of her anorexic rituals, she is slowly experimenting with new forms of bodily activity:

It was internal and iron will, an absolute iron will, which is what separated me – and what kept me alive . . . When you contract, energetically contract, you appear smaller and when you begin to expand and open yourself to the world, you take up more space . . . I did quite a long workshop a while ago. We were doing dancing; chaotic movement. And I was really terrified to do it, thinking I would be self-conscious or whatever. And what came out of it was absolute pure joy. I just had such a revelation, that I'd been holding back. And what was I frightened of? I was frightened of joy; joy and pleasure!

Yoga

Yoga is also one of the rituals which several participants have discovered as a means of reinventing themselves and their bodies. Sheena, for example, has been practising yoga for twenty years and she believes it is one of the three things, together with acupuncture and a thirty-minute daily exercise routine, which have been most important in her ongoing recovery. They are her personal recovery rituals and they help unify her body, mind and spirit: 'Physically, yoga has had a very calming effect. It's my thing. Other people find something else that works for them – like meditation- but it's really been the physical side of yoga that's helped. But again, you can't separate the two things.' In addition, Sheena has learned specific yogic techniques for bringing awareness into parts of her body (especially the pelvic and genital areas) which she had been taught to disregard and to fear:

It was called remedial yoga; therapeutic yoga. And I just suddenly found myself with all these sexual feelings that I'd never had before. My body started speaking to me in ways that I hadn't had before. That's going about it (recovery) from the other end; just from the physical end. I think that bodies have all these huge potentials for probably feelings and experiences that we don't even know exist, and that's a realization that came to me from just physical exercise and yoga. The reason it's changed my life is not just because it made me feel better and look better too – and that's important – but it made me be more friendly with my body and made me like my body; and my body had always been an enemy.[5]

In yoga the emphasis is on what the body can do, rather than on its outward appearance or as the enemy; an appendage to the self. Yoga is a way of learning about parts of oneself and the feelings associated with them. It is performed in sacred time, outside of ordinary everyday activities. It places great stress on the breath as the connection between body and mind; that which enables both to realize soul. Yoga is still highly disciplined, in the sense that the more frequent and careful the practice, the greater the learning which takes place. But the discipline is that of substantive rather than instrumental rationality; it is about balance and connectedness, not weighing and measuring. Most importantly (and I pursue this further in chapter 12), the language and practice of yoga create a new imaginary body inseparable from self and the environment.

The imaginary body

The key to the bodily transformations of recovery and to their social source is the imaginary body; the culturally created body which is the object of the changes and without which the changes could not occur.[6] By 'imaginary body' I mean the significance to each person of 'the body as lived' (Gatens 1983). As well as the physical sensations participants experience in their new, positively oriented rituals, a major change has occurred in the way they conceive of their body. The two changes go hand in hand. As they recreate their bodies as 'recovered', rather than 'anorexic' bodies, they think of them in quite different ways, borrowing from 'technologies' (discourses and their associated practices) like yoga and Tai Chi (which several participants practised), and often from books of popular psychology and 'recovery' which allocate specific psychological meanings to different parts of the body.[7] Each of these discourses contains the idea that the body has its own rhythms, needs and meanings and that these can be 'discovered' as a means of living a life in greater harmony with 'nature'.

The 'imaginary' body, however, is not just the body as seen in the mind's eye, but as it is experienced by each of the senses.[8] Kate no longer imagines/experiences her stomach distorted by the food she eats, and her psychological state no longer depends on what she feels/imagines about her body. She says:

Now if my stomach's full of food, it's just full of food. There's no connotations. I'm free of those connotations. My body isn't linked in with all those systems any more, so that I'm not trapped or bound. I can have thoughts and emotions that are quite different to the state of my body. I have far more room to move.

This has not been Freda's experience at all. Before her eating disorders began, she wore size fourteen clothes. When she was anorexic, she took size eight or less. Today, she 'only eats junk food' and takes a size twenty-two. But Freda has the imaginary body of a thin person. She feels as if she takes up less space than she does: 'I always get a surprise when I see myself somewhere. Who's that fat person?' Her imaginary body gives her hope that perhaps this is the size she might one day become.

Vivienne has developed a very graphic imaginary body which she uses as a means of evaluating her well-being:

The way I experience my body is of being made up of two cones. And one of them kind of comes down from under my ribs to my navel, and then there's another part of my body which is a kind of cone as well. The two cones fit into one another. And it's like, when I experience myself as bedded down into my pelvis, I'm fine. I have a sense of proportion, I am not worried about what other people think about me. I have a sensuality and I move comfortably. When I kind of start to separate up – I move up into my head and away from my sensation. It's like I withdraw from my skin. I start getting problems with perception. I get vague hallucinations. I get problems with contact with other people, instead of having the experience that AA and analysis have given me, which is 'I am bigger than the day. I have the resources to do this.'

Meredith's imaginary body is being transformed to include new ways of experiencing sexuality, in her encounter with Tibetan Buddhism and the Hindu concept of 'kundalini energy' made available in New Age texts and teachings. Her ongoing recovery includes a reformulation of sexual feelings as 'life energy'. Cradling her belly in her hands, she says:

It's all connected with this belly part. That's where your life is. It's in this part of your body that your sexuality is. I mean that's your life-force in there. With anorexia you're out absolutely out of contact – you're denying that; that vitality in that part of your body. So later on, you might have recovered physically from anorexia, but it's going to manifest in another way.

For each of these participants, the imaginary body is a mediator between the social and the biological realities of physical being. The ritual practices which assist the transformations of recovery do so via the imagination; an imagination shaped by 'alternative' discourses and their accompanying practices which increasingly influence contemporary western culture (Heelas 1996).

Summary and conclusions

The story participants tell about the body in recovery is about a re-discovery of an 'authentic' body; *as if* we were coming closer to nature and 'natural' patterns of behaviour, as we move away from the rigid (presumably culturally imposed) control of the body that takes place in anorexia. It is also the story of 'the mind' re-connecting with, listening to and feeling 'the body'; *as if* the two were in some senses still separate. The body/mind, nature/culture dualism present in these stories, as it is in western philosophy, including existentialist and post-structuralist attempts to avoid it, has not necessarily prevented recovery, but it does illustrate some of the immense problems we face in constructing the myths that make recovery possible. Since we live in a culture which makes these differentiations, it is extremely difficult to avoid speaking in these terms.

In spite of living in this dualistic culture, people are still able to create patterns of relating to self and others which (often unconsciously or semi-consciously) manage to avoid the dualism inherent in our very use of language. At least part of the solution to this problem of dualism in *language* has been through non-dualistic *practices*. The bodily rituals (themselves, of course, cultural) in which participants engage mitigate against dualism even when it is unavoidable in the language they use. The key to the bodily transformations of recovery and to their social source is the imaginary body; the body as it is re-conceptualized through practices like swimming, dance and yoga and the language which accompanies them. The imaginary body assists in the creation of new meanings about body and self; through an expansion of 'rationality' beyond its instrumental form, to embrace other ways of knowing.

The meaning of 'spirit' in these bodily changes is this: when participants refer to an 'authentic' or 'true' self, to the 'voice' of their bodies and to the new bodily sensations of recovery, they are referring to a transforming energy. Durkheim would have said that this energy was generated by the power of the social and he would be partly correct, given the power of the (socially constructed) imaginary body in rituals of recovery. What Durkheim ignored, however, was the material reality of spiritual energy; the necessity for some life-force which brings into being both natural and social phenomena; neither of which exists *sui generis*. When participants speak of their changed bodily awareness in recovery as authentic, natural, a life-force and a form of liberation, they are not only expressing the 'new' meanings they have unconsciously selected from a smorgasbord of cultural possibilities; they are also describing their belief in a kind of energy which brings life itself into being. It is in this sense that the physical experiences of recovery are as much 'spiritual' as they are 'social' and, *pace* Durkheim, the two are not reducible to each other.

11 The sexual body

There is an interfusion between sexuality and existence, which means
that existence permeates sexuality and vice versa.

(Merleau-Ponty 1962: 169)

Introduction

'Relationship' was an essential element in participants' narratives of
recovery. It was through relationships that they touched and were touched
by the lives of others. Desire, focused on a narrow form of perfection while
they were anorexic, broadened again to embrace friendships, sexual
relationships and a stronger sense of their physical presence in the world.
The reawakening of this desire (for other people, for nature and for life
itself) was essential to the ongoing creation of the new 'non-anorexic' self.
'Sexuality' is our active engagement with the Other, and participants'
accounts of their sexuality in anorexia and recovery show that desire is
inseparable from spirituality, since both are the life-force which animates
existence.

Sexuality and spirituality: a theoretical framework

Even people who have recovered from the body/mind split of an eating
disorder are constrained in their narratives by their use of dualistic terms
like 'inner' and 'outer' bodies, that so closely resemble the existentialist
philosophy of Sartre, with its accompanying horror of the flesh. At the
same time, participants employ a language of connection – the language of
spirituality – to dissolve this very dualism. Just as the philosophy of Sartre
was helpful in understanding the entrenched nature of body/mind
dualism in western thought, so the work of Maurice Merleau-Ponty is
valuable as a means of explaining the nature of the 'connections'
participants found in recovery.[1] Merleau-Ponty resolves the problem of
dualism by using the term 'flesh'. 'Flesh', in his work, refers to the
embodied spirit, or the spirit-imbued body. This term offers a bridge

between the body-for-others and the body-in-itself (and the body-for-itself, which is the more self-conscious embodied self apparent in accounts of recovery) because it is flesh, the desiring body (or embodied desire) that makes *connection* possible.

Merleau-Ponty is also concerned to combat, on one hand the tendency of psychoanalytic theory to reduce all human sensuous experience to the sexual (1962: 159), and on the other, the inclination of existentialist psychology to reduce the body to a mere 'transparent integument of Spirit' (1962:160). He does so through the example of recovery from anorexia. He deals at length with the case of 'an anorexic girl',[2] to illustrate the way in which asexuality cuts one off from Being. The girl, forbidden to see the young man with whom she is in love, loses her appetite, and eventually her speech. She is 'unable to "swallow" the prohibition which has been imposed on her' (1962: 158). Merleau-Ponty concludes that: 'loss of voice does not merely represent a refusal of speech, or anorexia a refusal of life; they are a refusal of others or refusal of the future' (1962: 164). Referring to recovery, Merleau-Ponty mentions the importance of 're-discovery' (of '*re*-connection') and the way in which 'sexuality', in his extended sense of the word, *re*-creates the meaning of the body. 'The girl will recover her voice', he writes (and, I presume her willingness to resume eating),

not by an intellectual effort or by an abstract decree of will, but through a conversion in which the whole of her body makes a concentrated effort . . . when the body once more opens itself to others or to the past, when it opens the way to co-existence and once more (in the active sense) acquires significance beyond itself. (Merleau-Ponty 1962: 165)

'Sexuality' is necessary, therefore, to take the self 'beyond itself' toward the Other. 'Sexuality' is a very precise term for Merleau-Ponty; for although he says there is an 'interfusion' between sexuality and existence, he does not reduce existence to sexuality, nor sexuality to existence. Instead, he asserts the necessity of sexuality to our humanity, along with all the other 'facts' of human existence. Most importantly, he believes that it is not only these facts but their inter-relation ('their inter-communication, the point at which their boundaries run into each other') which is crucial to human existence (1962: 166). It is in this sense of sexuality; as that which can enable us to dissolve boundaries; to make profound connections, whether positively or negatively, that I use the word here; adding two qualifications: First, just as Merleau-Ponty is concerned not to present a disembodied version of sexuality (he is adamant that sexuality is to do with 'the sexual drama' of genital penetration), so I do not wish to sound as though sexuality in recovery is simply the reclaiming of the sensual pleasures of the entire body for the self (although it is also that). The sexual *connection* is essential to the human task 'to generate the divine in us *and between us*' (Irigaray 1986:3, my italics).[3] My second qualification is a corollary of the first: Clearly, genital sexuality is not the only means of physical relation or even of sexual relation between people. People can be 'passionately celibate', deeply physical and spiritual beings without genital sex (Cline 1993).

In writing about the spiritual nature of sexuality, Merleau-Ponty is referring to what Kovel has called 'the coming to consciousness of some part of the self's relationship to itself and to others' (1991: 45); the recognition of the essential sociality of human beings.[4] The sexual experience, in other words, is not only spiritual but, because it is about connection, it is also social. Social relations themselves are part of the constant process of becoming to which the term 'spirituality' refers and which sexuality expresses. Merleau-Ponty's conception of the self is not of an essentialist body or an essentialist human being, but of an historically created person being constantly transformed. In this passage, with its reference to salvation, his interpretation hovers on the edge of a spiritual conception of the self:

> Why is the body the mirror of our being unless because it is a *natural self*, a current of given existence, with the result that we never know whether the forces which bear us on are its or ours – or with the result rather that they are never entirely either its or ours . . . There is no outstripping of sexuality any more than there is any sexuality enclosed within itself. No one is saved and no one is totally lost. (Merleau Ponty 1962: 171)

This 'current of existence', the transhistorical 'natural self', is more aptly named *spirit*. Sexuality is the means by which this current of existence is shared with other human beings and with the whole of nature. In anorexia nervosa and other attempts to protect the self, the closing down of the sexual body also shuts out the free flow of the spirit. The body, constantly being transformed as it encounters different objective circumstances, is thus the active centre for both spirituality and sexuality and, consequently, for sociality. The material body is infused with life energy that is constantly shaped and reshaped within its natural and social environment.

This notion of sexuality offers a solution to the problem of body/spirit dualism as well as body/mind dualism. One difficulty in western religious thought and practice has been the splitting of sexuality from spirituality; of body from spirit. I have been arguing that while the two are not identical, they are inseparable. It is through the body and its passionate relation to the world that we experience our spirituality; our being. The place of spirit in sexual desire and of sexuality in spiritual growth is cogently articulated by Kovel in relation to the sexual/spiritual experience of Teresa of Avila. Kovel draws on Merleau-Ponty to argue that 'flesh is a spiritual body . . . composed of the matter of life, yet alive with spirit power and spirit-being' (1991: 115). In contrast to the hatred of flesh in so much of western philosophy and religion,

> Teresa recognizes that the body has a share ('and even a great deal') in her spiritual voyage, and she does not reject this so much as pass through it. She differentiates between the erotic and nonerotic phases of a spiritual path, and does not try to split the one from the other . . . In other words, spirit need not reject flesh, though it remains different from flesh; rather it passes onward. (Kovel 1991: 122)

For as Kovel also writes, 'to transcend does not mean to abolish, but to raise to another plane' (1991: 128).

Sexuality and recovery: participants' stories

Anorexia is often interpreted as a denial of sexuality and a fear of sexual connection. Conversely, recovery studies stress the importance of establishing sexual relationships, but rarely go into detail.[5] In their phenomenological recovery study, however, Beresin, Gordon and Herzog (1989) do deal briefly with the issue of (hetero)sexual relationships in recovery. They stress, as did many participants in my study, that 'one critical step in recovery is taking the risk of exposing one's self to others' and being accepted as one really is. For a third of their (female) respondents, 'falling in love with a man' was a landmark event in regaining acceptance and pleasure in the body (p. 121).

In my study, there were important differences in the ways participants spoke about their sexuality. All but two (Sue and Simone) said that during their severely anorexic phase they had no interest in sexual relationships in the commonsense meaning of the term. Those who continued to be sexually active seem to have used sex as a desperate means of trying to find some acceptability from others (Sue and Simone) and/or remained relatively anaesthetized to their own feelings in their sexual encounters (Jennifer, Victoria and Marilyn). All of them would agree that they were seriously 'cut off' from bodily enjoyment other than the satisfaction of confirming through touch that their bodies were shrinking, and the reassuring sensation of emptiness and lightness in their bellies – anorexic forms of bodily pleasure. It is not celibacy per se which is the problem in anorexia, however, but the lack of physical and emotional engagement with the world; for as Sally Cline (1993) emphasizes, celibacy only deserves the name when it is an active choice and not merely accidental or a retreat from engaging with others.

In the examples which follow, I trace the importance of the sexual element in the genesis of anorexia nervosa itself and then in recovery, as well as the transmutations in the meanings participants attach to their sexual experience. Participants who had not recovered spoke of having disengaged from sexual openness in Merleau-Ponty's sense as well as in its commonsense meaning. Participants who were recovering were aware of the importance of sexuality in recovery, but still experiencing great difficulties in sexual relationships. Those who had fully recovered all referred to sexuality as a pathway to, and an expression of, their recovery.

Early sexual experience

Three important issues emerged from participants' descriptions of the connection between their early sexual experience and later eating difficulties: first, that some form of sexual abuse may have been one predisposing factor; secondly, that anorexia was about hunger for understanding which they often equated with sexuality; and thirdly, that anorexia was a way of postponing sex for people who felt they were not ready for the 'sacred mysteries' of initiation into full adulthood (the rites of passage for which anorexia becomes a substitute). The first issue is not surprising. Sexual abuse is one of the traumas most likely to disrupt a person's sense of safety and connection with others and hence with the world in general. Anorexia is simply one of several possible responses to this disruption. The issue is relevant to recovery, however, because for that 'original' connection to the world to be re-established, participants had to create new meanings for their sexual experience in the present. In doing so, they frequently reviewed their sexual past, as the following extracts from the stories of Ilse and Eloise will show.

Ilse says: 'I'm positive that my anorexia had a lot to do with my not being able to manage my sexuality. I'm positive about it. In my family, sexuality really wasn't on. It was non-existent. It was nothing you talked about.' When she left home at seventeen to begin her nurse's training, Ilse was plunged into the sexual revolution of the 1960s and had a short affair with an older man, a doctor, even though she now says she was not ready for, or interested in, a sexual relationship. He forced her to have oral sex, and the experience left her traumatized and guilt-ridden. She links it with the onset of her anorexia. For Eloise as well, 'sexuality was definitely an issue'. She was 'afraid of growing up, afraid of being a woman and afraid of being attracted or attractive to boys' and her fear grew out of several unpleasant experiences of sexual harassment by men and boys which made her link sexuality with domination and made the opposite sex particularly unattractive.

The second issue is not surprising either. Many participants associated hunger with longing for sexual experience and to possess knowledge (the metaphorical 'phallus' of Lacanian psychoanalysis). In Ilse's story, for instance, the older doctor was chiefly attractive to her because 'he appeared so knowledgeable and I had a great hunger for knowledge'. Several participants spoke of passionate emotional, if not sexual, attachments to academics (of either sex) who represented the knowledge they craved. In Sally's case, even today, longing for spiritual understanding is also experienced as a strong sexual attraction to her spiritual teacher. Desire and knowledge are closely intertwined, and food often acts as a metaphor for both (for example, in the Biblical fruit of the tree of knowledge).[6]

The third important issue here concerns the mystical dimension of the knowledge acquired through sexuality; the 'knowledge' which is experienced, through direct union with another being, as direct union with the cosmos. This sacred dimension of sexuality subtends rites of sexual initiation and is implicit in many of the recovery stories in my study. For Sally, for example, sexuality represented a frightening loss of control; not only the 'domination' to which Eloise refers, but the abandonment of self to a power beyond rational understanding. She associated sex with 'a depth of commitment I wasn't ready for'. The metaphor she uses for sex ('devouring and all consuming') is a key to her choice of anorexia as a defence against the possibility of losing her identity in a sexual relationship, but also to her desire for that relationship. As she says, anorexia was a way of delaying the confrontation with the sacred for which she did not feel prepared:

It was the loss of control that was frightening about sex and something sort of devouring and all consuming. I didn't think you had to be married, but I guess what I did associate it with was a sort of depth of commitment that I wasn't ready for. I can look back and I can think: 'Well, that wasn't a bad thing in a way'. I mean, I really avoided sexual relationships for the whole time I was at college and I developed a lot of friendships and a lot of self-confidence. I guess what I'm trying to say is that emotionally I wasn't mature enough.

Simone's story helps explain why some women may remain sexually active during an anorexic phase. She also explains the force of sexuality (including auto-eroticism) in self-knowledge, which she sees as spiritual knowledge. When she was anorexic, her body bespoke a sexual hunger which she described to me later in the conversation as a spiritual hunger:

I've had sixty sexual partners in my life! It was the hunger. I had such a hunger! My mother was abused as a child. She couldn't *bear* to be touched or touch anybody. I grew up with an absolute aching hunger for intimacy and physical contact. And as soon as I discovered sex, after I got over the very puritan views about sex I had until I was about seventeen/eighteen – when I became a hippie, I guess – suddenly, I just threw myself into it with a vengeance. I must have intuited that here was a path, perverted as it was, towards (recovery). Sexual relations – celibate or auto-erotic – were one of the ways. But sexuality depended on feeling better about myself. So, although I do think (sexuality is) a relationship between people and others, you can do it in your own mind. It's a relationship with others through your own relationship with yourself.

'Disconnected' sexuality

Since sexuality is so much more than the sex act, it was not always genital sexual encounters *per se* which were the problem in anorexia or the solution in recovery. Several participants had continued to be sexually active while anorexic (though they made a strong distinction between the passive sexuality of their anorexic phase and the active, connected experience of sex which both assisted and constituted their recovery). Among those who were still anorexic, several were married: Jennifer describes her sex-life as if she were observing herself from outside her body, and with extreme cynicism about her husband. She consciously chose him, she says, because she believed he would not demand emotional involvement in their sexual relationship. Her real relationship, she makes clear, is with food and its control, including her abuse of laxatives. In Jennifer's account, the severe disconnection between body and self is highlighted by the way she speaks of her 'body' enjoying sex while 'she' doesn't care :

Take it or leave it. Physically you exist. Your body still exists. You get all the right reactions. He thinks it's wonderful. Take it or leave it. And I know myself, I'm obviously enjoying it, 'cause my body's enjoying it; but take it or leave it. I'm lucky I don't have a husband who pressures me. I didn't pick my husband for nothing! If I'm going through a non-eating stage and taking a lot of laxatives, I'm probably too tired, to be quite honest. As soon as I put my head on that pillow, I'm ready to sleep. I never get enough sleep. I'm always up at the crack of dawn , ready to go to the toilet [laugh]. And also, if I'm at a stage where I've eaten, I've had dinner, I'm not feeling good about myself; he hasn't got a chance. Even when eating doesn't come into it – and he might even comment how wonderful it was, or 'Gees, we have a wonderful sex life' and I say 'Yeah, we do, don't we?' and I think: 'It wouldn't worry me if we didn't have sex for two years!' And I find that sad. I think that's terrible. I could not tell my husband that it really would not worry me if we didn't have sex. But it wouldn't. Even though my body enjoys it. I really don't care.

Victoria and her husband Chito are a strikingly attractive couple ('all the girls at work told me I'd never catch him', says Victoria). They have three children, but she is still obsessed with dieting and body-hate. This is how she describes her sex life, dramatically contrasting the sexual body and the maternal body:

When I'm feeling fat and I don't want to know about him; if I don't feel good about my body, there's no sex. When we're overseas, I do feel a lot better and we have a fantastic sex life. We get back here and I go: 'Mothers don't do that sort of thing'. It's terrible. [Mimicking herself:] 'How could he possibly fancy me? I am a blimp tonight.' And if he touches me on a part that you're beginning to think is fat! I do my best to avoid it, because I just don't want to be seen, touched, anything. And yet when I feel good, then I don't mind in the least. That's when I might wear tighter clothes. That's when I might show off more of my body.

Women's insecurity about parts of the body and the way this interferes with sexual enjoyment is endemic in western societies,[7] but for people with eating disorders the problem is particularly acute (McFarlane & Baker-Baumann 1991). Victoria's own experience leads her to question the clinical criterion of 'normal sexual relations' as a measure of recovery, since what actually happens between sexual partners may be far from the sexual connection such a criterion seems to envisage:

It's been a constant gripe – it's not overwhelming, just a constant in my life, just a bit of a joke – that he gets pleasure but I don't. But I don't anticipate getting pleasure. We joke that my clitoris was moved when I had the second child, 'cause she was a Caesarian. I mean, the doctor must have misplaced it! It's a bit of a joke. I think I've finally got Chito believing that's true, because he can't believe I could go so long, I suppose. Oh what a thing! That's why that, as a guide to recovery, sexuality is so – well – that's why I laugh about that definition of recovery. How do you qualify? How do you measure? Have I got a normal sex life? I've got three children; how does it happen? But ask me if it's a normal sex life – (and I'll tell you) it's not, because I fluctuate so much.

Marilyn considers herself to be in the process of recovering, but in her sexual relationships, she describes a similar detachment from her body. She likens her attitude to sex to her attitude to food: 'I suppose sex for me is a bit like reading cookbooks; I have this great desire, but I can't actually do anything'. These examples of 'disconnected sexuality' demonstrate the anorexic denial of pleasure, construction of the body as impure/profane and fear of losing control of one's boundaries. Each illustrates a meaning of sexuality that changes in recovery.

Recovered sexuality

When recovered participants spoke of sexuality, they emphasized the importance of recognition from their partners and their friends. They described the way in which the other recognized their wholeness, instead of focusing on parts of the body, or on the body as distinct from the person. Pip, now forty-three years old, did not feel ready for marriage until two years ago. She says her sexual relationship with her husband is important chiefly because, within it, she feels accepted as a whole person; not as a body or as a mind. It creates and recreates her as a whole being:

After the first year or so of 'being in lust', things settled down a bit. Now there are a lot of cuddles in our relationship; particularly in bed. And I find that probably more satisfying than anything. It just indicates – it's all voluntary – it indicates that he likes me for what I am. That's the bottom line.

Naomi, who was sexually abused as a child, has never had what she would call a satisfying sexual relationship. Nevertheless, during her recovery, she did experiment with lesbian relationships, because they felt 'safer': 'At least', she says, 'I got some caring and some gentleness'. After the operation which ended her epilepsy, she felt 'these very strong urges to be heterosexually active that I'd never felt in my life'. Although she makes clear that she does not want a sexual relationship at present, Naomi's sexual feelings, which coincided with the beginning of her current period of intense artistic output, correspond to the kind of 'sexual' engagement of the body with the world to which Merleau-Ponty's analysis refers.

The maternal body

Pregnancy is a particular form of this 'sexual' engagement that can be an important part of recovery. Anorexia is often taken to be a conscious or unconscious aversion to and fear of the pregnant body and motherhood itself, as if motherhood were an inevitable consequence of womanhood and anorexia a retreat from being a woman and being a mother. Simone de Beauvoir described the fear of pregnancy and motherhood which many women experience as due in part to their lack of control over 'nature':

She feels it as at once an enrichment and an injury; the fetus is a part of her body, and it is a parasite that feeds on it; she possesses it, and she is possessed by it; it represents the future and, carrying it, she feels herself vast as the world; but this very opulence annihilates her, she feels she herself is no longer anything. (de Beauvoir 1953: 476)

Women's joy in their pregnant bodies, on the other hand, she describes as a kind of false transcendence:

It is especially noteworthy that the pregnant woman feels the immanence of her body at just the time when it is in transcendence . . . The transcendence of the artisan, of the man of action, contains the element of subjectivity; but in the mother-to-be the antithesis of subject and object ceases to exist; she and the child with which she is swollen make up together an equivocal pair overwhelmed by life. Ensnared by nature etc. (de Beauvoir 1953: 477)

The problem with de Beauvoir's account is that it equates transcendence with *action* upon the world, instead of a renewed *connection* with it. For her, immanence is passive. In contrast, Merleau-Ponty's 'sexual body' transcends the individual ego through the connection of self with other. The pregnant body and the maternal body are sexual because of the spirit energy that interpenetrates and links a woman and her child.

This passage from *The Second Sex* is embedded in a chapter on motherhood, a quarter of which is taken up by a discussion of abortion and the avoidance of pregnancy. In the historical situation she describes, where contraception was illegal and unreliable, a negative attitude to pregnancy and a sense of lack of control were very understandable; but this was not the situation for participants in my study, none of whom were anorexic before the 1960s. All would have known about contraception and (with the possible exception of participants from Catholic backgrounds) would have expected to use it to control their fertility. A fear of pregnancy cannot be adduced to explain male anorexia either. What is involved instead, is the fear of the sexual body as the body which is shared with others and whose boundaries are willingly opened to interpenetration with another being. Symbolically, and more than symbolically, since body and self are inseparable, this openness is also an openness to the being of another person, of other people, and to sharing their pain and their joy. To be open in this way requires a sense of wholeness the anorectic does not yet have: her fear of loss of self and of domination by another, even if it is a foetus or a child, is justified. It is only in recovery, as the sense of inner connection develops, that the openness which makes full parenthood possible is able to grow. It is the same openness which makes sexual relations possible (including, as I have argued, 'passionate' celibacy).

One reason for the anorexic ambivalence about pregnancy (and it *is* often ambivalence rather than outright rejection) is, therefore, a fear of the sexual body. In the second half of the twentieth century, the reasons for this fear are not the material conditions of conception and childbirth, but the less-understood cultural aversion to pregnant bodies as the embodiment of women's power to carry and bring forth life. The anorexic woman introjects this cultural ambivalence about the pregnant form together with all the other negative messages about large and sensual women's bodies. In recovery, these particular cultural messages are generally (but not always) dismissed in favour of other, more positive attitudes to pregnancy, whether or not participants choose motherhood.

Nicki, although she has overcome her eating difficulties, is still repelled by the idea of pregnancy and children. Her attitude is not necessarily representative of an 'anorexic stance' towards these experiences, because several participants (including myself) continued to hope, even while they were anorexic (to the extent that they could contemplate any future at all), that they would eventually have children. It does, however, illustrate some of the ambivalence or outright disgust many women feel as they contemplate the physical changes of pregnancy.[8] Nicki says:

I think the whole idea of being pregnant just sounds revolting. Kids don't grab me either, and I just think going through nine months of being pregnant would just feel awful. Maybe one day, I will . . . but having to put on weight makes you feel really fat and gross.

Most recovered participants who did have children described motherhood as a kind of confirmation and expansion of their sexuality; another opportunity for intense and physical relationship to another which in turn gave them a sense of connection with other women and with the rhythms of nature. Zoe stressed the way the birth of her daughter fuelled her desire for further spiritual understanding. Rosalie spoke of the 'visceral relationship'[9] of motherhood as akin to falling in love. For both, motherhood has taken them further in their (now 'positive') quest for self-transformation. For Victoria, however, the maternal body is still 'disgusting' and, although she has 'accepted' her three children, she found pregnancy and the early weeks of motherhood distressing. Motherhood has not, according to her, had any positive impact on her perception of her body or on her relationships with others and the world, because she has remained obsessed with her weight and size. My questions to her about motherhood elicited a great deal about dress size and self-loathing but no mention of positive changes in her relationship to others (including her children) or in her engagement with the world.

Given prevailing attitudes to the pregnant body, the associations between eating, weight gain, changes in bodily size and shape and pregnancy are fraught with shame, guilt and confusion for women. New images and practices are required before this association can be experienced positively. The words and actions of women who have recovered from eating disorders, given birth, and been able to transform the social ambivalence about pregnancy into a positive valuation, are powerful models for social change with regard to one of the most spiritual of all sexual experiences; the creation and nurturing of new life. In fact, stories of recovery from anorexia contain a great deal of valuable knowledge about the relationship between body, self, spirit and society which, like many other 'emerging discourses' on the body, holds real power for positive social transformation.

12   The knowing body

The anorexic reality had at least an equivalent vividness and naturalness as the reality in which I now live as a non anorectic . . . Why then did I give it up?

I need to go back to the inside of me, into my flesh, into my fat, my muscle, my bones, my veins. I need to listen to my body. Let my body talk of itself. Let my body tell me its story, about its pain, its rage, its tears, and about its love.

. . . The story of my body? . . .
. . . What then, bridges the gap between me and my body? . . .
. . . What is the 'gap'?

(extracts from Mukai 1989: 635–6)

Introduction[1]

Stories of recovery from anorexia contain important understandings about 'reality' and 'knowledge'; especially about the ways we come to know, and about the role of the body in this knowing.[2] Takayo Mukai raises, but does not answer, a series of questions about the part her body has played in her story, and about the knowledge she says it holds. I have tried to answer her questions by consulting the story of my own body.

Why did I abandon an 'anorexic reality'? Because the 'vividness and naturalness' of recovery expanded my knowledge, whereas anorexia (however 'real' it seemed) constricted my access to others and to the world. *How can my body 'know' and 'speak'?* Because its language (its bodily symptoms) is metaphorical and all language relies on the body for its metaphors. *How can my body hold a story?* Because my experience is written on and in my body; scars and habitual pathways of pain, interior and exterior, constantly remind me of that story. *What bridges the gap between my 'body' and my 'self'?* The feeling of energy flowing between myself and my physical surroundings, so that I am fully present in my body. *What is the gap?* It is the gap created by 'dualistic discourses' separating body and mind, and the experience of 'disconnected sexuality';

173

the absence of spiritual energy. This chapter examines the epistemological changes that take place in recovery from anorexia, and the discourses through which participants often articulated them.

Rationality and the New Age

'Rationality' has traditionally been contrasted with bodily feelings as a superior pathway to knowledge; yet people recovering from eating problems speak of their bodies as the truest means of knowing. Is this just another aspect of the New Age Movement – a privileging of emotion over reason – or have these people found a way of knowing that includes both reason and emotion; mind and body? It is no accident that the dominant forms of knowledge in western societies are informed by counting, weighing and measuring, whereas the cultivation of inner bodily awareness has come mainly from eastern philosophies. These dominant ways of knowing were embraced by the entrepreneurs who set capitalism in motion in the seventeenth century and have informed capitalist society since then.[3] Such 'instrumental rationality' (including its present form; economic rationalism) is, therefore, essential to the continuation of the capitalist sytem and continues to pervade contemporary life in the west at the expense of 'substantive rationality'. At the same time, other sources of rationality/knowledge which Kovel (1991) would call manifestations of spirit (or being) emerge in those discourses that escape from the dominance of instrumentality.[4] New Age discourse, itself groping towards mystical knowledge, has this potential, but not all New Age thinking avoids instrumentality: Heelas (1996) amply demonstrates that the 'New Age Movement' includes a spectrum of attitudes ranging from the counter-cultural rejection of capitalism to the instrumentality of its 'prosperity wing' (which holds that spirituality is quite compatible with, and should be used for, material purposes like the accumulation of wealth).

In the stories of this book, people often drew upon New Age ideas to explain the spiritual component of their recovery.[5] Lauren, for instance, spoke of affirmations, visualizations, universal energy and relaxation techiques; 'working on reconnecting my body and my mind, because a lot of these new Age books that I've been looking into do emphasize that'. Simone drew on the language of the Human Potential Movement, to which she belonged in the 1960s, and on the nature worship of the 'new' paganism and neo-paganism. Aleisha found meaning in goddess worship and crystals, simultaneously referring to 'synchronicity' and other ideas of the Jungian society she regularly attends.[6] It is important to note that each of these women has at least one post-graduate degree and is quite capable of critically appraising her own language. New Age discourse seems to co-exist relatively comfortably, in their minds, with other forms of rationality. Meredith, Sally and Vivienne used western adaptations of Buddhism to describe their spirituality. Ariel, a recent convert, drew on her understanding of Judaism, and a Jewish heritage informed Susanna's and Jacqueline's accounts of their spirituality. Zoe was influenced by the mystical tradition in Catholicism (especially St John of the Cross and Teresa of Avila), and Rosalie by a more recent variety of charismatic Christianity. 'The New Mysticism' (Johnston 1995), of which these people's spiritualities are examples, takes from Eastern, Christian and pagan religions, intersecting with and drawing upon, but not reducible to, New Age forms of spirituality.

There are several theories about the appeal of New Age thinking to educated western middle-class people. The most convincing (Heelas 1996: 153) is that the New Age *both* provides alternatives to the conventional world (thereby promising to handle difficulties arising from mainstream modern culture) *and also* belongs to central aspects of our times (thereby serving to cater for, or advance, people's interests and expectations): in sum, 'that the New Age is embedded in, whilst exemplifying, long-standing cultural trajectories':

New Age teachings can be (relatively) plausible and perhaps more attractive than other alternatives on offer (because), generally speaking, intending participants do not have to handle a yawning 'cultural gulf' between what they already know or expect and at least some of the things which the New Age has on offer. Continuities – between the more conventional and the more radical – serve to ensure that people are (sometimes) encouraged to gravitate into the New Age, seeking a more complete or 'finished' version of familiar values and experiences (as well as, frequently, hoping to solve their problems). (Heelas 1996: 154)

But is New Age thinking 'anti-rational'? In the latest edition of her witty commentary on the recovery and co-dependency movements, Wendy Kaminer writes: 'Listening to the weird New Age babble of bliss-speak, techno-talk, and personal development proverbs, while the experts bemoan the excessive rationality of our culture, I wonder' (Kaminer 1993: 117). The writings and teachings of the New Age do often seem 'anti-rational', exhorting us to think with the heart instead of the head. 'Why', writes Kaminer, 'can't the experts tell us to think with our hearts *and* our heads?' (1993: xviii). I am suggesting that many of the recovered participants in my study are doing both.

When participants refer to 'spirituality', although some may use language and ideas borrowed from the New Age and recovery movements, it is not these movements themselves which have been responsible for their recovery. Instead, in a society which simultaneously offers appeals to instrumental rationality and to 'intuitive' 'inner' knowing, participants are actively choosing their own pathway through the maze of conflicting discourses on what to think and how to behave.[7] Some turn to New Age spirituality in search of 'becoming', but for others it simply provides a common language for communication about spiritual matters in modern society. For example, my conversations with participants usually took place within a shared understanding of the meaning of 'spirituality'. The term held similar connotations for us. Its increasing use in everyday language is connected with the rise of New Age and 'recovery' phenomena. Many participants had read a good deal of this recovery literature. It has given them a vocabulary with which to talk of their own transformations, but it is not 'responsible' for their recovery; especially since they usually adopted the language of New Age *after* the major events in their transformation. New Age ideas *can* be 'irrational' when they are accepted uncritically, but are not *necessarily* so when they are used as a kind of 'transitional object' (Winnicott 1965), like a toy or game, in personal and social development. This is how many participants in my study seemed to use New Age discourse.

Another reason why stories of recovery from eating disorders draw upon New Age terminology is that it provides a ready-made language about the sacredness of the body,[8] and this in itself, together with some of the bodily practices on offer in the New Age movement, is an essential part of recovery. New Age discourses and practices[9] often understand and treat people as 'embodied spirit'; they spiritualize the body and acknowledge that spirit is embodied. They recognize the way in which spiritual energy/ life force/ existence itself creates emotions and knowledges in the body. Many of the practices that are currently referred to as New Age actually derive from the theories of Wilhelm Reich (1897–1957) about cosmic energy and its flow within the body (e.g. Reich 1949, 1973).[10] New Age therapies are also inspired by Eastern philosophy and practice which avoid the extremes of western body/mind/spirit splitting. Yoga, for example, relies on an understanding of the self as having five inseparable bodies corresponding to the social, the physical, the emotional, the imaginary and the spiritual. The practice of yoga includes each of these bodily manifestations which are transcended (not denied) in turn, to experience mystical knowledge.[11]

All of these 'techniques' or 'means of healing' (depending on one's perspective) assume that one may come to 'know' through the body and that such knowledge is 'holistic' rather than fragmented. They also assume that much of this experiential knowledge is inexpressible in words. I would contest this, however, for two reasons: firstly because words are constantly used in the teaching of these 'techniques' and they help to construct the experience itself, locating it in a western system of meaning;

and secondly, because if mystical knowledge were truly inexpressible, people would have no idea that it exists unless they had experienced it themselves, and this is clearly not the case. The very poetry of language is what makes it possible to describe, from an infinite number of perspectives, the experience of being at one with existence. It is when an imaginary barrier is put up between bodily sensations and language (as it is in some 'New Age speak' and much academic jargon) that mystification results and meaning is reduced.

To illustrate the first point: It is not 'merely' poetic to say that yoga recognizes the intelligence of the body; the way one can learn from the body, and the inseparability of body from spirit. In all language it is the poetic imagination which makes the links between body and spirit and hence bridges the gaps between intellectual, bodily and spiritual ways of knowing.[12] For example, Irigaray (1986: 6) refers to the knowledge of the body in a poetic language which resembles that of yoga teaching. My yoga teacher says: 'Let the body be proud; not letting the mind be proud of the body, but letting the body itself have the pride.' She is referring to pride the virtue, not the vice. Irigaray writes: 'Women have rarely used beauty as a weapon for themselves, and especially as a spiritual weapon. The splendour of the body has rarely become a tool for self-love, for the achievement of the self'. My yoga teacher says: 'the body remembers, even when the mind forgets'. Irigaray writes: 'It is not impossible to imagine that the body can be, and above all can *become*, intelligent or stupid.' What each of these forms of language strives to express is the relationship between body and mind; the thought that the body gives rise to meaning and vice-versa.

Poetic and bodily knowing

The relation between language and the body is crucial in understanding how people effect their own transformation from anorexia to recovery. It is like the relation between myth and ritual, since myth is expressed in language and ritual always involves the body (and, at least in recovery from anorexia, its transformation). The split between body and mind which characterizes anorexia nervosa is also a split between forms of rationality; an attempt at instrumental control which ignores bodily, metaphorical, poetic ways of knowing.

The reciprocity of body and language

My argument for a 'rationality of the body' (upon which recovery depends) is that the body gives rise to meaning and meaning in turn influences the body. This idea is most fully explored in the work of Lakoff and Johnson (1980) and Johnson (1987). My discussion here is confined to the latter reference. In *The Body in the Mind* (1987), Johnson is concerned with the ways in which bodily schemata (our awareness of concepts like in/out, inside/outside, balance, etc.) are fundamental to language. These bodily schemata, he says, give rise to the linguistic metaphors through which we make sense of our existence. Thus, rather than discourse determining our bodily experience, bodily schemata already constrain discourse; because our understanding is 'our way of being in, or having, a world'; and 'this is very much a matter of one's embodiment, that is, of perceptual mechanisms, patterns of discrimination, motor programmes, and various bodily skills' as well as being historically and culturally specific (p. 137). In other words, language itself arises from bodily experience.[13]

The language of yoga illustrates both the knowledge to which bodily experience gives rise and the way in which language is used to enhance or develop this awareness. When teachers talk about 'inner and outer bodies'; of 'turning the awareness' inward or outward, they assist the student to return the mind to the body. When they say: 'take more distance' or 'take less distance', they make students conscious of the body's location in space. When they speak of 'going deep into the layers of the body', they provide a metaphor for the unconscious and they refer to the possibility that repressed memories are locked into body tissue as it grows (for example, when a habitual tensing of particular muscles in response to stress results in spasm and eventually permanent hardness in those muscles).[14] When we practise 'balance' in yoga, it is more than a physical metaphor for daily life. The experience of physical balance is carried into other aspects of daily living, which we then discover depend as much on bodily awareness as on intellectual agility.

Analogy links biological, imaginary and social bodies

This reciprocity of body and language is effected through metaphor. Poetic, analogical language is used to create the links between body and mind, self and nature, and self and others (the wider society, whether conceived as 'community', as 'social structures' or in other ways). In 'Thinking through the Body', Michael Jackson (1983) argues, as I do here, that bodily metaphors are not mere 'vehicles' for the 'tenor' of the body, but that they represent a true interdependency of body and mind. Jackson refers to non-western systems of thought to show how analogical modes of understanding link personal, social and natural 'bodies' (p. 127). In the *I Ching* (Wilhelm edn 1988) for instance, personal and political fate is closely connected with occurrences in the natural world. In

Hinduism (hence also in the yoga I am describing) 'controlled movement of energy in the field of the body becomes a means of resonating with and re-cognizing the ultimate ground of all Being' (Bharati 1965, cited in Jackson 1983).

Poetry has this capacity to merge the world of things with the world of Being. Poetic metaphor is 'a corporal, sensible way of reading the world as corresponding to the body' (p. 130). Jackson shows how these metaphors become part of a cultural repertoire of ideas for individual autobiographies. His argument is similar to Brumberg's (1988) that 'fasting girls' draw upon a range of culturally available symbols to signal their distress as women in that particular culture. I have been arguing that in the process of recovery too, people make use of metaphors that circulate in their own society. The expressions I heard many times in relation to recovery: 'I am a part of nature', 'I listen to my body', 'I fell in love' are all metaphorical means of expressing and creating ways of thinking and being which make recovery possible.

The sexed body

Different kinds of bodies, however, give rise to different kinds of metaphors and to different understandings of the body; a possibility which neither Johnson nor Jackson considers. Race and ethnicity, youth and age, masculinity and femininity mark the body and how others perceive it. In turn, they determine our subjectivity; the ways we come to know the world. Moira Gatens (1983) draws particular attention to the importance of the 'sexed' body as opposed to the 'gendered' body. The concept of 'gender' stresses the social construction of femininity and masculinity. It suggests, therefore, that the body is a neutral site upon which 'feminine' or 'masculine' characteristics are inscribed through the process of 'socialization'. Against this position, Gatens argues that the body and the unconscious are also actively involved in the formation of subjectivity. There are two parts to this argument. First, Gatens stresses, the body is never neutral:

There are at least two kinds of bodies; the male body and the female body . . . The very same behaviours (whether they be masculine or feminine) have quite different personal and social significances when acted out by the male subject on the one hand, and the female subject on the other. (Gatens 1983: 148)[15]

Next, since male and female bodies are fundamentally different, male and female subjectivities must be fundamentally different. In conclusion, Gatens argues that theories of 'gender' perpetuate a Cartesian mind/body dualism in which the mind is privileged over the body. They suggest that changes to human subjectivity always occur through rational, conscious processes. Instead, she shows that the imaginary body (the body as it is experienced by the subject), and not the biological body, is deeply implicated in our choice of masculine or feminine ways of being. Given that the vast majority of anorectics are women and girls, but that men may also become anorexic, it is important to examine the differences in perception and in action between differently sexed bodies.

In her essay 'Throwing like a girl', Iris Young (1989) considers the difference between men's and women's forms of bodily comportment and the perceptions of the world that result from each. She refers to 'different feminine and masculine "modalities" of the structures and conditions of the body's existence in the world', to argue that:

> the woman who enacts her subjectivity in patriarchal society lives a contradiction: as human she is a free subject who participates in transcendence, but her situation as a woman denies her that subjectivity and transcendence . . . The modalities of feminine bodily comportment, motility and spatiality exhibit this same tension between transcendence and immanence, between subjectivity and being a mere object. (Young 1989: 55)[16]

These differences in the 'lived experience' of male and female bodies help explain why the body is perceived so negatively by so many women in western society and why women are more likely than men to exert control over the body, instead of using the body to control space. Men whose experience has also given them a lack of confidence in their ability to control their environment are therefore more likely than other men to be anorexic. It follows from Young's arguments that experiences which provide women (and men who have felt disempowered) with the sense of a new relation between their bodies and space, their bodies and others, will also encourage greater personal control over their social and political environment. This is one of the changes which takes place in recovery. It is therefore intimately associated with changed perceptions of the body. A few examples will illustrate my point.

Young speaks of women's 'ambiguous transcendence'; their inability to move out into the world of action in the fluid motion of transcendence without being aware of their body as a burden, unprotected and constantly observed. In my ongoing recovery, it is the bodily experience of yoga which is gradually teaching me to counteract this ambiguous transcendence as I learn to let go of my conscious awareness and let my body flow where the teacher's voice tells me to go; to focus on that position rather than on the trajectory my body must take to reach it. The 'inhibited intentionality' which 'makes women stiffen their bodies against the performance of the task (Young, 1989: 60) evaporates when I do a successful handstand; in trusting my body's memory, I am able to move gracefully into an inverted position (something I could not do until I learned it through yoga). Young's 'discontinuous unity' of women with their surroundings dissolves when I identify with the name of a yoga pose ('mountain pose', 'dog pose', 'cobra', 'tree'); for yoga also provides a poetry of the body that links me imaginatively with the natural world. But it is not these actions by themselves that bring about the transformed relation of the body to the world, but always the meaning attached to them; in this case, my conscious linking of growing bodily confidence with confidence in less physical 'movings out into the world'. While only some participants in my study practised yoga, I have used it as an example of the way new uses of the body give rise to new meanings of the self and its relation to the world. Young argues that

> Women in sexist society are physically handicapped. Insofar as we learn to live out our existence in accordance with the definition that patriarchal culture assigns to us, we are physically inhibited, confined, positioned, and objectified. As lived bodies, we are not open and unambiguous transcendences which move out to master a world that belongs to us, a world constituted by our own intentions and projection. (Young 1989: 65)[17]

Much recent theory of the body has been concerned with the ways in which our bodies are controlled, marked, and 'inscribed' by the operations of power upon them (as objects) and the ways (as subjects) they resist power. This approach has tended to regard anorexia itself as a form of unconscious bodily resistance to power. I am interested in how we also 'resist' this social inscription through recovering from anorexia (or not becoming anorexic);[18] in the means by which people teach themselves to experience and use their bodies, with conscious self-direction, in life-enhancing ways. In several feminist analyses, 'anorexia nervosa' itself has been regarded as a metaphor for women's social position.[19] For what, then, is recovery the metaphor?' I have been arguing that recovery involves the conscious development of greater openness and more 'moving out' into a world we increasingly 'constitute by our own intentions and projections' and that it is recovery from anorexia nervosa which is, among other things, a metaphor for resistance. I have shown how myth and ritual are used in this process. I have also been suggesting that recovery involves a transition to wider forms of rationality which take account of 'bodily knowledge'.

In anorexia, therefore, the split between body and mind is also a split between forms of rationality; an attempt at instrumental control which ignores bodily, metaphorical, poetic ways of knowing. Recovery takes place through the reclamation of this knowledge; of these forms of rationality. At the same time, just as the body gives rise to knowledge, so an expanded rationality has effects on the body; giving it new meanings, hence new feelings, new possibilities for experience and, above all, greater acceptance of the fact of one's embodiment. Nowhere is this more present than in changes to participants' use of food as metaphor.

Knowledge and food metaphors

The meanings of food in different cultures, and for different individuals within a culture, can demonstrate a great deal about people's relation to the world. A contrast between these meanings during and after anorexia therefore illustrates many of the ideas I have been exploring in this chapter concerning the links between language, the body, society and nature. Food and eating provide metaphors for these links, but they are also (together with breathing) our strongest links to the material world. In denying them, we not only cut ourselves off from sociality (Visser 1991: 220) and from the sensual experience of taking in part of the natural world; we also deny life which *is* the materiality of our living bodies. In recovery, a reclaiming and a greater awareness of the body is accompanied by a celebration of food and eating. There is a huge contrast between the meaning of food in the anorexic phase and its connotations in recovery.

When I was anorexic, food represented the spiritual connection I both desired and fearfully rejected. As I recovered, food remained my strongest symbol; the ideal meal continued to be like a holy communion[20] and usually as unattainable as the holy grail. Eating was reified; it became something more than it could bear. Today, this obsession has gone and the energy which it required has been channelled into other pleasures and other creative endeavours. But occasionally I still experience hunger as a total absence of meaning; just as it was in anorexia. The sense of lack of meaning both produced and was reinforced by self-starvation.[21] This is the refrain which occurs over and over in accounts of anorexia: 'There's no meaning . . . there's no meaning . . . there's no meaning. I can't find my relationship to God and all the world recedes', wrote Anne, a twenty-two year old woman treated for anorexia nervosa by Marion Woodman (1980: 78, her ellipses).[22] If we deprive our bodies of food, their ability to move outward and engage with the world is correspondingly reduced. The absence of this engagement is not only symbolized by self-starvation; starvation also produces it. The vacant stares of malnourished children in Ethiopia attest to the withdrawal and loss of interest in living which accompanies lack of food.

Food is necessary for ongoing participation in life. In this sense it is not simply symbolic of spirituality, it is itself sacred. The words of The Lord's

Prayer: 'Give us this day our daily bread', express this inseparability of spiritual and material nourishment. When participants in my study spoke about food, this symbolic relationship and its changed meaning in recovery was prominent. During their anorexic stage, they described food as 'a terrible master' (Rosalie) and something that ruins their lives (Victoria). Philip described the metaphors involved in his eating problems like this: 'When I was unhappy I didn't eat. It was when I was happy that I was eating; but now I find it's sort of the opposite; I go for a binge. It's a mysterious thing.' As they recover, they come to understand food metaphors, as does Sheena when she says 'Sexual appetite and the appetite for food are so closely related; especially for women'.

Food metaphors do not work according to the 'rationality' of science. Instead they are part of the imaginary body, as Margaret explains:

> I think of food as taking up space in my body and making my body take up more space and sort of look fatter. I think a hunk of meat is going to take up that much space and also because of the fat content of it. It's very primitive sort of thinking, because I know it's illogical and mad, because the food is really all digested and mushed up.

Food metaphors can also be linked with other behaviours, to express one's relationship to existence: Lesley says 'my strong willpower hasn't been limited to food; I've used it with study and work too. It's just part of my personality.' There are also parallels between the use of food and other attempts to escape the self: Patricia, who has switched from anorexia to binge eating, says 'it's not just food I binge with. I used to do it with housing. I used to buy property. It was the same sort of thing. I'd go on a binge – binge-buying – then I'd panic and sell'. But for participants who had moved beyond anorexia, food has acquired a positive sacredness. It is still powerfully metaphorical for them, but now that they have access to knowledge of and through their bodies, they understand its metaphoric significance. Jodie says: 'My current attitude to food is positive; I enjoy it and I'm not scared of it.' For Aleisha, eating is ' a constant confirmation of my commitment to living . . . in the fullest sense' and Meredith, who has become a food writer, says not only: 'Food is life, isn't it? Food is a symbol of life', but also: 'more and more I see that symbolism of food: it's a spiritual symbol; spiritual nourishment.'

Epilogue

It is now time to draw together the threads of a complex argument and point to some of its implications. My substantive conclusions, like the stories from which they are drawn, will be of greatest interest to readers interested in their own recovery or that of others they care about, while my theoretical arguments will be of use to students and teachers of social theory and to health and welfare practitioners of many kinds; but the substantive and the theoretical inevitably overlap. The way I have told the story of recovery cannot be separated from the story itself: firstly because it includes so much of my own experience, both implicitly and explicitly; secondly because that experience has itself been shaped by academic associations; thirdly because each of the conversations I held with participants was told as a story which contained its own theoretical assumptions; and lastly because theory itself always takes a narrative form.

The form of the book

In the opening chapters of the book I alluded to a number of issues which concern its shape; the way I have introduced my ideas to readers and sought to convince them of the 'truth' and importance of my arguments. The most important of those ideas was the pact I made with participants and with readers. My writing of imaginative truth (my 'authenticity') relied upon a similar form of authenticity in what participants would tell me and in the reader's good faith. As a result, the knowledge available in this book has been co-created with participants and readers. A related idea was that I would adopt a number of different personae at different points in the thesis; as student, critic, researcher, theoretician, biographer and storyteller; but never as masks for the autobiographer. In this way, I have woven my 'personal' and my 'academic' self into the text along with my interpretations of data and theory. During the book's long gestation, my auto-critique disrupted the previous coherence of my own story and forced me to write some of it over again.

My text has also been shaped by desire: the desire of participants to understand themselves, the desire for truth (and perhaps power) of each theoretician whose work I have used, my own desire to understand them all as well as to know myself and to create a document which would hold their varied perspectives in a unified whole. The book in its entirety, as well as the separate stories which make it up, is offered as an alternative to the narratives which currently dominate people's thinking about anorexia and (if they think of it at all) about recovery. Storytelling is a political act and, as an intervention in the discourses on eating disorders, this book is a political document: it intends to destabilize current thinking in this field in order to make way for new understandings.

Substantive conclusions

As I wrote, the most frequent question people asked about my work was, of course; 'how *do* people recover?' (often preceded by '*do* they recover?). They expected my answer to include not just a list of the activities people undertake to recover but also the conclusions I have reached about the relative importance of different elements in recovery. In other words, the mere listing of reasons is not enough to satisfy even the most naive listener. What follows is a summary, in story form, of what I have learned in the course of my research.

Most stories we hear about eating disorders (in the media, anecdotally and from doctors and psychiatrists) are about 'anorexia nervosa' (as if it were more serious or more common than bulimia or compulsive eating, and as if the same person could not experience several of these difficulties). People usually speak of anorexia as an *illness in search of a cure*. Even books about recovery devote most of their length to descriptions of symptoms and possible causes; biological, psychological and social. Although these books use the words of 'anorectics' themselves, they select those that deal with the horror of the experience in preference to those which tell of the rewards of recovery. In my study, I asked people *not* to tell me about how they became anorexic or what it was like, but about the changes which took place as they stopped 'being anorexic'. The usual story about anorexia is that all women are potential *victims of media pressure* to be thin. Even sociologists and feminist theorists blame social forces of various kinds for the way women starve themselves or binge and purge. No one seems to ask *how* the same people manage to escape from this 'oppression'; to find pleasure in eating again, to live active and productive lives and to have satisfying relationships in contrast with their anorexic period. If we heard more stories of recovery, perhaps more people would recover, and perhaps fewer might become anorexic in the first place.

I found, when people told me their recovery stories, that the more they felt they had recovered, the more *coherent* were their stories; that it is through the creation of these stories, whether or not they are entirely historically accurate, that they also create their own recovery. All these narratives seemed to include the same 'myths'; they were like the age-old stories of death, birth and resurrection told in many different cultures. They always involved some kind of descent into an 'underworld' of chaos and suffering, then a return to a fuller life, almost as a new person.

When I asked myself and thirty-three other people at various stages of recovery (but mostly recovered) what they thought recovery meant, they mentioned several *elements* they believed to be essential. 'Feeling normal' was one; and this did not necessarily mean looking and eating like everyone else around them, but feeling as if they had found a way of eating and living which was comfortable for them in a quite different way from their earlier anorexic lifestyle. Losing their obsession with food was another. Believing that they were worthwhile people and that their lives had meaning was another change which they all associated with their recovery in contrast with the period of their 'anorexia'.

Enjoying and no longer being afraid of social situations was yet another. For some, recovery seemed to be faster than for others, but they all spoke of it as an *ongoing process*, rather than a sudden change; most of them felt that it was a kind of knowledge and that learning about it never stops; often the same issues would come up again at different points in their lives and they would solve new parts of the old puzzle.

When they spoke about the *stages and turning points* in their recovery, they described changes in their perceptions of space and time. They began to feel part of the natural world and part of the society in which they live; they began to feel 'connected' again. Some of them (but by no means all) had had psychotherapy or other forms of treatment. Many felt that treatment had not helped them at all, but when it had, it was always because a strong relationship had been established with a therapist (or a nurse, another 'patient', a dietician, a friend or a lover); a relationship in which the many aspects of themselves apart from their anorexic behaviour were acknowledged and nurtured. This person also provided a model for a non-anorexic way of life. Often, travel allowed them to explore reality beyond the boundaries of their known selves. They also mentioned creativity; their involvement in music, art, writing and gardening as parts of their recovery. The most important element of recovery was their conviction that, unlike recovered addicts or alcoholics, once recovered they would never be tempted to do it again. At the same time, they all said they had learned something very worthwhile from the experience. What was it?

Most of them said that their anorexia had been a kind of search and a way of testing themselves and their limits. Several said it was a *spiritual quest*, and certainly a *quest for meaning*. What they found was something they felt they had already experienced much earlier; a sense of being at peace with themselves and at one with nature and with other people. One of the powerful 'myths' which has helped them recover has been this story of a lost and found inner unity and communion with the outer world. Their descriptions of recovery were just like descriptions of a religious *conversion experience*, with the same accompanying joy, peace and certainty, following a period of despair and suffering. Like conversion experiences, they usually included a belief in some force beyond themselves and of its active participation in their recovery.

One of the questions often asked about anorexia is: 'if we are all subject to the same cultural forces, why aren't we all anorexic?'. So it is also worth asking: 'if the means of recovery are also available to us, *why don't all anorectics recover?*' First of all, we are not, of course, all subject to exactly the same social pressures (which is why fewer men than women are anorexic, for instance). Similarly, we are not all equally exposed to the factors that make recovery possible; especially not to recovery stories. But there is another reason why some people and not others become anorexic and why some recover while others do not. It has to do with *agency*. Not just 'choice', because often people do not consciously 'choose' to recover or not; but agency in the sense of taking certain steps rather than others. So, to recover, you not only need to start telling your life story differently, but at the same time it seems that you must act differently too; plunge into alternative *practices* to those you followed into anorexia.

The practices that contributed to recovery for the participants in my study I have called *rituals* because, like the ritualistic behaviour of anorexia, they are performed over and over again and they maintain and deepen recovery just as those of anorexia nervosa sustained and exacerbated suffering. The rituals of recovery are healing rituals and they almost always include, and bring about changes to, the body. For these people, they included swimming, surfing, bike-riding, yoga, meditation, gardening, singing, playing musical instruments, writing, painting, all kinds of craftwork and cooking. Not that people did not indulge in these activities when they were anorexic, or sometimes before then, but in recovery they took on a quite different *meaning*. Through these rituals, people expressed and found new parts of themselves, new ways to live and especially the sense of connection I've described; within themselves, with nature and with other people.

Although I never started our conversations with any mention of '*spirituality*', this is the term I have used to describe what participants found, because it is the word the majority used themselves. Even when they did not, most accepted it as one way of speaking about their experience. The reason they have been able to find the words and the practices that led them to recovery is that they have read and heard about them, sometimes almost by accident and often through popular psychology or New Age therapies. Sometimes their sources were more 'intellectualized'; they studied the work of Carl Jung; or delved into the many 'alternative' practices arising from the teachings and experiments of Whilhelm Reich (Bioenergetics, Biodynamics, Alexander Technique, Feldenkrais, Rolfing, Rebirthing and so on). Often they were pursuing an interest in eastern philosophy and religion and its accompanying practices like Yoga and Tai-Chi. Some were Christians, Jews and Buddhists and others were humanists. All of them, however, had found myths (or sacred stories) that gave meaning to their lives, and activities that continued to *transform* them.

When I tell people this story, they often ask 'but how different is all that from what most people do during their lifetime anyway?' To which I answer that it is not very different at all. People use myth and ritual as their means of self-transformation and of recovery in many different situations. I have focused on one situation in which people's suffering revolves around food and eating, but a great deal of what I have found to say is applicable to the human search for better ways to be, in all its manifestations.

Theoretical conclusions

In seeking to *explain* the story of recovery I have just told, I have used ideas from many writers; as stimuli in the development of my own theories or as a kind of framework for my arguments and evidence. These writers' thoughts have also come to me in narrative form, for example as 'sociological stories'. Writing my own narrative; providing explanations and discerning patterns in the sometimes conflicting accounts of participants has required me to address several theoretical problems which I now outline together with the provisional solutions I have reached in this book. Some of these problems were present in the growing sociological literature on eating disorders while others – like the central question of how recovery is possible in the same society which produces eating disorders – were my own.

The three major theories underlying the rest of my arguments are as follows: from Durkheim, I have developed the concept of anorexia and recovery as the negative and positive phases respectively in a rite of passage which involves a confrontation with death, and I have also used his notion that the social *is* the spiritual, to explain the social significance of spirituality. From Kovel, I have taken the idea of spirit as that which exists both within and apart from history and society and is essential to liberation from individual and social suffering. From Weber, I have used the concept of alternative rationalities to argue that mystical knowledge, which comes through the body and the emotions, is also 'rational'; that is, not separate from other forms of knowledge.

Autobiography as a source of understanding

In studying the relationship between individual people and the society of which they form part, it is difficult to know how best to use 'anecdotal' material, whether about oneself or another person. Through this book as a whole, and especially in its chapter on autobiography and narrative, I have tried to show how vital this material can be as a source of theory, as well as evidence. Treating experiential knowledge and its subject's reflections upon it as sources at least equivalent to those of academic or clinical 'experts', and recognizing that membership of these groups often overlaps, brings us closer to understanding that experience, to making it more widely accessible and to finding solutions to personal and social problems.

The epistemological status of memory

The autobiographical data used in my research consist of memories which I have taken to be 'real' in the sense that the reconstruction of the past represents the *meaning* of those events for that person in the present. Since autobiography and this book are attempts to elucidate the present, not the past, questions about the 'validity' of factual memory have not been strictly relevant. Recovery involves changes in the meanings attributed to one's behaviour as much as it does the adoption of new behaviours, including refusing an 'anorexic' identity. It also 'returns' the recovered person to an imaginative memory of an original 'mystical' experience of unity and connection with the Other; a memory whose traces are present in the material body. Access to this re-cycled mythical memory is the 'beginning' of recovery, rather than its 'origin'. Whatever their epistemological status, however, I have argued that the memories dealt with in my phenomenological approach have more to contribute to an understanding of recovery than do attempts to measure recovery in empirical ways.

Defining 'recovery'

I have not been completely satisfied with the word 'recovery' to describe what this book is about because it suggests a kind of linear evolution from a primitive to a more advanced level of development – in medical terms, a reduction in pathology; in psychology, the achievement of a retarded 'developmental goal' or, in spiritual terms, a greater degree of 'holiness'. These are not the connotations I have tried to express. Nevertheless, as with the problem of mind-body dualism (to which I return below), the word and its accompanying concepts is entrenched in our language and can serve as a useful shorthand for some of the changes I have described. One solution to this problem has been to understand recovery as one aspect of the same rite of passage that includes anorexia, instead of as its triumphant defeat. Another has been to ask participants how they would define their experience of no longer needing to starve, or (if they were still starving or bingeing) how they might define their expectations in that direction. What they have had to say in reply has expanded the notion of recovery, rather than confirmed commonsense perceptions of it. I have used the word because it makes some kind of sense to participants and potential readers, but I have stressed that it need not be associated with notions of linear progress; that it is not only an ongoing process, but also a cyclical one; a return to previous experience and a constant redefining of the meaning of that experience.

Recovery as rebellion

One of the most prevalent characterizations of anorexia nervosa in social theory is as a form of rebellion against the imposition of power. This theory fails to explain that the rebellion is ineffective in changing either the individual or the society for the better. It makes 'anorectics' into victims of their own behaviour. Instead, I have argued that the real rebellion against the construction of 'docile bodies' is recovery itself (or not becoming anorexic in the first place). This formulation allows self-starvation to be a necessary stage in a greater self-transformation which eventually resists the western social imperative to slenderness and rigid control. Especially, it gives 'anorectics' greater agency in their own actions; sometimes consciously, but always as they are inspired by a liberating spirit at the level of the body and the emotions. Recovery is one form of praxis which is ongoing, cyclical, and constantly renewed to present greater and greater positive resistance to social control and self-objectification.

Medieval asceticism and contemporary anorexia

Many of the sociological problems which 'anorexia' presents converge in the question of continuity or discontinuity between medieval and contemporary self-starvation. In particular, the question of whether to remain anorexic is to choose a distorted form of spirituality. My focus on recovery suggests a solution to these problems. If voluntary fasting is the initial stage in an existential confrontation with death, and recovery is the dénouement and integration of this confrontation, then both medieval and modern fasting are important individual and social rituals brought on by encounters with mortality. Each era, however, has placed a different interpretation upon such fasting. While medieval fasting served as a respected form of symbolic social suffering, contemporary anorexia is regarded as a medical and psychiatric phenomenon. For this reason, the more socially valuable rituals today are the rituals of recovery, and stories of recovery therefore need to be more made more widely known.

The ontological and theoretical status of spirit

All societies have myths that speak of the individual's 'symbolic resonance with the social and the planetary microcosm' (Kleinman 1988); his or her links with natural and social reality. This resonance, this *connection*, is part of what I have referred to as spirit; and I have found it, in one shape or another, in the stories of all participants. Spirit is a necessary condition for life and for knowledge. I have also, however, written of spirit as a *material force*, because it is experienced through the material body and because it brings about physical as well as emotional and ideational change ('conversion' and 'transformation'). At times in the book, I have appeared to make a distinction between 'existentialist' theories and those which take account of the spirit; but in fact, all philosophies which are concerned with Being (and poststructuralism is not excluded, as my discussion of Irigaray makes clear) seek answers to questions about the nature of spirituality. I have chosen to use the term because it was familiar to participants in my study and because, in doing so, I hope to open up new questions about its meaning.

The place of the body in recovery

Part of this book has been about the relation between the myths and the rituals it describes; between *language* and *bodily awareness and action*. In my discussion, I have taken the body to be irreducible to language, but greatly influenced by the meanings which language confers upon it. I have used the concept of the *imaginary body* (the body we think and feel we have) as the body which is malleable through language and transformed through the rituals of recovery. I have described the process of bodily transformation as a reciprocal one in which language arises from the experience of the body and the body is in turn changed by the meanings which are ascribed to it through language.

A major problem in any discussion of the body is the *body/mind dualism* which pervades western thought. It was present in my own and in participants' accounts, and in the theoretical works to which I referred. I have tried to counteract these scars of instrumental rationality by continually referring to the self as an *embodied self*. The self, in this book, has many parts (including the physical) which, in recovery though not in anorexia, are united in an 'imaginary' whole. Merleau-Ponty's notion of *the sexual body* has been invaluable as a way of expressing the interfusion between the body, *desire*, spirit and existence; for the sexual body is the body which is alive with spirit-power and spirit-being (Kovel's terms). The body, in my text, is also the source of knowledges which are alternative (though complementary) to the 'instrumental' rationality that dominates late modernity. I have used Foucault's concept of subjugated knowledges to speak of the awareness of the body which comes through recovery rituals and counteracts some of the prevailing myths about anorexia. This in turn suggests that knowledge can be retained in the body itself; that the body is a source of mystical awareness which Weber includes among the forms of rationality.

Social sources of recovery

Spirituality, as Durkheim so strongly argues, is indeed a social phenom-enon. My problem has been to find its sources in contemporary society. Most participants referred to a sense of participation in a community, and at the very least individual relationships, as essential to their recovery. The community can be an 'imagined' one, known through the media and one's upbringing; or a more tangible group like Overeaters' Anonymous, a religious or political group. Through the stories of participants, I have reached the conclusion that although the rituals of anorexia and recovery are largely carried out alone, they depend on understandings reached through exposure to a variety of discourses. These understandings are present, though sometimes in 'distorted' form, in certain 'New Age' ideas and practices, the 'western' interest in eastern mysticism, neo-Reichian therapies, Jungian and transpersonal psychology; and in the Christian Church and its attempts to alter its own rituals and meet contemporary needs. These are all discourses that include the subjugated knowledges of the body, the emotions and the spirit, as well as those of the mind. They are present in participants' stories of recovery, which is why these stories are so important.

Political implications of this text

One of my aims has been to create a counter-discourse to the hegemony of psychiatric and psychological stories about *anorexia*, through personal stories of *recovery*. Given the cultural importance of myth, and the significance of metaphor in self-transformation; the more stories and models of recovery become available, the more likely recovery becomes. The more recovery rituals are practised, the less will be the prevalence of anorexia; since (as Durkheim emphasized) ritual itself creates reality on personal and social levels. Participants sometimes spoke of existing accounts of anorexia and bulimia (even the 'good' ones) as 'how-to' manuals to which they referred for further ideas about how to starve. I have sought to offer a different kind of 'how-to' manual; the kind which provides credible alternatives, not in the form of step-by-step instructions, but in the much stronger medium of narrative.

I have argued that the theoretical stories of anorexia which are currently available (even or especially feminist theories) are politically conservative. We need theories which address the existential and spiritual questions that are fundamental to anorexia nervosa, as it is defined by the participants in this study. The most valuable theories are therefore those which articulate the meaning, not of the problem, but of the solution. Given the political importance of recovery stories, I can think of no better way to close these pages than in the way I opened them; to pay tribute once more to those who so frankly, compassionately and often humorously shared them with me; and to hope that their contributions will have the effects for which they have committed so much of themselves.

Appendix A   Participants' profiles

These tables are intended to provide background information and not statistical evidence. All information is from the participants' self-description and self-report. Words in inverted commas are those of the participants themselves. The tables use the following abbreviations: AN = anorexia nervosa; BN = bulimia nervosa; CE = compulsive eating; ED = eating disorder; OA = Overeaters Anonymous.

Table A1. *Group 1: Not recovered*

Name	Age	Occupation	Tertiary Education	Marital Status	No. of Children
Freda	44	radio technician	BA	single	0
Jennifer	27	fashion sales	none	married	0
Lauren	31	teacher	MA	single	0
Michael	44	stylist	BA	single	0
Patricia	43	not divulged	BA	single	0
Philip	40	teacher	BA Dip Ed	single	0
Victoria	35	receptionist	food school	married	3

Name	ED	Age of Onset	Treatment for ED	Rel/Phil. background	Rel/Phil. affiliation	'Spiritual seeking'
Freda	AN & CE	20	none	Humanist	none	no
Jennifer	AN & laxatives	14	none	Christian	'Christian'	no
Lauren	AN	19	none	?	none	yes
Michael	AN&BN	15	none	?	none	yes
Patricia	AN&CE	13	none	?	none	no
Philip	AN,BN & laxatives	29	none	Evangelical	Evangelical	?
Victoria	AN	17	none	Anglican	children Catholic	no

Table A2. *Group 2: Recovering*

Name	Age	Occupation	Tertiary Education	Marital Status	Children
Ariel	35	nurse & model	Registered nurse	single	0
Jacqueline	38	part-time journalist	BA	separated	2
Joanne	41	unemployed secretary	none	married	3
Lesley	26	doctor	MB/BS	married	0
Margaret	39	teacher	BA/ Dip Ed	married	4
Marilyn	33	training consultant	BA	separated	0
Marjorie	60	physiotherapist	BA and Dip physio	separated	4
Nicki	29	hotel management	BA	single	0
Susanna	36	management consultant	MA, MBA	single	0
Sheena	44	copywriter	BA in progress	divorced	0

Name	ED	Age of onset	Treatment for ED	Rel./Phil. background	Rel./Phil. affiliation	'Spiritual seeking'
Ariel	AN&BN	16	hospital & psychiatric	Anglican	Judaism	yes
Jacqueline	AN	16	hospital & psychiatric	Jewish	none	yes
Joanne	AN	15	none	Anglican	none	no
Lesley	AN	13	psychiatric for depression	Lutheran	'Christian'	no
Margaret	AN	17	none	Methodist	'Christian'	?
Marilyn	AN	16	none	Catholic	none	no
Marjorie	AN	56	hospital & psychiatric	Agnostic	Agnostic	no
Nicki	AN&BN	16	hospital & psychiatric	Presbyterian	'Christian'	yes
Susanna	AN	27	psycho-therapy	Jewish/atheist	none	no
Sheena	AN	24	'alternative' therapies	Catholic	none	Eastern religion

Table A3. *Group 3: Recovered*

Name	Age	Occupation	Tertiary Education	Marital Status	Children
Aleisha	36	student/ex-prostitute	2 BAs,MA in progress	single	0
Eloise	33	youth worker	BA	single	0
Ilse	34	nurse	RN/MA	partner	0
Jodie	28	music teacher	BSc	married	0
Kate	33	writer	MA	partner	0
Meredith	41	food writer	BA	divorced	2
Miranda	44	librarian	BA/Dip Ed.	widowed	2
Naomi	39	public servant	2BAs	single	0
Pip	42	nurse	Reg'd Nurse.	married	0
Rosalie	36	pub. serv./now full time mother	BSc/DipEd		3
Sally	43	marital counsellor	BA	married	2
Simone	43	research consultant	PhD	single	0
Sue	41	film industry	none	married 2x separated	3
Vivienne	31	psychotherapist	PhD in progress	partner	0
Zoe	43	teacher	Dip Art/Dip Design	divorced	1

Name	ED	Age of onset	Treatment for ED	Rel./Phil. background	Rel./Phil. affiliation	'Spiritual seeking'
Aleisha	AN, BN&CE	14	None	Catholic	'All'	Yes
Eloise	AN	14	None	?	None/Humanist	No
Ilse	AN&BN	17	None	'Pantheist'	'Pantheist'	No
Jodie	AN&BN	19	psychiatric	?	Humanist	No
Kate	AN&BN	18	hosp & psychiatric	Anglican	Anglican	No
Meredith	AN	16	psychiatric	Anglican	Tibetan Buddhism	Yes
Miranda	BN	14	None	Anglican	None	Yes
Naomi	AN	19	None	?	'Nothing definable'	'alot by that name'
Pip	AN	17	hospital	Anglican	None	Eastern Religions
Rosalie	AN	18	None	Presbyterian Uniting Ch	Pentecostal	NA
Sally	AN	17	None	?	Zen Buddism	Yes
Simone	AN	18?	None	Presbyterian	None	Yes

Name	ED	Age of onset	Treatment for ED	Rel./Phil. background	Rel./Phil. affiliation	'Spiritual seeking'
Sue	AN	19	hospital	?	None	No
Vivienne	AN, BN&CE	11	psychiatric and OA	None	Buddhism	Yes
Zoe	AN	22	None	Catholic	Catholic	Yes

Appendix B   Interview questions

My interactions with participants were conversations in which they took the lead, rather than formal interviews. The following questions were prepared in advance as a checklist. They were not asked in order. The information I have used most in writing the thesis came directly from participants without my questioning. I began most conversations by asking for the participant's story of recovery and mentioning my interest in the general areas covered by 'Prompt questions' below.

My focus question (not asked)

What knowledges are implied in narratives of recovery from anorexia nervosa:
> about the body?
> about society?
> about spirituality?
> about the relation between them?

Prompt questions

(a) Narrative
> 'I'd like to hear the story of how you gave up being anorexic'(or, for participants who said they had not recovered: 'what do you think recovery will involve?')

(b) Defining recovery
> How long did it take?
> When did the recovery begin? Were there turning points? stages? key factors?
> What do you think you were(/are) recovering from? i.e. what do you now, in retrospect, think anorexia was about for you?
> Would you describe it as recovery or would you use another word?
> Do you think there are degrees of recovery?
> Or that you are never fully recovered?

How do you know/would you know that you had 'recovered'? i.e.
what are you criteria for recovery?)

Why did you need to be anorexic? and why don't you need it now?

What has changed since you were anorexic? Do symptoms recur?
Do you expect them to?

Do you feel like the same person you were when anorexic? Before
anorexia?

(c) Social influences on recovery/or not

How much reading have you done about anorexia? What have
you read?

Do any of the accounts you know of resemble your own
experience and insights? In what ways?

Did you have treatment for anorexia? How do you think it
affected you?

What have been the strongest forces in your recovery (what has
influenced your recovery most strongly?)

(d) Concerning spirituality (if not already mentioned)

Do you have any particular religious or philosophical beliefs?
Have they helped at all in your recovery?

Appendix C   Codes used for analysis

Achievement
Addiction

Balance
Birth Injury
Body
Bulimia

Catherine
Children
Control
Coping
Creativity

Desire
Death / Mourning
Dieting

Exercise

Family
Feminism
Food

Guilt

Identity
Immediacy
Introjection

Knowledge about
  AN

Location

Masculinity
Meaning
Media
Memory
Metaphors (food)
Methodology
Mirrors
Motherhood /
  Parenthood

Normality

Other Anorectics

Perfection
Pleasure
Postpartum
  Depression
Purity

Quest

Rebellion
Recovery
Relationships
Ritual

Sexuality
Social
Spirituality
Stages
Suicide

Time
Travel
Treatment
Turning points

Notes

2. RESEARCHING RECOVERY

1 The glossary explains the sense in which most participants used the word spirituality and the way I have employed it myself. As this book is an extended consideration of the meaning of 'spirituality' in recovery, each chapter reveals and develops another aspect of its significance.

2 As well as the authors referred to in the text, the following have influenced me: Roberts (1981), Stanley and Wise (1983), Bowles and Duelli Klein (1983), Reinharz (1983), Harding and Hintikka (1983), Bell & Roberts (1984), Harding (1986), Finch (1984), Stanley (1990), and Smith (1974, 1977, 1979, 1992). Some of Kondo's (1986) anthropological reflections on this subject parallel mine: e.g. informants are also actors/agents negotiating meaning with the ethnographer (p. 75); although various kinds of 'closeness' to informants can be advantageous, some degree of remove from the Other is necessary in order to recover meaning from the (shared) experience (p. 84); 'our quest for anthropological understanding should be animated by an openness to Otherness, even if it exists in the Self' (p. 86).

3 See glossary for the relationship between anorexia nervosa, bulimia nervosa and compulsive eating and why I have chosen to use 'anorexia' as a blanket term.

4 Appendix A, 'Participants' profiles', gives details of the personal data I summarize and comment upon here.

5 Articles about anorexia in men include (in chronological order): Beumont et al. (1972), Crisp & Burns (1983), Andersen & Mickalide (1983), Burns & Crisp (1984), Sterling & Segal (1985 ; a useful review article), Hall et al. (1985), Crisp & Burns (1986), Goodwin & Fairburn (1987) and Hsu (1989). A book on the subject has been edited by Andersen (1991). See also note 2 to chapter 9.

6 Once they resume eating, for instance, hospitalized 'anorectics' from less affluent areas are generally less fussy about their food; less likely than their counterparts from higher socio-economic groups to avoid fat and sugar (Jan McCullough, Eating Disorders Nursing Association, personal communication).

7 For Naomi Wolf (1991), fashion and the worship of a particular kind of beauty *is* a religion; a notion which accords with my arguments about anorexic rituals and their social foundations elsewhere in this book. While the media are important in shaping the desire for slenderness, their role in the genesis of

anorexia is usually overestimated. Blaming the media is a popular, but one-dimensional perspective on the aetiology of anorexia nervosa, as I argue in part II.

8 Some eating disorders are, however, less 'visible' than others. There are probably many undetected sufferers (and recovered sufferers) in all social categories in many different societies. On the issue of whether eating disorders are culture bound, see Banks (1992) and Lee (1996).

9 Thanks to Helen Hayward-Brown for this point.

10 See Appendix B for the questions I used in our conversations.

11 In my view, it can be artificial to conceal participants' views from each other and helpful to encourage them to make comparisons with each other's ideas. This 'cumulative' approach makes them genuine participants instead of objects of the research.

12 I have drawn on psychoanalytic terms for general suggestions, well aware that in their own context they are very complex and often strongly challenged.

13 See Appendix C for a list of the codes I used. Computer packages for qualitative analysis (N.U.D.I.S.T. or Ethnograph) did not seem appropriate for this project as I was not aiming to 'validate' my analytical findings and wanted to do more than show correlations between variables. I chose to let the writing itself reveal essential connections in the material, even after my own coding and analysis. A computer package might be helpful for finding one's way around the data of a larger project, but genuine 'theorizing', I think, can only be achieved in the writing process.

14 The way in which I coded and analysed data in this project was influenced, to a certain extent, by Grounded Theory (Glaser & Strauss 1967; Strauss 1987); but, as Strauss insists, his work merely formalizes what most good social scientists do anyway. It follows common intellectual patterns; ways in which thinkers make sense of data. More important influences have been: C. Wright Mills (1959/1965) on intellectual craftsmanship and Reinharz (1983), Harding (1986), Stanley & Wise (1983) and Stanley (1990) on the importance of personal experience in research. Crawford et al. (1992) introduced me to the cliché as a sign of cultural conditioning.

15 I discuss this 'chaotic' condition from the point of view of narrative in chapter 3 and of ritual in chapters 8 and 9. Chapter 9 also includes Naomi's story.

3. AUTOBIOGRAPHY, NARRATIVE AND HEALING

1 But see 'Stories' in Game and Metcalfe (1996) for discussion of this very point and Wilkins (1996) for the centrality of emotions to the research process and to sociological understanding.

2 'The feminist standpoint epistemologies argue that because men are in the master's position *vis-à-vis* women, women's social experience – conceptualized through the lenses of feminist theory – can provide the grounds for a less distorted understanding of the world around us.'

3 These three references reveal the mutual influence of poststructuralism and feminism – the first two being primarily feminist and Lupton primarily poststructuralist.

4 Some of these reasons have been adapted from Olney (1980/1966), Benstock (1988), Heilbrun (1988) and The Personal Narrative Group (1989).

5 *The Interpretation of Dreams* (1900/1985a) and *The Psychopathology of Everyday Life* (1901/1985b) demonstrate the way self analysis may form the basis of new theories about human behaviour in its social context.

6 Another theory of narrative (Frank 1995) suggests that there are three 'basic plots' in all stories; chaos, restitution and the quest. Following this idea, 'recovered' and 'recovering' stories in this book appear to be structured as quests while 'unrecovered' narratives, especially when the protagonist (like Freda, Patricia and Michael) is devoid of hope, are chaos stories (thanks to Helen Hayward-Brown for our conversation on this topic).

7 The form favoured by most autobiographical accounts of anorexia this century has been existential (in contrast to the 'spritual' letters and biographies of the medieval fasting saints, whom I discuss in chapter 8). Bruch (1973, 1978, 1988), Palazzoli (1974) and McLeod (1981) see anorexia as an existential problem. The existential is hard to separate from the spiritual, whichever term the writer chooses, since both are about ultimate meaning. MacLeod's story is, therefore, also about what people in my study called 'spirituality' and about the influences of religion in her life.

8 The assumption that spirituality cannot flourish in a society most of whose institutions are secular ignores the fact that 'spirituality' is perennial; constantly reappearing in different guises, from the life-distorting to the life-enhancing.

9 Though spiritual autobiography has provided the background for psychological typologies of the spiritual experience (like James' *The Varieties of Religious Experience* 1958) and for reflections on the nature of memory (Crites 1989).

10 Spitzack (1990), for example, gives a Foucauldian critique of this trend in the 'anti-diet literature' of late twentieth-century North American culture.

11 Kondo, for instance, claims that 'the narrative authority of the text gives [academic writers] the power to 'know' and to 'represent' as we see fit' (1986: 83). I disagree. Every academic knows his/her text will be subject to peer review so, at least part of the time, we write as if critics were reading over our shoulders.

12 Along with autobiography, poetry has been the preferred form for the literary expression of spirituality. 'Poetic' truth is the truth of the apt metaphor; that which opens us to new ways of representing reality and so takes us closer to it.

13 One important reason for the 'unreliability' of participants' memories of the eating disorder itself is, as Becky Thompson points out, that 'many of them experienced one trauma right on top of another, giving them little chance to make sense of events or to recover from them' – also a reason why sexual abuse is often 'forgotten' and only retrieved years later. 'These gaps in memory', writes Thompson, 'left them unable to explain or understand their feelings of shame, fear, depression and loss.' (Thompson 1994: 100). In further support of my use of narrative to present the 'realities' of recovery, it is important to remember that 'the coldly distant, so-called objective language of social science' can do real violence to the richness of human experience (Kondo 1986: 83).

14 Like many of the protagonists who have lost their memories in the stories of

Oliver Sacks (1984).

15 Some Australian examples include Moore (1992) (a surgeon's recovery from his car accident), Henderson (1993) (overcoming adversity in a rural setting), Shepherd (1997) (a young woman's recovery from accident – used as a 'motivational' story in corporate training seminars).

16 For critiques of these movements see e.g. Masson (1990), Kaminer (1993) and Noll (1996) and for their effectiveness see Heelas (1996).

4. REINTERPRETING 'ANOREXIA'

1 The latest clinical definitions of these terms can be found in the *Diagnostic and Statistical Manual* of the American Psychiatric Association (1987) and in the World Health Organization (1992) *Classification of mental and behavioural disorders*.

2 The debate about continuity or discontinuity between these practices and 'anorexia nervosa' is addressed in chapter 8.

3 For a detailed historical account of the naming of anorexia nervosa, see Brumberg (1988: 111ff and notes).

4 See Brumberg (1988), Wolf (1991), and Robertson (1992).

5 See Ehrenreich and English (1973), Foucault (1973), Illich (1976), Willis (1983), Brumberg (1988), Robertson (1992).

6 Significantly for feminist arguments, until recently medical discourse has generally ignored the eating problems of men, in spite of its early encounters with male anorexia (Brumberg 1988) and such famous examples as Byron and Kafka (Vandereycken and van Deth 1994).

7 As any meeting of Overeaters Anonymous will also demonstrate. I attended one of these and have spoken with several people who have been on a regular basis.

8 For detailed descriptions of compulsive eating, a problem which is not necessarily related to obesity, see Woodman (1980), Roth (1982, 1992) and McFarlane and Baker-Baumann (1991).

9 These diagnostic manuals are continually being revised, partly because psychiatrists encounter forms of disordered eating which they cannot neatly fit into previous diagnostic specifications and partly because of changes in the patterns of eating problems themselves; e.g. more patients combine anorexia and bulimia which once seemed to be distinct disorders, and eating disorders now usually include a compulsive exercise component related to contemporary discourses on diet and exercise (B. Turner 1982; Crawford 1978, 1986; Colquhoun 1989a, 1989b; Tinning 1985; Hargreaves 1986; Wright 1991). Some psychiatrists believe that a single word 'anorexia' should now replace the two separate categories 'anorexia nervosa' and 'bulimia nervosa' (Beumont & Touyz 1991).

10 For exceptions (e.g. Hall 1993), see chapter 6.

11 e.g. Garner & Garfinkel (1982: 123–6); Brumberg (1988: 30).

12 John Collins, Psychology, Macquarie University, personal communication, 1983.

13 The object-relations school originated with the work of Winnicott (1965) and

also posits an 'authentic self' hidden behind a 'false self'.

14 Another theory that relies on the notion of an 'authentic self' comes from a combination of self psychology and object-relations theory used in the treatment of eating disorders by the followers of Masterson (1981, 1985).

15 In exploring the parallels between anorexia and spirit possession, I encountered Boddy's (1989) equally useful definition of the self as 'a creative energy or process which actively engages the world, integrating the human biological organism with its physical and sociocultural environments, continually moving, becoming, maturing, making and organizing meaning' (Burridge 1979: 5; Kegan 1982: 2–15 and Elster 1986 are cited as contributing to this definition).

16 Existentialism refers to a group of doctrines, some theistic, some atheistic, deriving from the writings of Kierkegaard (1813–1855) (see essays in the collection Kierkegaard 1873), who stresses the importance of existence as such and of the freedom and responsibility of the finite human individual (*Macquarie Dictionary*). Its relation to 'spirituality' is discussed further in part III.

17 Other transpersonal/spiritual approaches which have informed but not been incorporated into my discussion include Brown, Peterson & Cunningham (1988); Brown & Peterson (1991); Clemmons (1991); Krystal & Zweben (1988); Helminiak (1989); Mariz (1991); Pancner & Pancner (1988).

18 For further discussion of the use of metaphor in recovery, see Garrett (1996a).

19 Work in progress in this area was presented to the 1995 European Council on Eating Disorders General Meeting by Brian Lask (for a report of the conference, see Garrett 1995a).

20 Freud's studies of hysteria include over twenty publications in the period from 1886–1933 and he constantly revised his theories concerning its aetiology.

21 The arguments which follow are drawn from B. Turner 1984: 2, 112–3, 197–200.

22 Alternatively, advanced capitalism may be blamed for perpetuating the 'beauty myth' (Wolf 1990) which in turn allegedly produces anorexic behaviour. Wolf's analysis, not particularly 'poststructuralist', centres on the economic imperative behind the 'beauty myth' and suggests a kind of cultural conspiracy theory.

23 Turner 1984: 180, 185, 201–2. Turner's insights into the ascetic dimension of anorexia, on the other hand, when they are linked with theories of religion which he has developed elsewhere (1983), are highly relevant to my project of understanding recovery, as I will show in chapter 8.

24 Susan Bordo's feminist appropriation of Foucault also argues that anorexia is an attempt to rebel which only succeeds in being a capitulation; 'Anorexia, hysteria, and agoraphobia may provide a paradigm of one way in which potential resistance is not merely undercut but *utilized* in the maintenance and reproduction of existing power relations' (1989: 16) She does not take the next logical step, which is to assert that *recovery* is the most effective rebellion. She also (problematically) attributes a form of false consciousness to the anorexic woman who, she writes, 'is, of course, unaware that she is making a political gesture' (p. 20).

25 For a detailed and powerful account of class, race, sexism and homophobia in

the lives of women with eating problems, see Thompson (1994). Although race and ethnicity did not seem to play any part in 'my' stories and no one in my study identified him/herself as homosexual, there are many similarities between Thompson's stories and mine, including the emphasis on emotional and sometimes sexual abuse.

26 I am not suggesting that these are restricted to the culture of poverty but, as Thompson (1994) shows, they can often be some of the ways in which oppressed people attempt to cope with their lives.

27 Echoing the subtitle of *Anorexia and Recovery* (Way 1993).

5. REINTERPRETING 'RECOVERY'

1 Brumberg (1988: 20) cites alarming figures from the Anorexia Bulimia Association, but it must be remembered that associations like these are more likely to exaggerate the extent and severity of eating disorders in order to attract the support they need to help their members. Similarly, Wolf (1990: 179ff) selects the highest available figures from clinical outcome studies to support her own polemical points.

2 In thirty follow-up studies from several countries, some spanning over forty years, estimates of mortality from anorexia nervosa and bulimia nervosa vary between 0 per cent and 22 per cent, with over half the studies reporting 4 per cent or less (Herzog et al. 1988). Herzog et al. found only seven outcome studies of bulimia nervosa and none reported any deaths. Deaths from bulimia are, however, occasionally noted in the media (e.g. the death of a Sydney University student in 1992), provoking deep anxiety but offering no real guidance towards prevention or recovery.

3 Gull (1874: 22–8), cited in Brumberg (1988: 124).

4 My comments are based on a close reading the following studies (including two very useful review articles: Hsu 1980 and Herzog et al. 1988): Dally (1969); Morgan & Russell (1975); Halmi, Broadland & Rigas (1975); Crisp (1980); Hsu (1980); Schwartz & Thompson (1981); Theander (1983); Vandereycken and Pierloot (1983); Abraham, Mira & Llewellyn Jones (1983); Burns & Crisp (1984); Keck & Fiebert (1986); Russell et al. (1987); Herzog et al (1988), Sohlberg et al. (1989); Beresin, Gordon & Herzog (1989); Takaoka et al. (1990) and Casper (1990). The earliest example of this genre was written in 1954 (Beck & Brockner-Mortensen) and there have been thirty such studies since then. Herzog et al. counted only seven (all recent) follow-up studies of 'bulimia nervosa'.

5 Examples of autobiographical and fictionalized accounts of anorexia include: Liu (1979); Boone-O'Neill (1982); Place (1989); Shute (1992); Jones and Crawford (1995).

6 E.g. 44 per cent good outcome, 26 per cent intermediate outcome, 30 per cent poor outcome (Burns & Crisp 1984) – roughly parallel with the findings of my study.

7 Exceptions include review articles, such as Hsu (1980) and Herzog et al. (1988). Indeed, Herzog et al. refer to this very problem.

8 Review articles grouping these studies have compared their results under the

headings of: (a) mortality, (b) nutritional outcome, (c) menstrual outcome, (d) eating difficulties at follow up, (e) psychiatric outcome, (f) psychosexual outcome, (g) psychosocial outcome, (h) effects of treatment, and (i) outcome predictors. The tables in Herzog et al. (1988) provide detailed comparisons of thirty studies. These tables, like the list above, clearly show what is missing from 'clinical/empirical' recovery studies.

9 Appearing in such journals as the *International Journal on Eating Disorders* and *Eating Disorders: The Journal of Prevention and Treatment*.

10 This literature is peppered with words like 'mystery' (Russell 1977, cited in Theander 1983: 168; Keck & Fiebert 1986: 432), 'obscure' (Sohlberg et al. 1989: 249) and 'victim' (Keck & Fiebert 1986: 432).

11 Vandereycken and Vanderlinden (1983) comment that 'we can trust the patient (only) as far as she or he can trust us' and Sohlberg et al. warn researchers to beware of the patient's 'denial of illness . . . particularly when self-report questionnaires are used' (1989: 256).

12 In a rare and valuable journal article about a 'phenomenological' clinical study, Beresin, Gordon and Herzog (1989) spoke with thirteen former patients (not their own), without a predetermined list of criteria, to elaborate a sensitive account of the recovery process. They describe recovery as 'becoming real' (experiencing oneself as real) through 'real' (totally accepting) relationships and they draw attention to 'the therapeutic value of experiences in daily life' (1989: 20).

13 For my own analysis of the contributions of Bruch and Palazzoli to an existential theory of recovery, see Garrett (1996b).

14 The chapter by Fallon and Peters is the exception.

15 Sheila MacLeod (1981) also believes that 'full recovery is practically impossible' (p. 145) and describes herself as a 'controlled' or 'residual' anorexic for twenty years (p. 148). My desire to elaborate the notion of an 'irreversible' recovery (even if it is never 'complete') stems in considerable part from my disappointment that an author I admire has denied its possibility. Like MacLeod, I recognize traces of anorexia in my own behaviour from time to time but, like other anorectics who have recovered, my identity and commitment are no longer tied up with an 'anorexic' existence.

16 For existential dimensions of changes in space and time during recovery, see Garrett (1996 b).

17 See also Root (1990); Fallon & Peters (1994) who also show that 'recovery . . . is not a static state'; Way (1993: 100) and Thompson (1994: 124), who describes recovery as a 'dynamic, evolving process'.

18 My story (chapter 1) already makes this point. See also Way (1993: 85).

19 Freud's concept of 'the return of the repressed' and Vico's (1968) historical notion of 'ricorso' perhaps best name this aspect of recovery over time. See also Said (1975) on the difference between 'origins' and 'beginnings'.

20 Thompson also refers to major life crises as turning points (1994: 109) and Way (1993: 96) found that facing the return of repressed feelings is part of recovery.

21 E.g. Cardinal (1975); Moore (1992); Hull (1990); Danieli (1988); Cole et al. (1992).

22 Freud's theories of hysteria have been used in many feminist theories about the female body in society (e.g. Grosz 1987); explicitly in theories about anorexia (Celermajer 1987; Sayers 1988); implicitly in analyses of anorexia proceeding from object-relations theory – see chapter 4 and notes.

23 For a clear exposition of similarities and differences between the various mystical traditions, see Johnston (1995). As Nicholas Lash points out, 'mystical life' is really nothing other than Christianity, or Judaism, Hinduism, Islam and some forms of Buddhism lived to their maximum intensity, but always shaped by the narrative tradition of each religion (pp. 18, 167,171).

24 Said is commenting on Vico's *New Science* (1968/1774) which argued that the study of humanity must take place poetically (through language and the imagination) and that both social and individual histories (the *corso*) followed a pattern of constant return to unresolved patterns (the *ricorso*). Consequently, there are no 'origins' but only 'beginnings'. It follows that finding the beginnings of recovery is more realistic than looking for the origins of eating problems.

25 See chapter 11 for an extended discussion of the meaning of sexuality and its part in recovery.

26 E.g. Laing (1960) and Szasz (1973, 1974, 1979) are critical of psychiatry and Masson (1990) believes that psychotherapy is also irretrievably flawed. Much of the published criticism of behaviourist clinical interventions in anorexia nervosa has come from feminist psychotherapists including those at the Women's Therapy Centre in London (Orbach, Lawrence, Dana, etc.) and most contributors to Fallon, Katzman and Wooley (1994).

27 E.g. the poet Anne Sexton committed suicide at the age of forty-six after an adult lifetime of madness and addictions. At a memorial gathering, her fellow-poet Denise Levertov commented 'We should make clear, as she could not, the distinction between creativity and self-destruction, The tendency to confuse the two has claimed too many victims . . . To recognize that for a few years of her life Anne Sexton was an artist even though she had so hard a struggle against her desire for death is to fittingly honor her memory' (Middlebrook 1992).

28 'Technologies' of the self include discourses and practices involving body and psyche. The word is particularly appropriate to the complex of beliefs and actions involved in health maintenance and in recovery. (Thanks to Toni Schofield for this insight).

6. RECOVERY STORIES

1 The stories are not 'complete' but made up of selections from our taped conversations. Different selections from the same conversations have been made for inclusion in other chapters of this book.

2 For Persephone/Proserpina see Homer (1965), Ovid (1955) and Grant and Hazel (1973).

3 Inanna's story is also about the connection between sexuality and spirituality (Kovel 1991). This myth is of particular relevance because it is about death

(my chapter 8), rebirth (chapter 6) and ritual inititiation (chapter 9) – all integral to anorexia and recovery. It is also about initiation into full *woman-hood*. Corresponding birth and resurrection myths for men are likely to be useful to the 10 per cent of 'anorectics' who are men.

4 The avoidance of the first person in the personal narratives of people with eating disorders is mentioned in Kress, Lohrey and Place (1990).

5 For this French fairytale, see Picard (1955) and Byatt (1990).

6 A variety of theologies may be invoked to explore the questions of life and death which are fundamental in anorexia (see chapter 8). Indeed, critics of Weber's notion of the Protestant ethic, in a collection edited by R. W. Green, have adduced evidence of anxieties and exhortations similar to those he claimed for Calvinism; in Catholics (Robertson), Jews (Sombart) and other Protestants (Tawney); at least during the same historical period. (Green 1973: ix-xi).

7. SOCIETY AND SPIRIT

1 Parts of this and the following chapter have been published as Garrett (1996 c) and Garrett (1997).

2 Thanks to Morny Joy (Religious Studies, University of Calgary) for this insight.

3 Self, as emphasized elsewhere in this book, does not imply an 'authentic' or 'essential' self, but a many-sided being engaged in a continual process of transformation in association with the natural and social environnment.

4 Existential and transpersonal psychologies are briefly outlined in chapter 4.

5 Sheila MacLeod (1981: 182) points out this paradox and the contradiction she has been unable to resolve in her own life.

6 See Lash (1996), in which he argues that the emergence from 'modernity' makes possible the reintegration of God into daily life, instead of isolating 'religion' from the rest of modern life and thought and culture (p. 174). At the same time, Lash warns against the contemporary interest in 'spirituality' which does not stretch the mind or change behaviour.

7 See Johnston (1995). Johnston defines mysticism as 'the science of Love' and locates it in social action as well as in contemplation. Johnston warns, however, that meditation and mysticism are not separate from the teachings of the great religions; that you cannot have spirituality without doctrine or vice-versa. Hitler, too, felt an 'inner light' (Mystical Theology workshop, Sydney, 10–13 January).

8 Kovel's notion of 'flesh' is derived from Merleau-Ponty, as I show in chapter 11.

9 I return to Weber in part IV. The ideas discussed here are his, but the links among them are mine.

10 In Christian literature, for example, humans 'hunger and thirst after right-eousness'; 'find in the Lord a sweet savor'; 'taste and see that he is good'; and 'spiritual milk' is 'drawn from the breasts of both testaments' (James 1958: 27). See also Bynum (1987) for the significance of such imagery in the Middle Ages.

11 For further reading in the sociology of emotion, see Hochschild (1979, 1983), Barbalet (1994), Freund (1988, 1990), de Rivera and Grinkis (1986), Kemper (1978, 1981, 1990).

12 These statements are suffused with emotion; with a longing for a wisdom transcending the form of their own discourse. Yet mystical wisdom is only a problem if it is artificially set apart from other forms of knowledge. Mystics throughout history have encountered this challenge and resolved it by concluding that both ordinary, commonsense knowledge and scientific, scholarly knowledge are perfected by the mystical vision (Johnston 1995: 306–10). Similarly, people aspiring to mysticism must recognize its part in motivating social action; by identifying with the sufferings of the world (human and environmental) and allowing love to work through them to transform it (Johnston 1995: 345–64).

8. RITUALS OF SELF-TRANSFORMATION

1 'Spiritual masters' however, have always seen the danger and ambiguity of excessive penance (*Dictionnaire de la Vie Spirituelle*, 1987: 61 Edition du Cerf). In many religions, spiritual fasting has been 'a defence against taboo powers and a means of obtaining mana'. Modern Christian theology takes fasting to be an exercise in sharing and love of neighbour and in integrating the the body into the life of faith' (Zalba 1968; Rahner et al. 1968: 335). My thanks to Margaret O'Sullivan for these references.

2 As portrayed in the film *The Karen Carpenter Story* (Weintraub Entertainment Productions, Inc, 1988) and numerous magazine articles.

3 Eating Disorders Nursing Association, Sydney (personal communication). See Garrett (1991).

4 Historians have distinguished women's 'holy fasting' from men's in a variety of ways: Bell and Weinstein (1982) and Bell (1985: 16) suggest that gender differences in ascetic practices stem from different perceptions of the locus of sin: for women sin was internal, for men it was 'an impure response to an external stimulus'. Bynum (1987: 93) shows that 'food was *a* theme, not *the* theme in male lives and sensibilities' and comments in detail on the differences between the fasting of St Francis and St Clare of Assisi based on the medieval idea that women's bodies were themselves food (pp. 100, 114, 269) and that while holy men renounced power, women could only renounce food (p. 295). Men in my study became anorexic when they felt powerless.

5 The life of the Buddha displays the same structure of 'recovery' from extreme asceticism.

6 Bynum makes it clear that there were several different ways of interpreting unusual fasting during the medieval period (as, in fact, there are today): It could be viewed as fraudulent, as attention-seeking or as an illness. St Catherine of Siena (like Simone Weil) spoke of her inability to eat as an infirmity, not a voluntary religious practice (1987: 196).

7 An interpretation with which Bynum does not disagree (personal communication, Sydney, August 1993).

8 Heelas (1996), the most comprehensive sociological account of the New Age

movement, illustrates how easily accessible New Age ways of thinking have become today and points to many of their locations.

9 This much has already been suggested in relation to anorexia, in the work of Kim Chernin (1986). The recovery phase, equally amenable to this kind of anthropological interpretation, has received far less attention, and this may be one reason why recovery is far from automatic.

10 As Csordas argues; 'a comprehensive account of therapeutic effectiveness must find its locus elsewhere than in the transference activated in dyadic patient-therapist interaction' (pp. 336–7).

11 Shorter discusses the ritual initiation stories of five women encountered in her therapeutic practice. She stresses the religious nature of self-initiation rituals, their close connection with the body, their inseparability from relationships with others, the way in which they authorize 'letting go' of past attachments to embrace more appropriate new ones, and the presence of 'dark gods' (the father principle, Zeus and his brother Hades who takes the girl to the underworld and initiates the rupture with her former life). She acknowledges the importance of men's symbolic initiation, but also explains the differences between men's and women's psychic processes: Male initiation rituals are also replete with death and rebirth imagery, but the test for a woman is to discover and relate to a spiritual principle (birth, growth) already implanted symbolically in her own body: 'Transformation is not sought as desirable in and of itself; it is a command of her being'. As the rituals of descent into anorexia demonstrate, ritual per se does not ensure a safe passage through self-initiation, but it does ensure that the passage is signified (Shorter 1986: 52). For another account of women's spiritual quest and initiation rites in American literature, see Judith Christ (1980). For a Jungian view of 'women's mysteries', see Harding (1971).

9. SPIRITUAL STORIES

1 The metaphor of the self-imposed cage for anorexia has been used by Hilde Bruch (1978) and by Kafka (1952) in 'A hunger artist'.

2 For articles on anorexia in men see note 5, chapter 1. There were three men in my study; roughly the same proportion as in the population of people diagnosed with anorexia. I have included the stories of two of these men, to demonstrate their similarities with women's stories of eating disorders and the way they fit the pattern this book describes. One of the first recorded cases of anorexia nervosa in medical literature involved a male (Morton 1624, cited in Sterling and Segal 1986), and medical studies stress that despite the rarity of anorexia in men (the incidence is usually given as 5 per cent of cases), they exhibit the same clinical symptoms as anorexic women. Sterling and Segal's review article (1986) emphasizes that in men, the analog of female anorexia is definitely male anorexia and not the phenomenon of obligatory running or other forms of compulsive behaviour. Psychological/psychiatric studies of male anorexia have been especially interested in four questions: (1) sexuality, (2) body size prior to anorexia, (3) family background and (4) why so few men are anorexic. With respect to (1) Crisp and Burns (1983: 5), for example, postulate that anorexia in

men (as in women) serves to shield them from issues of personal identity and sexuality which they find too challenging. In relation to (2) most sutides have found that the men were often much fatter or thinner than their peers, whereas a greater proportion of anorexic women were originally within a normal weight range. As with women, anorexic behaviour in men was often a consequence of peer criticism and some males also perceive similar demands for slimness, but especially in competitive sports. (3) While some writers believe there is no evidence that the disorder in males only develops in the presence of greater psychological disturbance (Burns and Crisp; 1985: 323), others (Sterling and Segal 1985) found that in comparison to the families of female anorectics, there were more instances of pathology in the families of male anorectics (p. 566). (4) These researchers suggest that the sex difference in the incidence of anorexia nervosa is attributable to the fact that most adolescent girls diet, whereas very few adolescent boys do (Burns and Crisp 1985: 327). Michael, Philip and Dominic's stories illustrate these points, but also include their views on *recovery*, not covered in the literature on men and eating disorders.

3 Naomi, reading this account, adds: 'the flashbacks often came on Thursday, despite all the tricks Jane [her counsellor] and I tried to tell them to wait till Friday'.

4 Signer and Benson (1990) have noted other instances of anorexia occurring with epilepsy. They suggest that the 'affective disorders and dysmorphic delusions' caused by the epilepsy were contributing factors to anorexia nervosa. Their explanation relies on the theory of anorexia as a perceptual disturbance in body image which I have questioned in chapter 4. It also relies on a physical causation model of anorexia. Naomi's story suggests a more complex, social aetiology. Six years after our first meeting, Naomi is now conducting her own postgraduate research project on the connections between epilepsy and post-traumatic stress syndrome.

5 This is a familiar theme, included, for example, in Hans Christian Andersen's tale of the seven brothers turned into swans, whose sister knitted shirts of nettles in a race against time to restore them to human form. Naomi did not remember this particular story, but may have encountered analogues elsewhere.

10. RECREATING THE BODY

1 Elizabeth Grosz, in *Volatile Bodies* (1994), goes further still. For her, the 'inside' and 'outside' of the body are seamlessly connected, like the two sides of a Mobius strip.

2 This is one of the problems addressed by Jan Horsfall in a review of Joanne Finkelstein's *The Fashioned Self* (1991) (Horsfall 1993).

3 This awareness therefore partakes in the three forms of rationality identified by Max Weber (see chapter 7) as those which have been neglected in western society: poetic/artistic, substantive (concerned with ultimate ends) and ethical (directed towards self-perfection).

4 Parts of this chapter have appeared in Garrett (1996a).

5 I return, in chapter 11, to the idea of yoga as an alternative way to knowledge, and to Sheena's idea that recovery starts with the body, rather than the mind.

6 The concept of the imaginary body is familiar to readers of Lacan (appearing, for example, in 'The Mirror Stage', where he emphasizes its cultural construction). Gatens (1983), drawing on Lacan and Merleau-Ponty, writes of the imaginary body as 'developed, learnt, connected to the body image of others and not static . . . The imaginary body is socially and historically specific in that it is constructed by: a shared language; the shared psychical significance and privileging of various zones of the body . . . and common institutional practices and discourses . . . on and through the body' (Gatens 1983: 151–2). The imaginary body is perhaps best known in the phenomenon of the phantom limb (e.g. Sacks 1986). In anorexia, as Gatens mentions, the imaginary body is of vital importance, since the body is experienced (in spite of 'rational' evidence to the contrary) as larger than it really is. This is not a perceptual distortion, but an 'imaginary' one. In recovery, the most important transformations are those of the imaginary body. Recovery is not about 'correcting distorted perceptions', but about imagining the body in new ways. The way Sheena speaks about her new bodily awareness under my heading 'yoga' is an example of this.

7 In Hay (1990), one such book which several participants mentioned, the mouth represents taking in of new ideas and nourishment (p. 50); abdominal cramps are caused by fear and 'stopping the process' (p. 10); the back represents the support of life (p.16). Overweight (p. 32) means oversensitivity: in the arms it is anger at being denied love; in the belly it is anger at being denied nourishment; in the thighs it is childhood anger, often against the father, etc.

8 For this reason, a preferable term might be 'the anticipated body' (thanks to Andrew Metcalfe for this suggestion).

11. THE SEXUAL BODY

1 My method is therefore compatible with Merleau-Ponty's phenomenology, which also moved from the *experience* of 'being' to attempt to explain 'Being'. Since Merleau-Ponty's work arose as a critique of Sartre's, it deals with many of the same questions; engaging in 'a search for Being which takes place from within Being' (Merleau-Ponty 1964: 268) and attempting to go beyond Descartes' *Cogito* to an embodied understanding of human existence. Merleau-Ponty's approach to the question of being is inseparable from the development of his critique of Sartre. The similarities between the ideas of the two thinkers, however, are usually ignored (Whitford 1982).

2 Merleau-Ponty's example is from Ludwig Binswanger's *Uber Psychologie* (1935). Binswanger, founder of 'existential psychiatry', was a student of Jung. One of his patients was Bertha von Pappenheim, the famous 'Anna O' who also displayed signs of anorexia, in Freud and Breuer's *Studies on Hysteria* (1974). Binswanger's account of the life of Ellen West is used extensively in the literature on eating disorders, e.g. in Chernin (1981: 162–79), Orbach (1986), Brumberg (1988) and Jackson & Davidson (1989: 10–12).

3 And, Irigaray argues, between men and women in particular. This is not to deny the importance of same sex sexual relations, but to emphasize the need to bridge the divide between the sexes and the importance of a spiritualized sexuality in this task.

4 The importance of connection with others is what is often ignored in popular versions of 'self-spirituality', which place personal development ahead of relationships.

5 As we have seen, most of these studies are coy about the specific nature of sexual relationship; studiously ignoring lesbian relations, usually arguing against male homosexuality as a predisposing factor in men's anorexia and therefore equally silent about homosexuality in recovery.

6 Kovel explains the relationship between desire and knowledge in psychoanalytic terms which I find more persuasive than Lacan's, since Kovel's approach concerns the 'connections' within and of the self, and Lacan's the 'splits'. Kovel suggests that the child's 'original' experience of desire is for the mother, who herself desires the child, both as other and as extension of herself. Hence the child 'experiences the central Other as a desire for itself'. Since this is the 'elementary basis of knowing', 'the root of knowledge is desire and not logos' (Kovel 1991: 127). Kovel does not mention the mother's breast – the final link in this particular 'hunger knot' (Chernin 1986).

7 For example, a 1993 article in *Dolly*, a magazine for young women from thirteen to twenty, concerned 'Common Sex Fears'. One of the most widespread fears appeared to be 'my body will be a turn-off' (breasts too big/small, fat thighs, big abdomen, body odour, etc.).

8 Ella Dreyfus' book of photographs, *The Body Pregnant* (Dreyfus 1993), discusses this very point and gives us startlingly new images of pregnancy 'as women actually experience it'. Her work is influenced by Jo Spence (e.g. 1986; 1990), who also sought to present images of the body which were not the sanitized images of advertising or art photography.

9 A term she consciously borrowed from Germaine Greer (1970).

12. THE KNOWING BODY

1 Some of the arguments and illustrations in this chapter have been used in Garrett (1996a).

2 Since the early 1980s, there has been a renewed academic interest in 'the body' as an object of study and as a way of understanding both the self and society in philosophy, sociology, cultural studies and theology. To mention just a few important texts which have developed this approach: Turner (1984), Finkelstein (1991), Grosz (1994), May (1995), Lupton (1996). Another area where theories of the body are being developed is in the Sociology of Health and Illness (see, for example, articles in *Annual Review of Health Social Sciences* (1996) vol. 6: 'Reconstructing Health Knowledge') . . . See Garrett (1995b) for the ways in which I have used theorists of the body in my own work.

3 This is the Weberian explanation given in chapter 7.

4 My argument is also influenced by Foucault's concept of subjugated knowledges. In 'Two Lectures', Foucault (1980) refers to the potential for criticism (of established regimes of thought) which is contained in 'popular knowledges'; those which have been marginalized by powerful discourses like psychiatry. Foucault makes specific mention, here, of the knowledge of the psychiatric patient, the ill person, the doctor and the nurse as 'knowledges that

have been disqualified as inadequate to their task or insufficiently elaborated'. They are also 'those blocs of historical knowledge which were present but disguised within the body of functionalist and systematising theory and which criticism – which obviously draws upon scholarship – has been able to reveal' (p. 82). His arguments apply to the kinds of 'bodily knowing' which are the concern of this chapter. Although Foucault might have disapproved, I believe his arguments can be extended to the alternative rationalities of Weber's writings and to 'mystical knowledge' itself and that scholarly criticism is, indeed, able to reveal them.

5 These ideas and practices (including the Human Potential Movement, paganism and neo-paganism) are comprehensively discussed in Heelas (1996). From my point of view, the major problem with most New Age spirituality is that it remains self-preoccupied because it does not challenge fundamental social structures. In this, it escapes full rationality, since a full rationality must contain an ethical dimension; the dimension of care for the Other (for people and for the Earth). As Kovel and Christian Liberation Theology point out, the task for contemporary spirituality is to develop a communal spiritual practice which seeks to change social 'structures' themselves (1991: 204–12). Some participants in my study were aware of this need and others not.

6 For a fascinating critique of the 'cult of Jung' and its relation to the New Age, see Noll (1996).

7 For, as Kaminer emphasizes, the self-help texts of the recovery movement themselves purvey a new form of authoritarianism (1993: 23).

8 Not all New Age discourses achieve body-mind-spirit integration; some exalt one or other facet of this particular trinity, but they make it easier than does, for example, academic discourse.

9 'Holistic therapies' (e.g. Reiki, Yoga, Tai Chi, Aikido, Shiatsu) are often also spiritual practices. For brief accounts of these, see Martin (1989) and Kovel (1978).

10 While Reich's work was discredited during the 1950s as a result of his experiments with 'orgone therapy', his influence has been strong in a range of therapies which came into being before the use of the term New Age. To mention only those which I have experienced: Biodynamic massage (Boyesen & Boyesen 1980; Boyesen 1985) draws on the Reichian insight that 'cosmic' energy (a 'spiritualized' renaming of Freud's libido and of Eastern 'kundalini' energy) moves through the body and is capable of powerful emotional and physical effects. The practice of Reiki also depends on the ancient belief in healing through the laying on of hands. It can be felt, even by those who do not share a belief in its efficacy.

11 For detailed information about the philosophy and bodily practice of Iyengar Yoga, see Iyengar (1991). No book, however, adequately conveys the subtlety and range of the language used by experienced yoga instructors.

12 The parallels between the breath (inspiration) of a single person and the breath (poetic creativity; Divine Energy) which animates the imagination are illuminated in Coleridge's *Biographia Literaria* (Coleridge 1951). Coleridge distinguished between the poetic imagination and philosophical reasoning,

but he believed that both exist as manifestations of the 'living principle'; that 'the poetic and the philosophic genius' are two manifestations of a single power. This power he called The Primary Imagination. It is 'the prime Agent of all human Perception and a repetition in the finite mind of the eternal act of creation in the infinite *I am*' (p. 263). For Coleridge, the imagination is a metaphysical energy which partakes of the Divine. The poet, who is part of the natural world, is similarly animated by this energy which, like the wind, is a material as well as a metaphysical force, as Coleridge suggested in 'The Aeolian Harp':

And what if all of animated nature
Be but organic Harps diversely framed,
That tremble into thought, as o'er them sweeps
Plastic and vast, one intellectual breeze,
At once the Soul of each, and God of all?

13 Anthropologist Naomi Quinn (1991), in a critique of Lakoff and Johnson, insists that they overemphasize metaphor at the expense of culture. She argues that 'metaphors, far from constituting understanding, are ordinarily selected to fit a pre-existing and culturally shared model'. I see no conflict between my arguments concerning the role of the body in knowledge and Quinn's emphasis on culture since I have stressed the role of culture (society and social practices) in recovery. Another way of putting this is to say that in recovery, people shift their understanding of the body from one sub-cultural model (which objectifies the body) to another (which understands the body as continuous with self and spirit). Metaphor plays an important part in this shift, whether or not it is articulated in words (it can be expressed, for instance, in movement and in ritual symbolism).

14 This possibility was posited by Reich and is assumed in bioenergetics (Lowen 1976), biodynamic massage (Boyesen 1980; Boyesen & Boyesen 1985) and many similar therapies.

15 As Gatens points out (1983: 58, n. 30), we live in a society which will only tolerate two kinds of bodies, but even at the biological level we must also acknowledge the existence of sex as a continuum and bodies as multiple, given (for example) the existence of hermaphrodites.

16 Young uses transcendence to mean 'subjectivity' (the possibility of engaging with the world), and immanence to mean 'objectification'.

17 Many writers in the field of physical education are documenting the ways girls learn to be 'physically handicapped' in sexist society (e.g. Tinning 1985; Hargreaves 1986; Moriarty, Moriarty and Ford 1990; Wright 1991, 1992; Kenway & Willis 1990; Kenway 1992). It is not too fanciful, therefore, to suggest that the introduction of more 'holistic' exercise like yoga and Tai Chi might give young women the confidence in their bodies and themselves which would help prevent anorexia. In some hospital eating disorders units, treatment programs include anaerobic exercise which begins to give anorexic women a greater sense of the potential of their bodies and of the space they should legitimately take up in the world (see also Garrett 1991). As Jan Wright (1991) has shown, the language used by teachers and students in this attempt is fundamental to the way in which women learn to experience their bodily selves.

18 I am indebted to conversations with Deborah Lupton for the last part of this point.

19 Notably Orbach (1986), Bordo (1988), and others mentioned in my discussion of anorexia as metaphor in chapter 4.

20 As it sometimes can be, as in the film *Babette's Feast* (based on Karen Blixen's short story), where the ritual of eating a lovingly prepared meal was the means of creating bodily bliss, spiritual serenity and new bonds among those present.

21 As it is whenever blood sugar levels drop (in diabetes, before an insulin coma and in people who suffer from hypoglycaemia).

22 For further discussion of the 'loss of meaning' in anorexia, see Robertson (1992), Woodman (1980), and my review of both (Garrett 1992c).

References

Abraham, S. F. 1982, 'What can be learnt from eating disorders which may help the understanding of drug dependency syndromes', *Australian Alcohol and Drug Review*, vol. 1, no. 1, January, pp. 56–9.

Abraham, S. F., Mira, M. & Llewellyn-Jones, D. 1983, 'Bulimia: a study of outcome', *International Journal of Eating Disorders*, no. 2, pp. 175–180.

American Psychiatric Association 1987, *Diagnostic and Statistical Manual of Mental Disorders*, 3rd edn, American Psychiatric Association, Washington, DC.

Andersen, A. E. (ed.) 1991, *Males with Eating Disorders*, Brunner Mazel, New York.

Andersen, A. E. & Mickalide, A. D. 1983, 'Anorexia nervosa in the male: An underdiagnosed disorder', *Pschychosomatics*, no. 24, pp. 1066–75.

Atkinson, P. 1990, *The Ethnographic Imagination: Textual Constructions of Reality*, Routledge, New York.

Atwood, M. 1996, *Alias Grace*, Bloomsbury, London.

Baker, M. R. 1997, *The Fiftieth Gate: A Journey Through Memory*, Harper Collins, Sydney.

Banks, C.G. 1992, '"Culture" in culture-bound syndromes: the case of anorexia nervosa', *Social Science and Medicine*, vol. 34, no. 8, pp. 867–84.

Barbalet, J. 1994, 'Ritual emotion and body work: a note on the uses of Durkheim', *Social Perspectives on Emotion*, vol. 2, pp. 111–123.

Baumann, G. 1992, 'Ritual implicates "others": reading Durkheim in a plural society', in D. de Coppet (ed.), *Understanding Ritual*, Routledge, London.

Beauvoir, S. de 1953, *The Second Sex*, trans. & ed. H. M. Parshley, Knopf, New York.

Beck, J. C. & Brockner-Mortensen, K. 1954, 'Observation on the prognosis in anorexia nervosa', *Acta Medica Scandinavia*, no. 149, pp. 409–30.

Bell, C. & Roberts, H. (eds.) 1984, *Social Researching: Politics, Problems and Practice*, Routledge, London.

Bell, R. and Weinstein, D. 1982, *Saints and Society: The Two Worlds of Western Christendom*, 1000–1700, Chicago.

Bell, R. M. 1985, *Holy Anorexia*, University of Chicago Press, Chicago.

Ben-Tovim, D.I. & Morton, J. 1989, *The Anorexia Nervosa and Bulimia Study Programme: A Report to the South Australian Health Commission*, see also South Australian Health Commission.

Benstock, S. (ed.) 1988, *The Private Self: Theory and Practice of Women's*

Autobiographical Writings. Routledge, London.

Beresin, E. V., Gordon, C. & Herzog, D. 1989, 'The process of recovering from anorexia nervosa', *Journal of the Academy of Psychoanalysis*, vol. 17, no. 1, pp. 103–30.

Berger, P. L. 1969, *The Social Reality of Religion*, Faber, London.

Beumont, P. 1992, 'Overview of the Australian experience', paper presented at the Rivendell Conference on Eating Disorders in Adolescence, Thomas Walker Hospital, Concord, Sydney, 18 September.

Beumont, P. J., Bearwood, C. J. & Russell, G. F. 1972, 'The occurrence of the syndrome of anorexia nervosa in male subjects', *Psychological Medicine*, no. 33, pp. 31–47.

Beumont, P. & Touyz, S. 1991, 'Confusion in the classification of eating disorders', paper presented at the fourteenth National Conference of the Australian Behaviour Modification Association, University of NSW, Sydney, 6–10 July.

Bharati, A. 1985, *The Tantric Tradition*, Rider, London.

Boddy, J. 1989, *Wombs and Alien Spirits: Women, Men, and the Zar Cult in Northern Sudan*, University of Wisconsin Press, Madison.

Boone, O'Neill, C. 1982, *Starving for Attention*, Dove Communications, Blackburn, Victoria.

Bordo, S. 1988, 'Anorexia nervosa. Psychopathology as the crystallization of culture', in I. Diamond & L. Quinby (eds.), *Feminism and Foucault: Reflections on Resistance*, Northeastern University Press, Boston.

Bordo, S. 1989, 'The body and the reproduction of femininity: a feminist appropriation of Foucault', in A. Jagger & S. Bordo (eds.), *Gender/Body/Knowledge: Feminist Reconstructions of Being and Knowing*, Rutgers University Press, New Brunswick.

Bowles, G. & Duelli Klein, R. (eds.) 1983, *Theories of Women's Studies*, Routledge, London.

Boyesen, G. 1985, *Entre psyche et soma: Introduction à la psychologie biodynamique*, Payot, Paris.

Boyesen, G. & Boyesen. M. 1980, *Biodynamic Theory of Neurosis*, Biodynamic Psychology Publications, London.

Brodzki, B. & Schenk, C. (eds.) 1988, *Life/Lines: Theorizing Women's Autobiography*, Cornell University Press, Ithaca.

Brown, H. P. & Peterson, J. H. 1991, 'Assessing spirituality in addiction treatment and follow-up: development of the Brown-Petersen Recovery Progress Inventory (B-PRPI)', *Alcoholism Treatment Quarterly*, vol. 8, no. 2, pp. 21–49.

Brown, H. P., Peterson, J. H. & Cunningham, O. 1988, 'An individualized behavioural approach to spiritual development for the recovering addict/alcoholic', *Alcoholism Treatment Quarterly*, vol. 5, no. 1/2, pp. 177–97.

Bruch, H. 1973, *Eating Disorders: Obesity, Anorexia Nervosa and the Person Within*, Basic Books, New York.

1978, *The Golden Cage: The Enigma of Anorexia Nervosa*, Harvard University Press, Cambridge, Ma.

1988, *Conversations with Anorexics*, ed. D. Czyzewski & M. Suhr, Basic Books, New York.

Brumberg, J. J. 1988, *Fasting Girls: The Emergence of Anorexia Nervosa as a Modern Disease*, Harvard University Press, Cambridge, Ma.

Bruner, E. and Turner, V. (eds.) (1986). *The Anthropology of Experience.* University of Illinois Press, Chicago.

Burns, T. & Crisp, A. H. 1984, 'Outcome of anorexia nervosa in males', *British Journal of Psychiatry*, no. 145, pp. 319–25.

1985, 'Factors affecting prognosis in male anorectics', *Journal of Psychiatric Research*, vol. 19, nos. 2/3, pp. 323–8.

Burridge, K. O. 1979, *Someone, No One: An Essay on Individuality*, Princeton University Press, Princeton, N.J.

Byatt, A. S. 1990, *Possession: A Romance*, Virago, London.

Bynum, C. W. 1987, *Holy Feast and Holy Fast: The Significance of Food to Medieval Women*, University of California Press, Berkeley.

Cardinal, M. 1984 (1975 in French), *The Words to Say it: An Autobiographical Novel*, trans. P. Goodheart, Allen & Unwin, Sydney.

Casper, R. 1990, 'Personality features of women with good outcome from restricting anorexia', *Psychosomatic Medicine*, no. 52, pp. 156–70.

Ceaser, M. 1977, 'The role of maternal identification in four cases of anorexia nervosa', *Bulletin of the Menninger Clinic*, vol. 41, no. 5, pp. 475–87.

Celermajer, D. 1986, 'Anorexia nervosa', unpublished BA Hons thesis, General Philosophy, Sydney University, Sydney, Australia.

Celermajer, D. 1987, 'Submission and rebellion: anorexia and a feminism of the body', *Australian Feminist Studies*, no. 5, pp. 57–70.

Chernin, K. 1982, *The Obsession: Reflections on the Tyranny of Slenderness*, Harper & Row, New York (originally published in 1981 as *Womansize*, Virago, London).

1986, *The Hungry Self: Women, Eating and Identity*, Virago, London.

Christ, J. 1980, *Diving Deep and Surfacing.* (2nd edn), Beacon Press, Boston.

Clemmons, P. 1991, 'Feminists, spirituality and the twelves steps of Alcoholics Anonymous', *Women and Therapy*, vol. 11, no. 2, pp. 97–109.

Clifford, J. & Marcus, G. E. (eds). 1986, *Writing Culture: The Poetics and Politics of Ethnography*, University of California Press, Berkeley.

Cline, S. 1993, *Women, Celibacy and Passion*, Deutsch, London.

Cole, E., Espin, O. & Rothblum, E. (eds.). 1992, *Refugee Women and their Mental Health*, The Haworth Press, London.

Coleridge, S. T. 1951, *Selected Poetry and Prose of Coleridge*, ed. D. Stauffer, Modern Library Editions, Random House, New York.

Colquhoun, D. 1989a, 'Healthism and health-based physical education: a critique', unpublished PhD thesis, University of Queensland, Australia.

1989b, 'Healthism, the sociology of school knowledge and the curriculum', paper presented to The Australian Sociological Association Conference, La Trobe University, Melbourne.

Coopman, V. 1991, *Private Party*, Women's Redress Press, Marrickville, Sydney.

Coppet, D. de (ed.). 1992, *Understanding Ritual*, Routledge, London.

Cotterill, P. 1992. 'Interviewing women: issues of friendship, vulnerability and power', *Women's Studies International Forum*, vol. 15, nos. 5/6, pp. 593–606.

Cottom, D. 1989, *Text and Culture: The Politics of Interpretation*, University of Minnesota Press, Minneapolis.

Counihan, D. M. 1989, 'An anthropological view of western women's prodigious fasting: a review essay', *Food and Foodways*, vol. 3, no. 4, pp. 357–75.

Crawford, R. 1978, 'You are dangerous to your health', *Social Policy*, January/February.

1986, 'A cultural account of 'health': control, release and the social body', in J. B. McKinley (ed.), *Issues in the Political Economy of Health Care*, Tavistock, London.

Crawford, J., Kippax, S., Onyx, J., Gault, U. & Benton, P. 1992, *Emotion and Gender: Creating Meaning from Memory*, London, Sage.

Crisp, A. H. 1980, *Anorexia Nervosa: Let Me Be*, Academic Press, London.

Crisp, A. H. & Burns, T. 1983, 'The clinical presentation of anorexia nervosa in males', *International Journal of Eating Disorders*, no. 2, pp. 5–10.

Crisp, A. H., Burns, T. & Bhat, A. V. 1986, 'Primary anorexia nervosa in the male and female: a comparison of clinical features and prognosis', *British Journal of Medical Psychology*, no. 59, pp. 123–32.

Crites, S. 1989, 'The narrative quality of experience', in S. Hauerwas & G. Jones, (eds.), *Why Narrative?: Readings in Narrative Theology*, Eerdmans, Grand Rapids, Michigan.

Csordas, T. J. 1983, 'The rhetoric of transformation in ritual healing', *Culture, Medicine & Psychiatry*, no. 7, pp. 333–75.

Dally, P. 1969, *Anorexia Nervosa*, Grune & Stratton, New York.

Dana, M. 1987, 'Boundaries: One-way mirror to the self', in M. Lawrence (ed.), *Fed Up and Hungry: Women, Oppression and Food*, Women's Press, London.

Danieli, Y. 1988, 'Treating survivors and children of survivors of the Nazi Holocaust', in F. M. Ochberg (ed.), *Post-Traumatic Therapy and Victims of Violence*, Brunner/Mazel, New York.

de Rivera, J. and Grinkis, C. 1986, Emotions as Social Relationships. *Motivation and Emotion*, vol. 10, no. 4, pp. 984–1014.

Dictionnaire de la Vie Spirituelle, 1987, Edition du Cerf, Paris.

Dittmar, H. & Bates, B. 1987, 'Humanistic approaches to the understanding and treatment of anorexia nervosa', *Journal of Adolescence*, no. 10, pp. 57–69.

Douglas, M. 1966, *Purity and Danger: An Analysis of Concepts of Pollution and Taboo*, Routledge, London.

Dreyfus, E. 1993, *The Body Pregnant*, Penguin & McPhee Gribble, Ringwood, Victoria.

Dunbar, M. 1986, *Catherine: The Story of a Young Girl who Died of Anorexia*, Penguin Books, Harmondsworth.

Durkheim, E. 1976 (1915), *The Elementary Forms of the Religious Life*, George Allen & Unwin, London.

Ehrenreich, B. & English, D. 1973, *Witches, Midwives and Nurses*, The Feminist Press, Old Westbury, New York.

Elster, J. (ed.) 1986, *The Multiple Self: Studies in Rationality and Social Change*, Cambridge University Press (in collaboration with Maison des Sciences de l'Homme), Cambridge.

Epston, D. & White, M. 1989, *Literate Means to Therapeutic Ends*, Dulwich Centre Publications, Adelaide.

Fallon, P., Katzman, M. & Wooley, S. 1994, *Feminist Perspectives on Eating Disorders*, The Guildford Press: New York.

Falstein, L. H. 1981, 'Mourning postponed becomes anorexia', *Psychology Today*, no. 15, p. 26.

Finch J. 1984, 'It's great to have someone to talk to: the ethics and politics of interviewing women', in C. Bell & H. Roberts (eds.), *Social Researching: Policy, Problems, Practice*, Routledge, London.

Finkelstein, J. 1991, *The Fashioned Self*, Polity Press, Cambridge.

Foucault, M. 1973, *The Birth of the Clinic: An Archeology of Medical Perception*, Tavistock, London.

1977, *The Archeology of Knowledge*, Tavistock, London.

1979, 'What is an author?', in J. V. Harari (ed.), *Textual Strategies: Perspectives in Post Structuralist Criticism*, Cornell University Press, Ithaca, New York.

1980, *Power/Knowlege: Selected Interviews and Other Writings: 1972–1977*, ed. by C. Gordon, Harvester Press, Brighton.

Frank, A. 1995, *The Wounded Storyteller*, University of Chicago Press, Chicago.

Freud, S. 1900/1985a, *The Interpretation of Dreams*, Pelican Freud Library, vol. 4, Penguin, Harmondsworth.

1901/1985b, *The Psychopathology of Everyday Life*, Pelican Freud Library, vol. 5, Penguin, Harmondsworth.

Freud, S. & Breuer, J. 1893–5/1974, *Studies on Hysteria*, The Pelican Freud Library, vol. 3, Penguin, Harmondsworth.

Freund, P. 1988, Bringing society into the body, *Theory and Society*, 17, pp. 839–64.

1990, The expressive body: a common ground for the sociology of emotions and health and illness, *Sociology of Health and Illness*, vol. 12, no. 4, pp. 452–77.

Game, A. & Metcalfe, A. 1996, *Passionate Sociology*, Sage, London.

Garner, P. E. & Garfinkel, D. M. 1982, *Anorexia Nervosa: A Multidimensional Perspective*, Brunner/Mazel, New York.

Garner, D., Olmstead, M. & Garfinkel, P. 1983, 'Does anorexia nervosa occur on a continuum? Subgroups of weight-preoccupied women and their relationship to anorexia nervosa', *International Journal of Eating Disorders*, no. 2, pp. 11–c30.

Garrett, C. 1991, *Bread and Butter: Nurses' Work with Anorectics*, Monograph. Communication, Health and Education Research Centre, University of Western Sydney, Nepean, NSW, Australia.

1992a, *Men and Anorexia: A challenge to current theories*, Working Papers in Women's Studies, Women's Research Centre, University of Western Sydney, Nepean, Sydney.

1992b, *Anorexia as Personal and Social Ritual*, Working Papers in Women's Studies, Women's Research Centre, University of Western Sydney, Nepean, Sydney.

1992c, Thin voices, starved lives, *Modern Times*, September, p. 37.

1994, The Eating Disorders Smorgasbord, *Australian Journal of Communication*, vol. 21, no. 2, pp. 14–31.

1995a, 'Report on the European Council on Eating Disorders Dublin General Meeting', *Newsletter of the European Council on Eating Disorders*, Winter 1995–6.

1995b, *Anorexia Nervosa and Theories of the Body*, Feminist Cultural Studies

Series no. 2, Women's Research Centre, University of Western Sydney, Nepean, Sydney.

1996a, 'Remaking the self through metaphor: Recovery from anorexia nervosa'. *Annual Review of Health Social Sciences*, vol. 6, pp. 139–155.

1996b, 'Transformations of time and space: Social theory and recovery from eating disorders', *Eating Disorders: The Journal of Prevention and Treatment*, vol. 4, no. 3, pp. 245–255.

1996c, 'Recovery from anorexia nervosa: a Durkheimian interpretation', *Social Science and Medicine*, vol. 43, no. 10, pp. 1489–1506.

1997, 'Sociological perspectives on recovery from anorexia nervosa', *International Journal of Eating Disorders*, vol. 21, no. 3, (3), pp. 261–272.

Gatens, M. 1983, 'A critique of the sex/gender distinction', in J. Allen & P. Patton (eds.), *Beyond Marxism?: interventions after Marx*, Interventions Publications, Leichhardt, New Sourth Wales, pp. 143–62.

Geertz, R. 1988, *Works and Lives: The Anthropologist as Author*, Stanford University Press, Stanford.

Gennep, A. van, 1960 (1909), *The Rites of Passage*, with an introduction bt S. Kimball, Routledge, London.

Giddens, A. 1991, *Modernity and Self Identity: Self and Society in the Late Modern Age*, Stanford University Press, Stanford.

Glaser, B. G. & Strauss, A. L. (1967), *The Discovery of Grounded Theory*, Weidenfeld & Nicholson, London.

Glik, D. C. 1988, 'Symbolic, ritual and social dynamics of spiritual healing', *Social Science in Medicine*, no. 27, pp. 1197–1206.

1986, 'Psychosocial wellness among spiritual healing adherents', *Social Science and Medicine*, no. 22, pp. 579–586.

1990a, 'The redefinition of the situation: the social construction of spiritual healing experiences', *Sociology of Health and Illness*, vol. 12, no. 2, pp. 151–68.

1990b, 'Participation in spiritual healing, religiosity and mental health', *Sociological Inquiry*, vol. 60, no. 2, pp. 158–176.

Goodwin, G. M. & Fairburn, C. G. 1987, 'Dieting changes serotogenic function in women, not men: Implications for the aetiology of anorexia nervosa?', *Psychological Medicine*, vol. 17, no. 4, pp. 839–42.

Goody, J. 1977, 'Against 'ritual': loosely structured thoughts on a loosely defined topic', in S. F. Moore & B. G. Myerhoff (eds.) *Secular Ritual*, Van Gorcum, Assen and Amsterdam.

Grant, M. & Hazel, J. 1973, *Who's Who in Classical Mythology*, Weidenfeld & Nicholson, London.

Green, L. 1991, 'Hard and soft data: Gender discrimination in research methodologies', paper presented at the Australian Communication Association Conference, University of Technology, Sydney.

Green, R. W. (ed.) 1973, *Protestantism, Capitalism and Social Science: The Weber Thesis Controversy*, Heath, Lexington, Mass.

Greer, G. 1970, *The Female Eunuch*, Granada Publishing, London.

Grene, M. 1973, *Sartre*, Franklin Watts, New York.

Grosz, E. 1987, 'Philosophy of the body', seminar series in General Philosophy, University of Sydney, Australia.

1989, *Sexual Subversions: Three French Feminists*, Allen & Unwin, Sydney.

1994, *Volatile Bodies: Toward a Corporeal Feminism*, Allen & Unwin, Sydney.

Gull, W. 1874, 'Anorexia nervosa (apepsia hysterica, anorexia hysterica)', *Transactions of the Clinical Society of London*, no. 7, pp. 22–28.

Gusdorf, G. 1980, 'Conditions and limits of autobiography', in J. Olney (ed.), *Autobiography: Essays Theoretical and Critical*, Princeton University Press, Princeton, N.J.

Hall, A., Delahunt, J. W. & Ellis, P. M. 1985, 'Anorexia nervosa in the male: Clinical features and follow-up of nine patients', *Journal of Psychiatric Research*, vol. 19, no. 2/3, pp. 315–21.

Hall, L. 1993, *Full Lives*, Gurze Books, Carlsbad, CA.

Halmi, K., Broadland, G. & Rigas, C. 1975, 'A follow-up study of seventy nine patients with anorexia nervosa: An evaluation of prognostic factos and diganostic criteria', in R. D. Wirt, G. Winokur & M. Roff (eds), *Life History Research in Psychopathology*, vol. 4, University of Minnesota Press, Minneapolis.

Harding, S. 1986, *The Science Question in Feminism*, Cornell University Press, Ithaca.

Harding, S. & Hintikka, M. (eds.). 1983, *Discovering Reality: Feminist Perspectives on Epistemology, Metaphysics, Methodology and Philosophy of Science*, Reidel, Dordrecht.

Hargreaves, J. 1986, 'Schooling the body', Chapter 8 in *Sport, Power and Culture*, Polity Press, Cambridge.

Harmer, W. and Robinson, S. 1994, *What's the Matter with Mary Jane?*, performed at Sydney's Wharf Theatre and the Edinburgh fringe festival.

Haug, F. (ed.). 1987, *Female Sexualization: A Collective Work of Memory*, trans. from German by Erica Carter, Verso, London.

Haug, F. 1985, 'Women's experience and memory work', unpublished Visiting Fellow's paper given at sociology seminar, Macquarie University, Sydney, Australia.

Hay, L. L. 1990, *Heal Your Body*, Hay House, Santa Monica.

Heelas, P. 1996, *The New Age Movement*, Blackwell, Oxford.

Heilbrun, C. G. 1988, *Writing a Woman's Life*, Ballantyne Books, Random House, New York.

Helminiak, D. A. 1989, 'The quest for spiritual values', in *Pastoral Psychology*, vol. 38, no. 2, pp. 105–17.

Henderson, S. 1993, *From Strength to Strength*, Macmillan, Melbourne.

Henriques, J., Hollway, W., Urwin, C., Venn, C. & Walkerdine, V. 1984, *Changing the Subject: Psychology, Social Regulation and Subjectivity*, Methuen, London.

Herzog, D., Hamberg, P. & Brotman, A. 1987, 'Commentary: psychotherapy and Eating Disorder: an affirmative view', *International Journal of Eating Disorders*, vol. 6, no. 4, pp. 545–50.

Herzog, D., Keller, M. & Lavori, P. 1988, 'Outcome in anorexia nervosa and bulimia nervosa: a review of the literature', *The Journal of Nervous and Mental Disease*, vol. 176, no. 3, pp. 131–43.

Hochschild, A. 1983, *The Managed Heart: Commercialization of Human Feeling*,

University of California Press, Berkeley.

Homer. 1965, *The Odyssey of Homer*, trans. R. Lattimore, Harper & Row, New York.

Horin, A. 1991, 'A lost generation's anorexic nightmare', in *The Sydney Morning Herald*, Tuesday, 29 October.

Horsfall, J. 1993, 'Review of J. Finkelstein's *The Fashioned Self*, *Australian and New Zealand Journal of Sociology*, vol. 29, no. 2, pp. 259–61.

Hsu, L. K. G. 1980, 'Outcome of anorexia nervosa: A review of the literature', *Archives of General Psychiatry*, no. 37, pp. 1041–42.

1989, 'The gender gap in eating disorders: Why are the eating disorders more common among women?', *Clinical Psychology Review*, vol. 9, no. 3, pp. 393–407.

Hsu, L. K. G., Crisp, A. H. & Harding, B. 1979, 'Outcome of anorexia nervosa', *The Lancet*, 13 January, pp. 61–5.

Hull, J. 1990, *Touching The Rock: An Experience of Blindness*, Pantheon Books, New York.

Illich, I. 1976, *Medical Nemesis: The Expropriation of Health*, Pantheon Books, New York.

Irigaray, L. 1982, 'And one does not move without the other', *Signs*, vol. 7, no. 1.

1985, *Speculum of the Other Woman*, trans. Gillian Gill, Cornell University Press, Ithaca, New York.

1986, *Divine Women*, trans S. Muecke, Occasional paper no. 8, Local Consumption Publications, Sydney.

Iyengar, B. K. S. 1991, *Light On Yoga*, The Aquarian Press, London.

Jackson, C. & Davidson, G. 1986, 'The anorexic patient as a survivor: the denial of death and death themes in the literature on anorexia nervosa', *International Journal of Eating Disorders*, vol. 5, no. 5, pp. 821–35.

1989, *Appetite for Death: A Study of the Theme of Death in the 'Hidden' Literature on Eating Disorders*, Boolarong Publications, Brisbane (revised edition forthcoming).

Jackson, C. 1992, 'The themes of death and survival in the literature on eating disorders: clarifying the connections: clear answers to clear questions', unpublished resource materials to accompany Jackson & Davidson 1989.

Jackson, M. 1983, 'Thinking through the body: an essay on understanding metaphor', *Social Analysis*, no. 14, pp. 127–48.

James, W. 1958 (1901), *The Varieties of Religious Experience*, Penguin/Mentor, New York.

Johnson, M. 1987, *The Body in the Mind: The Bodily Basis of Meaning, Imagination and Reason*, University of Chicago Press, Chicago.

Johnston, W. 1995, *Mystical Theology*, Harper Collins, London.

Jones, A. & Crawford, A. 1995, *Shadow of a Girl*, Penguin, Ringwood, Victoria.

Kafka, F. 1952, 'A hunger artist', trans. Willa and Edwin Muir, in *Selected Short Stories of Franz Kafka*, intro. Philip Rav, The Modern Library, New York.

Kaminer, W. 1993, *I'm Dysfunctional, You're Dysfunctional: The Recovery Movement and Other Self-Help Fashions*, Vintage Books, Random House, New York.

Keck, J. & Fiebert, M. 1986, 'Avoidance of anxiety and eating disorders', *Psychological Reports*, no. 58, pp. 432–4.

Kegan, R. 1982, *The Evolving Self: Problems and Process in Human Development*, Harvard University Press, Cambridge, Ma.

Kemper, T. 1978, *A Social Interactional Theory of Emotions*, Wiley, New York.

1981, 'Social constructionist and positivist approaches to the sociology of emotions', *American Journal of Sociology*, vol. 82, no. 2, pp. 336–62.

1990, *Research Agendas in the Sociology of Emotions*, SUNY Press, New York.

Kenway, J. & Willis, S. 1990, *Hearts and Minds: Self-Esteem and the Schooling of Girls*, Falmer Press, London.

Kenway, J. 1992, 'The journey from 'hope to happening,' keynote address to Conference on girls' education and post-school options, NSW Department of School Education & Department of Education, Employment and Training, Sydney University, 7–8 February.

Kessler, C. 1985, 'The cultural management of death: individual fate and its social transcendence', in M. Crouch & B. Huppauf (eds.), *Essays on Mortality*, University of New South Wales, Sydney.

Kierkegaard, S. 1973, *A Kierkegaard Anthology*, ed. R. W. Bretall, Princeton University Press, Princeton, NJ.

Kimball, S. 1960, Introduction to van Gennep, A. *The Rites of Passage*, Routledge, London.

Kippax, S., Crawford, J., Benton, P. & Gault, U. 1988, 'Constructing emotions: weaving meaning from memories', *British Journal of Psychology*, vol. 27, no. 1, pp. 19–33.

Kirsner, D. 1991, 'Sigmund Freud', in Beilharz, P. (ed.), *Social Theory: A Guide to Central Thinkers*, Allen & Unwin, Sydney.

Kleinman, A. 1988, *The Illness Narratives: Suffering, Healing and the Human Condition*, Basic Books, New York.

Kondo, D. 1986, 'Dissolution and reconstitution of Self: implications for anthopological epistemology', *Cultural Anthopology*, vol. 1, no. 1, pp. 74–88.

Kovel, J. 1988, *A Complete Guide to Therapy*, Penguin, Harmondsworth.

1991, *History and Spirit: An Inquiry into the Philosophy of Liberation*, Beacon Press, Boston.

Kress, G., Lohrey, A. & Place, F. 1990, 'The language of people with anorexia nervosa', unpublished research report for the Australian Research Council, University of Technology, Sydney.

Kristeva, J. 1980, *Desire in Language*, trans. Leon Roudiez, Basil Blackwell, Oxford.

1984, 'Julia Kristeva in conversation with Rosalind Coward', *ICA Documents*, special issue on *Desire*.

Krystal, S. & Zweben, J. 1988, 'The use of visualization as a means of integrating the spiritual dimension into treatment: a practical guide', *Journal of Substance Abuse Treatment*, vol. 5, pp. 229–38.

Lacan. J. 1977, 'The mirror stage', (1949), in *Ecrits*, Tavistock, London.

Lagarde, A & Michard, L. 1962, *XIXeme Siecle*, Collection Textes et Litterature Bordas, Paris.

Laing, R. D. 1960, *The Divided Self*, Tavistock, London.

Lakoff, G. & Johnson, M. 1980, *Metaphors We Live By*, University of Chicago Press, Chicago.

Lash, N. 1996, *The Beginning and the End of Religion*, Cambridge University Press, Cambridge.

Lawrence, M. 1984, *The Anorexic Experience*, The Women's Press, London.

1987 , 'Education and identity: the social origins of anorexia', in Lawrence (ed.), *Fed Up and Hungry: women, oppression and food*, The Women's Press, London.

Lee, S. 1996, 'Reconsidering the status of anorexia nervosa as a Western culture-bound syndrome', *Social Science and Medicine* vol. 42, no. 1, pp. 21–34.

Liu, A. 1979, *Solitaire*, Harper & Row, New York.

Lowen, A. 1976, *Bioenergetics*, Penguin, Harmondsworth.

Lupton, D. 1996, *Food, The Body and the Self*, Sage, London.

MacLeod, S. 1971, *The Snow White Soliloquies*, Viking Press, New York.

1981, *The Art of Starvation*, Virago, London.

Maine, M. 1985, 'An existential exploration of the forces contributing to, sustaining and ameliorating anorexia nervosa: The recovered patient's view', PhD Dissertation, Saybrook Institute.

Maitland, S. 1987, 'Passionate prayer: masochistic images in women's experience', in L. Hurcombe (ed.), *Sex and God: Some Varieties of Women's Religious Experience*, Routledge and Kegan Paul, London, pp. 125–40.

1990, 'Rose of Lima: some thoughts on purity and penance', in A. Joseph, (ed.). *Through the Devil's Gateway: Women, Religion and Taboo*, SPCK & Channel Four Television Company, Great Britain.

Malouf, D. 1975, *Johnno: A Novel*, University of Queensland Press, St. Lucia, Queensland.

Mandel, B. J. 1980, 'Full of life now', in J. Olney, (ed.), *Autobiography: Essays Theoretical and Critical*, Princeton University Press, Princeton.

Mannheim, K. 1968 (1936), *Ideology and Utopia: An Introduction*, Routledge, London.

Mariz, C. L. 1991, 'Pentecostalism and alcoholism among the Brazilian poor', *Alcoholism Treatment Quarterly*, vol. 8, no. 2, pp. 75–82.

Martin, S. 1989, *Body and Soul: Physical Therapies for Everyone*, Penguin Arkana, London.

Masson, J. 1990, *Against Therapy*, Fontana, London.

Masterson, J. F. 1981, *The Narcissistic and Borderline Disorders: An Integrated Developmental Approach*, Brunner/Mazel, New York.

1985, *The Real Self: A Developmental, Self, and Object-Relations Approach*, Brunner/Mazel, New York.

May, M. 1995, *A Body Knows: A Theopoetics of Death and Resurrection*, Continuum, New York.

McAll, K. 1980, 'Ritual mourning for anorexia nervosa', report in *The Lancet*, 16 August, p. 368.

1988, 'Ritual mourning for anorexia nervosa', unpublished paper, available from Drs R. K. & F. A. McAll, Bignell Wood, Lyndhurst, Hants, SO437JA, United Kingdom.

McFarlane, J. & Baker-Baumann, T. 1991, *Shame and Body Image: Culture and the Compulsive Eater*, Health Communications Inc., Deerfield, Fl.

McGuire, M. 1988, *Ritual Healing in Suburban America*, Rutgers University Press, New Brunswick.

McMaster, R. 1993, 'Travellers in the land of paradox', a review of books by G. Moorhouse & W. Dalrymple, in *The Sydney Morning Herald*, Spectrum, Saturday 30 October, p. 10A.

Meehan, B. 1993, *Holy Women of Russia: The Lives of Five Orthodox Women Offer Spiritual Guidance for Today*, Harper, San Fransisco.

Merleau-Ponty, M. 1962, *The Phenomenology of Perception*, Routledge, London. 1964, *Le Visible et L'Invisible*, Gallimard, Paris.

Middlebrook, D. W. 1992, *Anne Sexton: A Biography*, Virago, London.

Mills, C. Wright, 1965 (1959), *The Sociological Imagination*, Oxford University Press, Oxford.

Mogul, S. L. 1980, 'Asceticism in adolescence and anorexia nervosa', *Psychoanalytic Study of the Child*, no. 35, pp. 155–75.

Moore, T. 1992, *Cry of the Damaged Man: A Personal Journey of Recovery*, Picador, Australia.

Morgan, H. G, & Russell, G. F. M. 1975, 'Value of family background and clinical features as predictors of long-term outcome in anorexia nervosa: four-year follow-up study of forty-one patients', *Psychological Medicine*, vol. 5, pp. 355–71.

Moriarty, D., Moriarty, M. & Ford, C. 1990, 'The role of sport/fitness and eating disorders: cosmetic fitness from starvation to steroids', paper presented at the International Congress on Youth, Leisure and Physical Activity, Brussels, May 1990.

Morton, R. 1694, *Phthisiologia; or a Treatise on Consumptions*, London.

Mukai, R. 1989, 'Anorexia nervosa from within', *Women's Studies International Forum*, vol. 12, no. 6, pp. 613–63.

Murray, M. 1981a, 'The jagged edge: a biographical essay on Simone Weil', in G. A. White (ed.), *Simone Weil: Interpretations of a Life*, University of Massachusetts Press, Amherst.

1981b, 'Simone Weil: last things', in G. A. White (ed.), *Simone Weil: Interpretations of a Life*, University of Massachusetts Press, Amherst.

Noll, R. 1996, *The Jung Cult*, HarperCollins, London.

Oakley, A. 1981, 'Interviewing women: a contradiction in terms', in H. Roberts (ed.), *Doing Feminist Research*, Routledge, London.

Olney, J. (ed.) 1980 (1966), *Autobiography: Essays Theoretical and Critical*, Princeton University Press, Princeton.

Orbach, S. 1986, *Hunger Strike: The Anorectic's Struggle as a Metaphor for our Age*, Faber & Faber, London.

Ovid, 1955, *Metamorphoses*, trans. R. Humphreys, Indiana University Press, Bloomington.

Palazzoli, M. S. 1974 (1963), *Self-Starvation: From the Intrapsychic to the Transpersonal Approach to Anorexia Nervosa*, Chaucer Human Context Books, London.

Pancner, K. L. & Pancner, R. J. 1988, 'The quest, gurus and the yellow brick road', *Individual Psychology*, vol. 44, no. 2, pp. 158–66.

Parkin, D. 1992, 'Ritual as spatial direction and bodily division', in D. de Coppet (ed.), *Understanding Ritual*, Routledge, London.

Perera, S. B. 1981, *Descent to the Goddess: A Way of Initiation for Women*, Inner City Books, Toronto.

Perrin, J. B. & Thibon, G. 1953, *Simone Weil as We Knew Her*, Routledge, London.

Personal Narratives Group, 1989, *Interpreting Women's Lives: Feminist Theory and Personal Narratives*, University of Indiana Press, Bloomington.

Peters, L. 1990, 'Recovery from bulimia: the woman's view', PhD dissertation, University of Washington.

Peters, L. and Fallon, P. 1984, 'The journey of recovery: dimensions of change', in P. Fallon et al., *Feminist Perspectives on Eating Disorders*. The Guildford Press, New York.

Pétrement. S. 1976, *Simone Weil: A Life*, trans. R. Rosenthal, Pantheon Books, New York.

Picard, B. L. 1972 (1955), *French Legends and Fairy Stories*, Oxford University Press, London.

Place, F. 1989, *Cardboard*, Local Consumption Publications, Sydney.

Quadrio, C. 1989, 'Hologram to Holocaust', paper given at the Australian and New Zealand Family Therapy Association Conference, Christchurch, NZ, reprinted in *Australian Association of Marriage and Family Counsellors Bulletin*, no. 34, October, pp. 4–29.

Quinn, N. 1991, 'The cultural basis of metaphor', in J. Fernandez (ed.), *Beyond Metaphor: The Theory of Tropes in Anthropology*, Stanford University Press, Stanford.

Rahner, K. et al. (eds.). 1968, *Sacramentum Mundi: An Encyclopedia of Theology*, vol II, Burns & Oates, London.

Raimbault, G. 1971, 'Le thème de la mort dans l'anorexie mentale', *Revue de Neuropsychiatrie Infantile et d'Hygiène Mentale de l'Enfance*. vol. 19, no. 11, pp. 645–9.

Rampling, D. 1985, 'Ascetic ideals and anorexia nervosa', *Journal of Psychiatric Research*, vol. 19, no. 2/3, pp. 89–94.

Reich, W. 1949, *Character Analysis*, 3rd edn., trans. T. P. Wolfe, Orgone Institute Press, New York.

Reinharz, S. 1983, 'Experiential analysis: A contribution to feminist research', in G. Bowles & R. Duelli-Klein (eds.), *Theories of Women's Studies*, Routledge, London.

Ring, K. 1980, *Life at Death*, Coward, McCann & Geoghan, New York.
1984, *Heading Towards Omega*, William Morrow, New York.

Rinpoche, S. 1992, *The Tibetan Book of Living and Dying*, Harper Collins, San Fransisco.

Roberts, H. (ed.). 1981, *Doing Feminist Research*, Routledge, London.

Robertson, M. 1992, *Starving in the Silences; An Exploration of Anorexia Nervosa*, Allen & Unwin, Sydney.

Root, M. 1990, 'Recovery and relapse in former bulimics', *Psychotherapy*, vol. 27, no. 3, pp. 397–403.

Roth, G. 1982 *Feeding the Hungry Heart: The Experience of Compulsive Eating*, Plume Books, Penguin, New York.

1992, *When Food is Love: Exploring the Relationship between Eating and Intimacy*, Penguin, New York.

Russell, G. F. M. 1977, 'General managment of anorexia nervosa and difficulties in assessing the efficacy of treatment', in R. A. Vigersky (ed.), *Anorexia Nervosa*, Raven Press, New York.

Russell, G. F. M., Szmukler, G., Dare, C. & Eisler, M. 1987, 'An evaluation of family therapy in anorexia nervosa and bulimia nervosa', *Archives of General Psychiatry*, vol. 44, December, 1987

Sacks, O. 1984, *A Leg to Stand On*, Picador, London.

1985, *The Man Who Mistook his Wife for a Hat*, Picador, London.

Said, E. W. 1975, *Beginnings: Intention and Method*, Basic Books, New York.

Sartre, J.-P. 1965 (1938), *Nausea*, trans. R. Baldick, Penguin, Harmondsworth.

1966, *Being and Nothingness: A Phenomenological Essay on Ontology*, trans. H. Barnes, Pocket Books, New York.

Sayers, J. 1988, 'Psychodynamic and feminist approaches to anorexia nervosa and bulimia nervosa', in D. Salt (ed.), *Anorexia and Bulimia Nervosa: Practical Approaches*, New York University Press, New York.

Schwartz D. M. & Thompson, M. B. 1981, 'Do anorectics get well? Current research and future needs', *American Journal of Psychiatry*, vol. 138, no. 3, pp. 319–23.

Shepherd, J. 1997, *Dare to Fly*, Sydney: Random House.

Shorter, B. 1987, *An Image Darkly Forming: Women and Initiation*, Routledge, London.

Shute, J. 1993, *Life-Size*, Mandarin: London.

Signer, S. F. & Benson, D. F. 1990, 'Three cases of anorexia nervosa associated with temporal lobe epilepsy', *American Journal of Psychiatry*, vol. 147, no. 2, pp. 235–8.

Slade, 1984, *The Anorexia Nervosa Reference Book*, Harper & Row, London.

Smith, D. 1974, Women's Perspective as a Radical Critique of Sociology, *Sociological Inquiry*, vol. 44, pp. 7–13.

1977, 'Some Implications of a Sociology for Women', in N. Glazer and H. Waehrer (eds.), *Women in a Man-Made World: A Socioeconomic Handbook*, Rand-McNally, Chicago.

1979, 'A Sociology for Women', in J. Sherman and E. T. Beck (eds.), *The Prism of Sex: Essays in the Sociology of Knowledge*, University of Wisconsin Press, Madison.

1992, 'Writing women's experience into social science', *Feminism and Psychology*, vol. 1, no. 1, pp. 155–69.

Smukler, G. & Tatum, D. 1984, 'Anorexia nervosa: starvation dependence', *British Journal of Medical Psychology*, no. 57, pp. 303–310.

Sohlberg, S., Norring, C., Holmgren, S. & Rosmark, B. 1989, 'Impulsivity and long-term prognosis of psychiatric patients with anorexia nervosa/bulimia nervosa', *The Journal of Nervous and Mental Disease*, vol. 177, no. 5, pp. 249–58.

Sommer, D. 1988, 'Not just a personal story: Women's testimonios and the plural self', in B. Brodzki & C. Schenk (eds.), *Life/Lines: Theorizing Women's Autobiography*, Cornell University Press, Ithaca.

Sontag, S. 1988 (1971), *Illness as Metaphor*, Penguin, London.

Spitzack, C. 1990, *Confessing Excess: Women and the Politics of Body Reduction*, State University of New York Press, Albany.

Stanley, L. (ed.). 1990, *Feminist Praxis: Research, Theory and Epistemology in Feminist Sociology*, Routledge, London.

Stanley, L. & Wise, S. 1983, *Breaking Out: Feminist Consciousnes and Feminist Research*, Routledge, London.

Steiner-Adair, C. 1990, 'New maps of development, new models of therapy: the psychology of women and the treatment of eating disorders', in C. Johnson (ed.), *Psychodynamic Treatment of Anorexia Nervosa and Bulimia*, Guildford, New York.

Steiner-Adair, C. 1990, 'The body politic: normal female adolescent development and the development of eating disorders', in C. Gilligan, N. Lyons, & T. J. Hanmer (eds.), *Making Connections: The Relational Worlds of Adolescent Girls at Emma Willard School*, Harvard University Press, Cambridge, Ma.

1991, 'When the body speaks: girls, eating disorders and psychotherapy', in Gilligan et al. (eds.), *Women, Girls and Psychotherapy: Reframing Resistance*, The Haworth Press, New York.

Sterling, J. W. & Segal, J. D. 1985, 'Anorexia in males: A critical review', *International Journal of Eating Disorders*, vol. 14, no. 4, pp. 559–72.

Strauss, A. 1987, *Qualitative Analysis for Social Scientists*, Cambridge University Press, Cambridge.

Sutherland, C. 1992, *Transformed by the Light: Life After Near-Death Experiences*, Bantam Books, Sydney.

Szasz. T. 1973, *Ideology and Insanity*, Calder & Byers, London.

1974, *The Myth of Mental Illness*, Harper & Row, New York.

1979, *The Myth of Psychotherapy*, Anchor/Doubleday, New York.

Tait, G. 1992, 'Anorexia nervosa: asceticism, differentiation, government', *The Australian and New Zealand Journal of Sociology*, vol. 29, no. 2, pp. 194–208.

Takaoka, K. et al. 1990, 'Clinical psychiatric study of recovery from 'pubertat-smagersucht' (anorexia nervosa)', *Japanese Journal of Child and Adolescent Psychiatry* (Japanese with English introduction), vol. 31, no.5, pp. 25–33.

Theander, S. 1983, 'Research on outcome and prognosis of anorexia nervosa and some results from a Swedish long-term study', *International Journal of Eating Disorders*, vol. 2, no. 4, pp. 167–84.

Thompson, B. 1992, ' "A way outa no way": eating problems among African-American, Latina and white women', *Gender and Society*, vol. 6, no. 4, pp. 546–61.

Thompson, B. W. 1994, *A Hunger So Wide and So Deep*, University of Minnesota Press, Minneapolis.

Tinning, R. 1985, 'Physical education and the cult of slenderness: a critique', *The Australian Council for Physical Education Research National Journal*, March, pp. 10–13.

Turnbull, E. 1997, 'Narcissism and the potential for self-transformation in the twelve steps', *Health: An Interdisciplinary Journal for the Social Study of Health, Illness and Medicine*, vol. 1, no. 2, pp. 149–66.

Turner, B. S. 1982, 'The discourse of diet', *Theory, Culture and Society*, vol. 1, no. 1, pp. 23–32.

1983, *Religion and Social Theory: A Materialist Perspective*, Heinemann Educational Books, London.

1984, *The Body and Society: Explorations in Social Theory*, Basil Blackwell, London.

1987, *Medical Power and Social Knowledge*, Sage, London.

Turner, V. 1977, *The Ritual Process: Structure and Anti-Structure*, Cornell University Press, New York.

Valle, R. & Halling, S. (eds.), 1989, *Existential-Phenomenological Perspectives in Psychology: Exploring the Breadth of Human Experience* (with a special section on transpersonal psychology), Plenum Press, New York.

Vandereycken, W. & Pierloot, R. 1983, 'Long-term outcome research in anorexia nervosa: the problem of patient selection and follow-up', *International Journal of Eating Disorders*, vol. 2, no. 4, pp. 237–42.

Vandereycken, W. & van Deth, R. 1994, *From Fasting Saints to Anorexic Girls*, The Athlone Press, London.

Vandereycken, W. & Vanderlinden, J. 1983, 'Denial of illness and the use of self-reporting measures in anorexia nervosa patients', *International Journal of Eating Disorders*, vol. 2, pp. 101–8.

Vico, G. B. 1963 (1744), *The Autobiography of Giambattista Vico*, trans. by T. B. Bergin & M. H. Fisch, Great Seal Books, Cornell University Press, New York.

1968 (1774), *The New Science of Giambattista Vico*, rev. trans. of 3rd edn by T. B. Bergin & M. H. Fisch, Cornell University Press, New York.

Visser, M. 1992. *The Rituals of Dinner*, Penguin, New York.

Walkerdine, V. 1984, 'Video replay: family, films and fantasy', in Henriques, J., Hollway, W., Urwin, C., Venn, C. & Walkerdine, V. (eds.), *Changing the Subject: Psychology, Social Regulation and Subjectivity*, Methuen, London.

Watson, E. & Mears, J. 1991, 'The ethics of feminist research', symposium presented at women's day, Annual Conference of The Australian Sociological Association, Murdoch University, Western Australia.

Way, K. 1993, *Anorexia and Recovery: A Hunger for Meaning*, Haworth Press, New York.

Weber, M. 1971 (1906, English trans. 1930), *The Protestant Ethic and the Spirit of Capitalism*, Allen & Unwin, London.

1978 (1951), *Economy and Society: An Outline of Interpretive Sociology*, Bedminster Press, New York.

Wilhelm, R. (ed.), 1988, *I Ching or Book of Changes*, 3rd ed., trans. C. F. Baynes, with a foreword by C. G. Jung, Routledge, London.

Wilkins, R. 1993, 'Taking it personally: A note on emotion and authobiography', *Sociology*, vol 27, no. 1, pp. 93–100.

Willis, E. 1983, *Medical Dominance: The Division of Labour in Australian Health Care*, Allen & Unwin, Sydney.

1995, *The Sociological Quest* (2nd edn), Allen & Unwin, Sydney.

Winnicott, D. W. 1965, *The Maturational Process and the Facilitating Environment*, The Hogarth Press, London.

Wolf, N. 1990, *The Beauty Myth: How Images of Beauty Are Used Against Women*, Vintage, London.

Woodman, M. 1980, *The Owl Was a Baker's Daughter: Obesity, Anorexia Nervosa and the Repressed Feminine*, Inner City Books, Toronto.

1982, *Addiction to Perfection: The Still Unravished Bride: A Psychological Study*, Inner City Books, Toronto.

1985, *The Pregnant Virgin: A Process of Psychological Transformation*, Inner City Books, Toronto.

1988, 'Addiction to perfection: an interview with Marion Woodman', by S. Bodian, *Yoga Journal*, Nov–Dec 1988, pp. 51–5, 112.

Woodward, K. 1988, 'Simone de Beauvoir: aging and its discontents', in S. Benstock (ed.), *The Private Self: Theory and Practice of Women's Autobiographical Writings*, Routledge, London.

Woolf, V. 1974 (1928), *A Room of One's Own*, Penguin, Harmondsworth.

World Health Organization 1992, *The ICD-10 Classification of Mental Disorders: Clinical Descriptions and Diagnostic Guidelines*, World Health Organization, Geneva.

Wright, J. 1991, 'The contribution of teacher talk to the production of gendered subjectivity in teacher education', unpublished PhD thesis, Wollongong University, Australia.

1992, 'Images of the body', in J. Kenway (ed.), *Gender, the State and Education*, Deakin University Press, Geelong, Victoria.

Young, I. M. 1989, 'Throwing like a girl: a phenomenology of feminine body comportment, motility, and spatiality', in J. Allen & I. M. Young (eds.), *The Thinking Muse: Feminism and Modern French Philosophy*, Indiana University Press, Bloomington.

Zalba, M. 1968, 'Fasting', in K. Rahner, et al. (eds.) 1968.

Index